Crimes Against Women:

Proceedings of the International Tribunal

I hope this book will give you some great ideas about actions you can do.

In sisterhood,

Diana E. H. Russell
March 7, 1996

Crimes Against Women:

Proceedings of the International Tribunal

Compiled and edited by

Diana E. H. Russell
Nicole Van de Ven

FROG IN THE WELL
430 Oakdale Road
East Palo Alto, CA 94303

1984

Cover design by Brenton Beck

Frog In the Well
430 Oakdale Road
East Palo Alto, CA 94303

First published by Les Femmes, November 1976
Made in the United States of America

Library of Congress Cataloging in Publication Data

International Tribunal on Crimes Against Women, Brussels,
1976.
Crimes against women.

1. Women—Crimes against—Congresses. I. Russell,
D.E.H. II. Ven, Nicole van de. III. Title.
HV6250.4.W65I57 1976 364 76-25356
ISBN: 0-9603628-5-1

(The appendices that appeared in the original edition have been omitted from this edition due to lack of space. Copies may be obtained by sending a sase to Frog In The Well, 430 Oakdale Road, East Palo Alto, CA 94303.)

To Lydia Horton and Laura Zelmachild

In the hope that this book will be a
weapon in our struggle against the
oppression of women everywhere.

NEW INTRODUCTION TO THE REPRINT EDITION

If like millions of others around the world, you have never heard about the International Tribunal on Crimes Against Women, you have been deprived of an important event in the evolution of feminism globally. Independently of governments, political parties, or any other existing institutions, it brought women together from many parts of the world to testify about their experiences of female oppression and violence against women and to denounce the abuse of women in its many forms. Organized on a tiny budget—smaller than the average annual salary of a professor in many countries—it attracted over 2000 women from 40 countries who raised their own money to go to Brussels because they wanted to make women's voices heard internationally. The women recalled painful memories and shared strategies, they argued over procedures and politics, they laughed and cried and planned for the future. They made history.

Yet, today, a mere eight years later, many feminists throughout the world have never heard about the tribunal. This conference which demonstrated the strength of feminism as an independent idea and movement and sparked the organizing of numerous women's projects is in danger of being lost from our collective memory. Precisely because it was independent of governments, it has been ignored by most of them, and many national accounts of the development of the women's movement do not include this ground- breaking event. Thus is history shaped and our heritage denied to us—even in our life times. Unless, that is, we write it ourselves. Feminists must make a conscious effort to record and analyze the events that have shaped our movement, particularly those that were activist oriented and did not depend on official sanctions for their survival. The International Tribunal on Crimes Against Women was such an event. I welcome the re-publication of its proceedings as important for that as well as other reasons.

This book records in painstaking detail not only the testimonies and proposals from the Tribunal itself but also the process of organizing it and the controversies that emerged during the sessions. It is thus several books in one: it is a moving statement of the terrible abuses against women in many parts of the world; it is a compendium of women's initiatives and strategies to fight those crimes; and it is an organizers' account of the issues involved in putting together such an event internationally.

TOWARD GLOBAL FEMINISM

In re-reading the testimonies of crimes against women included in this book, I was struck by their timeliness. Unfortunately, most of this testimony could have been given this morning. In the years since the Tribunal, few of these crimes have diminished or changed significantly. What has changed is what we know about them. Through the work of many women, we know in greater detail about such crimes, and thus, we know that what was denounced so eloquently in Brussels is only a beginning list of crimes against women committed in the world today. We also know more about the investment that men have in committing such crimes and the lengths to which patriarchal institutions will go to prevent us from eradicating them.

Let me illustrate from my work over the past few years of organizing internationally against female sexual slavery, forced prostitution, and trafficking in women. At the Tribunal, there was testimony about Japan of tours organized for Japanese men to Korea for the sole purpose of prostitution. Today, we know that this phenomenon, called sex tourism, is a vast multi-national business operating in both industralized and developing countries that involves travel agencies, hotels, individual pimps, police and customs officials. It forces women, particularly from the Third World, into prostitution through deceptive advertising and as their only survival option, and it is often promoted by governments as a form of national economic development.[1] This and other forms of trafficking in women are highly organized, and it is difficult to find victims who have escaped and survived who are willing and able to testify about it publicly. It is a testament to the importance that women accorded the Tribunal that—without resources to assist women or to guarantee them safety after testifying—it was still able to attract so much first hand testimony from women who were often taking great risks.

While there is no other collection that better documents the breadth and scope of crimes against women and their everyday character throughout the world, it must be noted that one would have liked to see more testimony from women from Africa, Asia, and Latin America at the Tribunal. I am sure that the organizers shared this desire. In 1976, however, independent women's movement in most countries in those regions were just beginning to emerge and no doubt most did not have the information or resources to attend. This is perhaps one of the largest problems in organizing global feminist events independently of existing institutions such as governments or universities—women from poorer countries and groups do not usually have the resources to attend such events unless special funds are available. Thus, the Tribunal, unlike U.N. conferences where government money (and control) is committed, was not able to insure a significant Third World presence. This seems too often to be the price women have paid for our independence and is an issue that requires more attention if we are to create a truely global, yet maintain a truely independent feminist movement. Nevertheless, it is important to add that the testimonies included in the book of women from Third World countries, while small in number, do foreshadow the issues and concerns that have emerged in the past few years as feminism has grown more visible in those regions.

There has been no one independent international feminist event since the Tribunal that has tried to cover so much territory. Appropriately perhaps, most of the international events since then have been more specialized, examining certain issues in depth, such as the International Women's Health conferences in Europe in 1981 and 1983 sponsored by ISIS and Self-Health Movement of the CAMS (Commission for the Abolition of Sexual Mutiliations) conference in Dakar in 1982, which tackled issues of violence against women. Another important development has been regional conferences, such as the Feminist Encuentro for Latin America and the Caribbean held every two years which covers most of the same topics as the Tribunal but is limited to one region. In these more specialized and regional events, feminists have faced many of the same questions of process and structure and controversies over leadership and politics that arose in Brussels. The discussion of organizing approaches and problems in this book is therefore a valuable resource for anyone putting together a large conference and/or an international gathering. In fact, a book devoted entirely to such organizing efforts is long overdue if we are to learn from each other's experiences and progress more quickly in our ability to be both more global and more effective in our work.

Perhaps the most important reason why we need this book is that the women's movement in most countries is still much too nationalistic and limited in its knowledge of women's situations and efforts in other parts of the world. Interest in the variety of women's experiences and global feminism has grown over the past few years. However, the effects of nationalistic thinking and ethnocentric media still limit our understanding of each other. This book comes out of one of our movement's earliest attempts to overcome those limitations. It only partially succeeds since it is primarily based on women's voices in industrialized countries. However it is a very moving start on that path toward global feminism.

Global feminism requires in the first instance indigenous movements in various parts of the world that define and develop what feminism means in each local political and cultural context. Fortunately, in the past few years, we have seen an enormous growth in such groups. But global feminism is also about an attitude, a world view, a way of seeing each local setting that takes into account the global implications and inter-relatedness of our lives today. This attitude depends on both the recognition of the commonality of women's oppression—that is that women are an oppressed peoples whose condition under patriarchy is similar—and at the same time, an understanding that the forms of that oppression vary considerably according to the particular cultural, economic, political, racial, and geographic circumstances. The Tribunal proceeded from this dual assumption, and thus provides us with much needed data for understanding both of these crucial tenets of global feminism.

Another requirement of global feminism is that it take seriously the oppressions of women based on domination by race, class, religion, sexual preference, and nationality. These are not only added onto the oppression of women by sex but shape the very forms by which we experience that oppression. Thus, we cannot simply add up the types of oppression that we suffer one by one as independent factors, but we must develop a feminist analysis of the forms of oppression in their inter-relatedness. To do this, feminism must be seen as about more than just a limited number of so-called "women's issues." Feminism is not just a list of concerns—no matter how long the list. Rather, feminism is a perspective on life, on any issue, based on an understanding of the oppression of women and the patriarchal dynamic of domination expressed in sexual politics and also reflected in all the ways that one individual or group is set against another on the basis of differences and domination. We must take our understanding of feminism as a transformational perspective into an analysis of any issues affecting human life—violence and militarism; racism and colonialism; development and poverty; environment and health, etc.

Most international women's events have involved a struggle to establish a core of agreement about how feminism is understood.[2] Some have broken down over this point by trying to define feminism too narrowly or too nationalistically or by simply becoming too pedantic in their approach. The Tribunal succeeded in this regard by both addressing very specific concerns of women and by taking a broad view of feminism as dealing with the struggle of individual women for control over their lives as well as with the social changes necessary in all institutions that affect women. Thus, it affirmed a transformational view of feminism as a perspective on all issues as reflected in its inclusion of testimony about how crimes against women manifest themselves in the areas of racism and apartheid, of torture and imprisonment, of poverty and migration, as well as in rape, sexuality, and motherhood.

Feminism must also struggle to determine what it means to be global in our time. In many ways, nationalism is the ultimate expression of the patriarchal dynamic of domination with its battle by groups for control over each other on the basis of territory. Yet, nationalism has also symbolized the struggle of oppressed peoples against the control of other nations over them (colonialism and imperialism) and against the growing global control of us all by transnational corporations. It is in this context that feminists must consider how to move beyond national boundaries. While seeking to be global in our perspectives, we must resist the idea that any of us knows what is best for everyone and work instead toward visions that affirm diversity so long as that diversity is not based on the domination of any person or group. This demands first that we realize that "reality" does not look the same from different frames of reference and therefore the desires of all women will not look identical. This book helps us to understand this better by giving us voices from women in various groups and parts of the world who tell about their view of reality and their visions for change. We need to listen carefully to these women and to many more for it is only on the basis of understanding or diversity that we can hope to shape a global feminist movement.

The development of global feminism is not a luxury activity for an elite but a necessity for effective action. It is not about travel and exotic experiences. Global feminism is about learning how our lives are globally inter-related, even in their diversity, because the world that we live in operates and controls us in a global way already. Increasingly local problems are determined by global forces and if we remain ignorant of them, we will not only narrow our visions but also doom feminism to eventual failure. Our movement must be based on specific local issues and grass-roots organizing, but we need to put those activities into a global framework if we are to work effectively to end crimes against women. The proceedings of this Tribunal begin this process by locating very specific personal crimes against individual women within a framework of world wide patterns of female oppression.

FROM WOMEN'S BIRTHRITE TO FEMINIST RIGHTS

I was not present in Brussels for the International Tribunal on Crimes Against Women. I did however participate in a Tribunal held in New York City in February of 1976, one of several local Tribunals in the USA held in preparation for Brussels. I testified there on the crimes of persecution against lesbians. At that time, I emphasized that part of the persecution of lesbians was based precisely on our attempts not to be victims, that is on our refusal to accept patriarchy's limited definition of and control over our lives. In refusing to accept the self-definition and sexual / emotional expression expected of all women, lesbians—whether consciously or not—are forced to become active in shaping our own lives without the patriarchal society's approval. Some lesbians remain victims of this persecution and are destroyed by it, but in fighting this victimization, many become self-confident and are able to develop strength in being a self-defined woman rather than a victim. By whatever means a women does this, I believe that the only hope we have of ending the oppression of all women is in refusing to be defined and limited by our victimization. While engaging in the process of struggle to shape our own lives, we are better able also to challenge the structures that make women victims.

I call then on all women to come together and assert our right to self-definition in all areas of our lives and to become actors against patriarchy rather than to acquiesce in society's tendency to make us victims. If you look at what is said about a woman's lot in most cultures, it is as if victimization was seen as the inevitable birthrite of woman. It is our feminist right—indeed duty—to challenge and reject this assumption, to shape our own lives, and to put an end to the crimes against women that have so defined our existence for centuries.

There is no reason to repeat the litany of crimes against women, to endure the pain and suffering recorded in this book, except as a step toward challenging that victimization. Many would rather not look at these crimes and pretend that they will just fade away. But it is not possible to end them without facing them directly and knowing their full horror. This book helps us to do both. It forces us to see and to remember in detail the oppression of women in its many insidious forms. But it does not leave us there as it also suggests strategies for change. This record of the first International Tribunal on Crimes Against Women is thus a valuable resource for all who want to take action to end such crimes and to build a world based on an end to the domination and victimization of people in any form.

- Charlotte Bunch,
NYC, January, 1984

FOOTNOTES

1. See "International Feminism: Networking Against Female Sexual Slavery," A Report of the Global Feminist Workshop Against Trafficking in Women, Rotterdam, The Netherlands, 1983. Available from the International Women's Tribune Centre (IWTC), 777 UN Plaza, New York, NY 10017.
2. For more discussion of this issue at other conferences, see "Women in Development: A Resource Guide for Organization and Action," ISIS, C.P. 50 (Cornavin), 1211 Geneva 2, Switzerland, and "Developing Strategies for the Future: Feminist Perspectives," Reports of the International Feminist Workshops in Bangkok (1979) and Stony Point (1980), available from the IWTC.

ACKNOWLEDGMENTS

We would like to be able to acknowledge here all the women who made the International Tribunal possible. Unfortunately, we don't know who all of them are. Those we do know about include the members of the coordinating committee who, along with the Belgian committee, were responsible for organizing the Tribunal. The women on this committee were: Mariam Baz zanella from Italy; Lily Boeykens from Belgium; Grainne Farren, an Irish woman who lives in Paris; Erica Fischer from Austria; Maureen Giroux, an American who lives in Paris (and who, together with Grainne, had the task of coordinating the various Tribunal committees); Lydia Horton, an American who lives in Brussels; Mireya Gutierrez, a Mexican woman who lived in Paris (now in Mexico); Jennifer Morris from Britain (her alternate being Marguerite Russell from Britain; later Jennifer dropped out and Marguerite became a regular member of the committee); Diana Russell from the U.S.A.; and Marit Winnem from Norway, later replaced by Lisbet Natland from Norway.

The names of the national contacts, whose task it was to organize Tribunal groups in each country, are: Laurie Bebbington (Australia), Erica Fischer (Austria), Lydia Horton (Belgium, Kamma Langberg, Signe Sylvest (Denmark), Marguerite Russell (England), Margot de Labar, Catherine Duchemin (France), Angelika Dietrich, Tina Perincioli, Barbara Schleich (Germany), Margaret Papandreou (Greece), Loes Emck, Meta Van Beek (Holland), Katrin Didriksen (Iceland), Savitri Nigam (India), Nuala Fennell (Ireland), Marcia Freedman, Joanne Yaron (Israel), Carmela Paloschi (Italy), Yuko Ijichi (Japan), Mireya Gutierrez (Mexico), Lisbet Natland, Inger Sand (Norway), Margarida Avelar, Helena Balsa (Portugal), Maria Santiago (Puerto Rico), Anne Mayne (South Africa), Christina Alberdi (Spain), Monica Engberg (Sweden), Jeanne Dubois (Switzerland), Diana Russell (U.S.A.).

We asked these national contacts to let us know whose work in each country should be acknowledged. However, presumably because of insufficient time and summer vacations, we only heard from France. So it must be remembered that there are many, many names missing from these acknowledgments.

The women who volunteered their skills as interpreters during the Tribunal were: Reina Ascherman, Stella Capelluto, Trudy Ernst, Lulu Eertwegh, J. P. Jans, Marjolein Juda, Caroline Kunstenaar, Elka Markuszower, Luise Moffat, Joke Oud, Susan Pawlak, Francoise Proost, Annie Putzeys, Francoise Raynaud, Marleen Roekens, Linda Rosen, Rita Rutten, Aideen Ryan, Agnes Schoevaerts, Nora Thybaert, Anita Vandamme, Lieven Van Elsen, Annemarie Wesselink, Mia Willard, Inge Susan Worm. Other women may have volunteered without giving us their names.

The women who worked so hard during the Tribunal at the reception desk, in the secretariat, at the doors, and at the Brussels Office were: Michele Alexander, Therese Chonquerez, Marie-Louise Coppens, Ingrid De Bie, Hetty Diepenbrock, Lydia "Babe" Horton, Kerstin Huygelen, Francoise Palante, Claire Raick, Berthe-Marie Reichardt, Greta Richter, Rita Schlitz, Mija Symoens, Ann Vandenberghe.

Other women who helped in a great variety of ways were: Rika De

Backer, the Belgian Minister of Dutch Culture, who offered the Tribunal the complete and free use of the Palais des Congrès for five days; Lily Boeykens who allowed a ten-month occupation by the Tribunal of her office; Hetty Diepenbrock, who took on the responsibility of housing the women attending the Tribunal; Moni Van Look, who took on the thankless task of moderating at the Tribunal and whose input in the 6 weeks prior to it were immensely valuable; Joy Chamberlain, who organized an international video team, and who, together with Mary Sheridan, has produced a half-hour videotape on the Tribunal*; the all-women crew who came from Britain to film the Tribunal: Mira Hammermesh (Director), Madeleine Most (Assistant Director), Diane Tammes and Madeleine Most (Camera), Mary Dickenson and Judith Freeman (Sound); "The Flying Lesbians," a German womens' rock band who played twice during the Tribunal for free; Anne Delcoigne, the artist who designed the Tribunal posters and buttons.

The women who transcribed the Tribunal tapes (aside from Nicole who did all the French, English, Italian and Dutch transcription) were: Stella Capelluto, Ingrid De Bie, Eva Henstead, Rita Schiltz.

Acknowledgments for sizable financial contributions are included in the section on our budget.

With regard to the help we have received in putting this book together, we would like to express our appreciation to the many women who have made this enormous undertaking possible. Firstly we want to thank the women who translated all the materials that had been transcribed from the tapes. They are: Michèle Alexander, Michèle Bosc, Stella Capelluto, Hetty Diepenbrock, Elisabeth Dodge, Margaret Freedman, Eva Henstead, Jean McNeal, Susi Muncey, Rita Schiltz, Marina Van Acker, Liz Woodcraft, and Anne Barham, who also helped greatly with some of the last minute typing.

A big thanks to Lydia Horton for responding to our numerous requests for information and material when we were working on the book in London; to Hetty Diepenbrock for her helpfulness in trying to locate whatever it was we needed; to Lydia "Babe" Horton who made herself available to help us regardless of how tedious the task, or how odd the hours; to Ann Vandenberghe and Mimi Coppens for helping us out in so many ways, particularly Ann for so generously permitting us to take over her apartment as our place of work for three whole weeks; to Melinda Coleman for her remarkably swift and competent editing job; to Lily Boeykens and Grainne Farren, the two members of the coordinating

---

*This half inch black and white videotape includes excerpts of testimony, workshops, and resolutions; it also gives a general introduction to the oppression of women and some of the problems entailed in developing solutions. Available from Just Us Women Video Collective, P.O. Box 7034, Berkeley, Ca. 94707 U.S.A., or from Mary Sheridan c/o The Other Cinema, 12–14 Little Newport Street, London W.C.2., England.

**This venture was made possible by the generous support of two film schools, and a friendly film company, who loaned the equipment as well as the free work of the crew. The expenses of travel and the 5-day stay were covered by V.A.R.A., Dutch Television, who in exchange for a ten minute report about the Tribunal, supplied 12 rolls of colored film and the lab cost for the developing and printing of this film. Mira, whose past films include a fine hour-long movie "Two Women" shown on British television, still hopes to complete a film about the Tribunal but has not yet been able to get the necessary financial support.

committee selected to read the manuscript, for their feedback and suggestions, almost all of which we have accepted; to Laura Zelmachild, Marcia Keller, and Lydia Horton for their helpful suggestions; and finally, our biggest thanks of all to Bernadette Jiru, for the incredibly rapid and expert typing she did in the most pressured of circumstances, and all for free.

We are also grateful to the committee on faculty research at Mills College for contributing $400 to the costs of editing this book. And finally, we would like to thank Les Femmes Publishing house for their enthusiastic support of our work, and for recognizing the importance of making this book available as soon as humanly possible.

CONTENTS

Preface

Over 2,000 women from 40 countries participated in the first International Tribunal on Crimes Against Women, which took place at the Palais des Congrès in Brussels, Belgium, from March 4–8, ending on International Women's Day, 1976. Unable to be present in person, Simone de Beauvoir sent these inspiring words to open the five day global speak-out:

> Dear Sisters, I am deeply sorry that circumstances do not allow me to be among you today, but I am present in my heart. I hold this meeting to be a great historic event. In contrast to Mexico where women, directed by their political parties, by their nations, were only seeking to integrate Woman into a male society, you are gathered here to denounce the oppression to which women are subjected in this society.
>
> To fight this oppression, for a long time now women have been gathering together in many countries; but these various groups were more or less ignorant of one another. For the first time they will join together, and women coming from all over the world will become conscious of the scandal of their condition. You are right to consider this condition the source of real crimes: the position imposed on women, whether under institutionalized forms or not, leads to unacceptable attacks against the human being; against these, in the vast majority of cases, there is no legal recourse. That is why it is urgent that women should mobilize themselves to combat these crimes by their own means.
>
> Strengthened by your solidarity, you will develop defensive tactics, the first being precisely the one you will be using during these five days: talk to one another, talk to the world, bring to light the shameful truths that half of humanity is trying to cover up. The Tribunal is in itself a feat. It heralds more to come. I salute this Tribunal as being the start of a radical decolonization of women.

Simone de Beauvoir expanded these stirring words in an article published in *Nouvel Observateur,* March 1st. "It is not by chance," she wrote, "that this Tribunal will open after the closing of the preposterous Year of the Woman, organized by a male society to confuse women. The feminists gathering in Brussels intend to take their destiny into their own hands . . . They are not appointed by parties, nor by nations, nor by any political or economic group; it is as women that they will express themselves. In effect, under whatever regime, law, moral code, social environment in which they find themselves, all women suffer from a specific form of oppression: they will be meeting in Brussels to denounce it.

"The liberty of the woman is attacked when unwanted pregnancies are imposed upon her: her body is horribly mutilated when she is sterilized regardless of her opinion, when certain medical or psychological treatment is inflicted on her, when she is subjected to the cruel operation of excision practiced in many Islamic countries. On the economic level, women are the victims of a discrimination just as unacceptable as the racial discrimination condemned by society in the name of the Rights of Man; unpaid work in the home is extorted from her, the most thankless duties are wished upon her and her salary is less than her male counterpart.

"In spite of the inferior role which men assign to them, women are the privileged objects of their aggression. In nearly every country, including the United States and France, rape is on the increase; physical cruelty is considered quite normal as well as the psychological or frankly brutal attacks to which they are exposed if, for example, they walk by themselves on the street.

"This widespread violence is unanimously unrecognized and passed off in silence. Even against specific acts of violence—rape, assault and battery—there is, in the vast majority of cases, no recourse in a court of law. It seems that women are destined to suffer and to keep quiet about it.

"It is this destiny which will be forcibly rejected by the women gathering in Brussels. When I consider the impetus given to the process of decolonization of women by this Tribunal, I think that it must be regarded as a great historic event."

PARTICIPATING COUNTRIES

Australia, Austria, Belgium, Brazil, Canada, Chile, Denmark, Egypt, England, France, West Germany, Greece, Guinea, Holland, Iceland, India, Iran, Ireland, Israel, Italy, Japan, Korea, Luxembourg, Mexico, Mozambique, the Netherlands Antilles, Norway, Philippines, Portugal, Puerto Rico, Scotland, South Africa, Spain, Sweden, Switzerland, Syria, Taiwan, the U.S.A., Vietnam and Yemen.

INTRODUCTION

The idea of having an International Tribunal on Crimes Against Women was conceived at Femø, during an international feminist camp in Denmark, August, 1974, as a feminist response to the U.N.—declared International Women's Year. It was actually born at a workshop of the International Feminist Conference held in Frankfurt in November, 1974, attended by over 600 women. The idea was further developed the following spring at an international planning meeting in Paris where an eight-women coordinating committee was formed to organize the Tribunal.

SISTERHOOD IS POWERFUL! INTERNATIONAL SISTERHOOD IS MORE *POWERFUL!* This slogan captures well one of the assumptions of those who organized the International Tribunal. Our struggle must not only be conducted within nations, but across national boundaries. Nations are man-made. "I belong to No-mans-land" proclaimed one of the buttons sold at the Tribunal.

Unlike a traditional Tribunal there was no panel of judges at the International Tribunal on Crimes Against Women. We were all our own judges. Moreover, the women present completely rejected patriarchal definitions of crime; all man-made forms of women's oppression were seen as crimes. Most of the crimes testified about are not recognized as such by patriarchal nations, indeed many of the crimes are enforced by our patriarchal laws. For example, many countries still make it a crime to use contraception or to obtain an abortion. If laws were made to serve women's interests instead of men's then it would be a crime, for example, to force women to be mothers against our will by outlawing contraception and abortion, or making them inaccessible.

Personal testimony was emphasized because of the belief that it is through sharing our personal experiences of oppression that we become politicized and motivated to struggle against that oppression and the societal conditions producing it, rather than by engaging in abstract theoretical debates divorced from our personal experiences. This focus seemed even more appropriate as a first step in moving our struggle into an international context. For us to recognize our common interests as women in combating the crimes we are subjected to, should help us more easily transcend differences in nationality, as well as culture, class, race, sexual preference, age, religion and politics. In contrast to the IWY Tribune in Mexico where these differences led to constant disruptions, the Tribunal's focus on our common problems did help to unite us.

This is not to say that there was no analysis, and no discussion of solutions, nor that there were no conflicts! During the first four days, four hours each day were set aside for prepared and spontaneous testimony. Workshops on these crimes, and others requested by participants, followed. This was where solutions and analyses were discussed; their conclusions were brought to the plenary session on the fifth and final day in the form of resolutions and proposals for change.

The conflicts related to the role of the organizers, the offering of daily press conferences for the male media (except for the opening half hour, no men were permitted into the plenary sessions or workshops), and the emphasis on personal testimony. In Parts III and IV of this book these conflicts will be described in some detail. In addition Parts III and IV will provide further information on the herstory of the International Tribunal, how it was funded, who organized it, what the critics and the media had to say about it, and finally, what it achieved.

Perhaps I should introduce myself at this point. I live in Berkeley, California. I have lived in the U.S. since 1963, though I am still a British citizen. For the last six years I have been teaching sociology, particularly the sociology of sexism, the sociology of social movements, and the sociology of oppression, at a women's college in the San Francisco Bay Area. In the fall of 1974 I took a five-month leave of absence from my college in order to go to Western Europe to try to find out what was happening in the women's liberation movements there. I spent from as little as four days to as much as five weeks in the following ten countries: Holland, France, Denmark, Sweden, Norway, Germany, Italy, Portugal, Belgium and England. These travels included 12 days at Femø where I became excited by the idea of the International Tribunal, and I travelled from London to the Frankfurt Conference specially to work on it. In fact, I talked about the Tribunal and the Frankfurt Conference everywhere I went after Femø, and I found that the idea of the Tribunal caught the imagination of many sisters. It was disappointing, then, to find only two other sisters from the Femø workshop at the Frankfurt workshop on the Tribunal, and few of the sisters who had been excited by the idea during my travels after Femø. But, of course, not many women are in a position to take leaves of absence from their jobs to travel wherever their politics take them.

Nicole Van de Ven, a Belgian journalist whose mother tongue is French, also speaks English, Dutch, Italian and Farsi, the language of Iran, where she was an art critic for many years. Nicole only heard about the International Tribunal in early November, 1975. Immediately excited by the idea, Nicole became heavily involved from that day on, finally giving up her job so that she could work full time on the Tribunal. After it was over, Nicole had the responsibility of seeing that the entire proceedings of the International Tribunal were transcribed from the tapes. In fact, she made the transcriptions of all the material in French, English, Italian and Dutch. Then she had the task of organizing the translations from six different languages into English.

I had the task of writing all but the chapter on "The International Tribunal Through the Eyes of the Media," which was written by Nicole. Since English is my native tongue, I also did the editing of the testimony and resolutions, but all substantive editorial decisions were made jointly.

Since this book constitutes the English language edition of the proceedings of the International Tribunal, some readers might be interested to know how we came to do this task. In January, 1976, I included in a letter to all the Tribunal's national contacts a request that anyone interested in working on a documentary publication in any language, should inform the coordinating committee. By the end of the Tribunal, we knew of no one interested in doing this, aside from ourselves. So, we went ahead. A contract was drawn up between us and the coordinating committee (see Appendix 1) which spelled out the guidelines for our work, and the rights and obligations of the coordinating committee and ourselves in this undertaking. Most salient, perhaps, is that any profits that might have accrued to us "should be donated to the International Feminist Network (described in Part II) or such other feminist cause designated by the coordinating committee."

Diana E. H. Russell

Berkeley, California
August 1976

Part I

The International Tribunal Begins

♀ ♀ ♀ ♀ ♀

Women from at least 40 different countries participated in the International Tribunal. I say "at least 40" because news keeps reaching us of participants from countries we had not known about. However, the amount of participation varied enormously from country to country, from over 300 women attending from Germany, to the Greek participation which was simply a tape and written testimony. For most countries, at least one woman, usually two, often three and sometimes more, gave prepared testimony about crimes against women in their respective countries. However, women from Egypt, the Netherlands, Antilles, Philippines, Luxembourg, Sweden and Taiwan presented no testimony. In the case of Korea, Greece and Mozambique the testimony was read by a sister from another country. And the testimony from Guinea was brought by women from France, but never actually heard in the plenary session.

Unfortunately, we do not have an accurate record of the number of women attending from each country. Quite a number of women did not register, for various reasons: fears for their security, objections to the registration fee of $3.75 (which covered the entire duration of the Tribunal), objections to the focus on women's issues, or just plain confusion. Some women registered illegibly. Incomplete though it would have been, we intended to draw up a list of the participants; however, the Tribunal participants still in Belgium decided after the Tribunal was over not to do so for security reasons. The Iranian and Indian embassies had called the office to enquire about the participants from their countries, which information was, of course, not given them. Even if one woman were to find herself in difficulties as a result of such a list, that would be too much; so the records were burned. Incidently, I received a call from the Library of Congress in the United States asking me for a list of attendees to the Tribunal. I was unable to find out why this information was requested.

Nevertheless, of the countries with the largest attendance we can say that there were roughly 300 women from Germany, 60 from Spain, 50 from the U.S., 40 from England, 40 from France, 30 from Switzerland and over 100 from Belgium.

Aside from nationality, it is rather difficult to say very much about who attended the Tribunal. A Brazilian journalist asked women to raise their hands if they had taken leave from their paid jobs to be there and many hands were raised; still this doesn't tell us much about the social class of those attending. We can say however that most of the women were not well-known in or outside of the feminist world. The exceptions known to me are Alice

Schwarzer from Germany, Lidia Falcon from Spain, Nuala Fennell from Ireland, Marcia Freedman from Israel, all well-known feminists in their respective countries, and Delphine Seyrig, a French movie actress who is also feminist. But for the most part, it was not a conference of leaders. It was a conference in which the willingness to talk about having been a victim of sexist oppression was the best qualification going. Ordinary women, who are actually extraordinary women, most commonly held our attention. Many had trouble raising the money to get there. Housed for the most part in youth hostels reserved by the Belgian committee, wearing casual clothing typical of women in the movement, the participants were indeed very different from those attending the IWY Tribune in Mexico, or the World Congress in East Berlin. This applies also to the organizers of the Tribunal. Lily Boeykens from Belgium is the only feminist among the organizers who is well-known in her country. This may explain why *Time* and *Newsweek* decided not to print even one paragraph about the Tribunal, though they hired women reporters and photographers to cover the entire event. The first question from a *Time* spokesman was, "What are the women wearing?"—the second, "Where are they staying?" Indeed, the first question on the lips of most of the non-feminist media people was "Who are the important women who are here?" We answered, "There are 1,400"—the seating capacity of the largest hall at the Palais.

Although I had been one of those on the coordinating committee who wanted an eloquent radical feminist to open the Tribunal, I ended up thinking that Simone de Beauvoir's message, read by someone else, gave us the best of all worlds. We had a moving, profound and radical statement of what the Tribunal was about, but without awestruck fans.

While we had been prepared to offer simultaneous translation in French, Spanish, English, and Dutch, there was a strong demand for German as well, after the Tribunal had begun. Women able to interpret to German gladly joined the other volunteers. For five exhausting days these women offered continuous simultaneous translations in five languages. (At the IWY Tribune, only three languages were offered, while at the enormously well-financed World Congress in East Berlin, October 1975, the number was six.) However, we have to admit that the translations were sometimes far from perfect which must have contributed to the misunderstandings and confusions that occurred.

There were many reasons for the uneven quality of the simultaneous interpretation. Some of the interpreters were students from a School of Interpreters in Brussels and this was their first real-life experience of simultaneous translation. Most worked nine to ten hours a day in suffocating booths without ventilation. Most of the women testifying forgot to say in which language they would speak, some would switch languages while speaking, and many spoke very fast, some appearing unable to slow down even when requested, probably out of nervousness. I am sad to say that with a few exceptions, the interpreters were far more often to receive angry reproaches than thanks for performing a difficult task in hectic circumstances; this surely could not have helped their performance.

On Thursday March 4, half an hour before the start of the International Tribunal, a woman was busy typing up the program for that first day! (Some of the women told us only at the last minute the crimes they were going to testify about and we were only able to complete the program at the last minute.) At 10:30 A.M., half-an-hour late, the Tribunal opened at the Palais des Congres, an enormous convention facility right in the heart of Brussels, with Nicole Van de Ven reading Simone de Beauvoir's message quoted in the Preface. I gave a short herstory of the Tribunal, followed by an apology for our "being stuck up here in a God-like position" by Marquerite Russell.* She explained that we were unable to sit on the same level as the other participants because the wiring of the microphones at the Palais was built into the podium. Moreover, women at the back of the hall would have had difficulty in seeing the moderators and speakers had we been on the same level. The very hierarchical structure of the hall was to lead to a great deal of antagonism, and no amount of apology or explanation could stop the feeling that those up there wielded enormous power.

Marguerite went on to say that it had been the coordinating committee's goal to set up the International Tribunal, but that each woman now had to decide what its purpose was for her, and to use it in whatever way she could in her struggle against oppression. Next, Lydia Horton gave a financial report, and finally, Lily Boeykens explained our policy towards the press, and announced where workshops would take place in the afternoon. She also invited women to initiate workshops on any topics which interested them.

There were workshops on most of the crimes about which prepared testimony was given; for example, inaccessibility of abor-

---

*Several women assumed that we were related, but this is not the case. The view was also expressed that the whole coordinating committee was a little clique of friends. However, most of us hadn't known each other before working on the Tribunal, and many of us still do not know each other well.

tion, medical crimes, economic crimes, double oppression of Third World women, on wages-for-housework, rape, wife beating, prostitution, pornography, persecution of lesbians, violence toward women political prisoners; other workshops covered medical self-help, elderly women, single mothers, feminist therapy, capitalism and women's oppression, anti-feminist socialism (as in Mozambique), the setting up of an international newsletter, the outcome of the Tribunal and a critique of the Tribunal.*

The best organized group at the Tribunal must have been the women involved in medical self-help. They came from Australia, Austria, England, France, Italy, the U.S.A., and West Germany. Three or four times every day they put on a self-help presentation with slides, accommodating different language groups and even different sexual orientations (they had a special workshop for lesbians). Many women had their first experience of self-examination at the Tribunal, much to the consternation of some Palais personnel, at least one of whom complained to the manager that women were teaching each other how to masturbate.

The second most organized group were the lesbians, who initiated a workshop on the first day, and every day thereafter.

In the days that followed, one of the many unscheduled events of the Tribunal was a huge lesbian demonstration on Saturday afternoon. A bomb scare had forced us to clear the hall in the midst of testimony on rape. Finding no bomb, we returned half an hour later. About 150 women with signs pinned on their backs and fronts announcing "I am a Lesbian," "J'aime les Femmes," "Ich bin Lesbich," swarmed onto the stage, a few with their heads covered for anonymity, sang a lesbian song, and explained their action. Testimony on persecution of lesbians had been scheduled near the end of the Tribunal, but they did not want to be invisible until the last moment. They wanted everyone to realize that the lesbian presence at the Tribunal was considerable, that they had suffered many of the crimes already dis-

*I very much regret that this book cannot include a report on some of these workshops. They were not taped, summaries were not written up, and the coordinating committee was so busy behind the scenes—answering questions, dealing with crises, discussing policy, and preparing the daily program (this continued to be a night-before undertaking)—that we didn't get to attend the workshops. This was exceedingly disappointing. I personally was eager to attend the workshops on the outcome of the Tribunal in particular, to discuss with other women ways in which the Tribunal's impact might be maximized. I am sure the other members of the committee felt equally deprived at not being able to pursue their particular interests. Most of the informal reports about the workshops that I received indicated that they were excellent. Many brought resolutions, action proposals, and strategy statements to the final session of the Tribunal; some impression of the quality can be gleaned from Part II.

cussed, and that a lot of lesbian energy had gone into making the Tribunal happen.

The demonstration was mounted in a friendly spirit, but became confused in some women's minds with yet another unscheduled event. After one of the group gave a fairly lengthy statement about the oppression of lesbians (which is included in the section on the persecution of lesbians), a French woman, Annie, came to the microphone and started to speak about her opposition to hierarchy; she also wanted to denounce the leader of one of the French women's movement groups as well as the leader of a French Trotskyite women's group. What she said had nothing to do with the persecution of lesbians, or rape (which was what had been scheduled for that time). Her insistence on testifying at that moment caused a great deal of commotion.

Many women simply didn't want to hear her and told her so. Some had grown impatient with the unscheduled events, and wanted to hear the testimony of the rape victims. Some objected that what she had to say was irrelevant. And others simply didn't understand a word of what she was saying as the translation soon broke down in all the commotion. But Annie persisted. Although members of the coordinating committee were on the platform, we had long since ceased to try to control what was happening. Other exasperated women came up onto the stage, at first trying to argue with her, and then trying to take the microphone away from her. She held on to it fiercely however, and managed to get herself into a fairly unreachable position, all the while continuing her denunciations. A woman then tried to wrench the microphone from her forcibly and Annie responded in kind. Finally the microphone was turned off. Annie continued. There was constant tumult in the hall, not all of it directed against Annie by any means. Many women were outraged at the way she was being treated. The perceptions of this incident varied immensely: some saw her as violently aggressive, others as the victim of violent aggression. Finally, Annie was persuaded to announce a workshop to be held immediately for those who wanted to hear more of what she had to say, and she left the platform.

Not permanently, however! The incident aroused tremendous feelings, and some women demanded that she be given time to speak again. This happened on the last day, after which a woman from one of the groups that Annie had attacked was given time to reply. She said Annie's accusations were slander not worthy of comment. None of these speeches have been included in this book since they seemed to relate more to conflicts within the French women's movement.

For many women the most enjoyable events of the Tribunal were two parties on Saturday and Sunday nights. Some coordinating committee members felt that it was important to have some good social times together, and so we had invited The Flying Lesbians, an extremely popular feminist seven-piece rock band from Germany, to play once or twice during the Tribunal.

While they were willing to play for free, as they always do for feminist events, they did need their transport costs. Because of our financial situation, we had delayed too long to rent a large enough hall for a party. So we ended up having two parties over the weekend in the far-too-small women's center, Maison des Femmes. Hundreds of women, gay and straight, danced exuberantly to The Flying Lesbians' music, and the crushed conditions didn't seem to bother anyone. In situations where language and cultural differences can so obstruct communication and feelings of solidarity, music, singing, and dance can be much more effective. The Maison des Femmes will never be the same after its first all-women dance, and the same is true for some of the partying women.

Testimony and Reports

CHAPTER 1

Forced Motherhood

The right of women in and outside of marriage to choose not to have children is still not recognized in many countries. Consequently, millions of unwanted children are born, and thousands upon thousands of women die every year from botched abortions. The countries represented by testimonies about this are: Ireland, Portugal, Belgium, Holland, Norway, Austria and Britain. Spontaneous testimony follows from Britain, Belgium, France, Israel, Switzerland and Canada.

Witness 1: Ireland*

While Europe is looking for the legalization of abortion, we in Ireland, as always behind the times, are looking for the legalization of contraception. Irish women are denied this right. It is known in Ireland as "artificial family planning." It is a criminal offense to sell contraceptives, to advertize them, or to sell literature on or even related to them. The only methods of family planning legally permissible are those advocated by the Catholic Church: abstention and the rhythm method. Despite this fact, 38,000 Irish women were using the pill in February 1974 because the pill, by typical Irish logic, can be prescribed as a "cycle regulator." Ireland should be listed in the Guiness Book of Records for the highest number of women in the world suffering from irregular periods!

A survey published in 1974 has shown that 68% of women of childbearing age wish to have the sale of contraceptives legalized in Ireland. In 1968, in Teheran, Ireland voted in favor of the United Nations Human Rights Convention which stated that couples should have the right to decide freely the number and spacing of their children, and the right to adequate information and education in this respect. Accordingly, the Irish High Court

*To accomodate those women who might prefer to remain anonymous, we have excluded all names except where we are sure that the woman is seeking publicity or in cases which have already been in the public eye.

decided last year that women could have artificial methods of birth control. It then became legal to *import* contraceptives into the country, but not to *advertise* them, and not to *sell* them. Thus in Ireland you can get contraceptives if you know about them, and if you can find out where to get them, but you can't find out where to get them if you don't know what they are in the first place! And you can't buy them because it is an offense to sell things which cannot be told about publicly, and which cannot be publicly found. The only way therefore to acquire imported contraceptives is in private family planning clinics, of which there are only a few, located in the three main cities. Thus, women in rural areas are denied even this means of contraception.

Efforts to introduce a family planning bill in the Irish Parliament last year—a bill which would have allowed free contraception to married couples only—was defeated by both Church and State. The Irish Prime Minister voted against the bill introduced by his own Minister of Justice, and the Catholic Archbishop of Ireland declared that artificial birth control is wrong, not just for Catholics, but for Protestants and atheists.

Ireland has the highest birth rate in Europe and the worst housing situation. It is mothers in the homes who suffer most from the denial of contraceptives, and many Irish women are forced to use abortion as a means of contraception, although abortion is of course also illegal. Because of the denial of contraception and the stigma attached in Ireland to the so-called unmarried mother, thousands of single Irish women are forced to go to Britain each year to seek abortions. Statistics show that 8,000 unmarried Irish women have had abortions in England since 1968. In 1973 one of every one hundred single Irish women went to Britain to have an abortion.

Witness 2: Portugal

Even though there are about 180,000 abortions a year, abortion is illegal in Portugal and liable to jail sentences of 2 to 8 years. The law dates from 1886 and is still in force. It punishes either the woman who aborts or the person who aborted her, as well as those who are considered accomplices. The conditions under which these abortions take place explain why about 2,000 women die every year as a consequence of abortion practices. Despair, and the firm decision of women who are unable, or unwilling, to have more children, leads them to the most diverse and most rudimentary procedures. When poverty and ignorance are equally great, women have recourse only through cabbage stems, parsley stems, knitting needles. If material means and the setting permit, women pay amateurs, or in the best of circumstances, midwives, who perform abortions for 1,500–4,00 escudos ($54–$143)* This sum is the equivalent of a month's salary for the majority of Portuguese workers. The law against abortion is enforced principally vis-à-vis those classes which are economically weakest and culturally the least enlightened. This situation has not changed since the revolution of April, 1974.

We know of women who have had more than 30 abortions during their lifetimes. In order to economize, women save on antibiotics, anesthetics and sanitary conditions. Clandestine abortions are supported by social hypocrisy and those who find it profitable. The clandestine way in which abortion is practiced in Portugal represents a further humiliation and unnecessary danger for women. The consequences are known: hemorrhage, septicemia, perforation of the uterus, sterility, and often death. Recently a doctor from Oporto stated: "In the main hospital of Oporto there are annually more than 1000 cases of abortion whose consequences would have been tragic if these women had not had recourse to our services." And this only in one hospital!

Since 1964, 223 women were sentenced, 134 for having aborted and 69 for having performed abortions. Among the condemned there was only one doctor; most were midwives, seamstresses, domestics. The majority had no profession. As for those who were aborted, most had no employment, immediately followed by domestic workers and agricultural workers. A woman journalist described a case which occurred in the central women's prison. As a result of being denounced, a woman was arrested several years after having aborted. At the time she was married and the mother of two children. Nevertheless, she underwent two years of prison. Several years after she was released, she again became pregnant. Fearing to have another abortion and thus face arrest again, the woman killed herself.

Three journalists, including myself, decided to make a film entitled: *Abortion is Not A Crime*. In this film there was a description of the vacuum aspiration method of abortion practiced by a group which performs free abortions at home on request. The episode was part of a community political action. The program was presented last February 4th. It provoked a wave of protest from rightwing organizations which cried, "Scandal!" and from the Catholic church. The Medical Association considered this

---

*Throughout this book conversion into dollars is calculated according to the exchange rate that applied on March 4, 1976.

method and its application as charlatanism. They accused the television producers of being imposters, anti-science, and common law criminals. Political parties such as the Christian Democrats and the Centrist Social Democrats asserted the program encouraged crime, and as such the people responsible for it should be punished. The popular Democrat party also took a position against condoning illegal abortions, and against legalizing the practice. The church, through the Council of Bishops, protested against the program as did the Catholic Council of Laymen who argued that the program incited crime. Television critics and the press were hostile to the program. Only a leftist critic dared to praise the program, considering it to be very courageous, and joined in solidarity with our fight. The parties of the left kept completely silent in this affair, including the Socialist Party, even though it is the only party of the left which mentioned the legalization of abortion in its platform. Only the weekly *Mulher* and a group concerned with abortion took a position in our favor.

The television network, having received such violent criticism for having presented the program, organized a televised debate between two doctors, a sociologist, a priest and the Prosecutor General of the Republic. All agreed the law on abortion should be anulled, but since it exists, they said it should be obeyed. The Prosecutor General ordered the judicial police to open an inquiry with a view to holding a trial of the journalists responsible for the program, the TV team which had made the film, and the television network itself for having shown the film. We still don't know the outcome of this affair. Considering the reaction of the right and the silence of the left, we fear a show trial will be used to postpone the question of the legalization or liberalization of abortion.

Despite the revolutionary movement, a cultural revolution is far from taking place in Portugal. The situation of the woman remains the same as it was before the 25th of April, 1974. What has happened on the issue of abortion is only one example. We are counting on the solidarity of the women of the whole world in order to advance the Portuguese women's liberation movement. As journalists we need your solidarity in order to continue our denunciation of prejudice and the crimes which weigh on women.

Witness 3: Belgium

In Belgium, the penal code of 1967, which is still in force, forbids abortion completely. One who disobeys the law is liable to serious sanctions. A prison sentence from two to five years is required for the woman who aborts voluntarily. The person who performs the abortion risks a similar sentence. Everyone who helps a woman to procure an abortion—by giving her an address for example, or supplying her with the money for an abortion, or by accompanying her to the place where she can obtain an abortion—is equally liable to legal sanctions. Some people risk even more serious penalties. Specialists such as doctors, midwives and pharmacists who, at the request of a woman, perform an abortion, risk sentences from 10 to 15 years. Save for a few idealists, doctors willing to run the risk ask exhorbitant prices. A medically guaranteed abortion costs, with few exceptions, between 30,000 and 50,000 Belgian francs ($750–$1250). So, this is the law. What of the practice?

To estimate the number of abortions is very difficult. Estimates range from 20,000 to 400,000 a year. The figure most cited is 40,000. Taking into consideration that an abortion usually involves several people, the woman, her partner, the abortionist, friends, and the family, we can see that a considerable part of the population is confronted with this problem each year, even though only a few are prosecuted. Most abortions come to the attention of the justice department by chance, for example, through a suspicious death or by anonymous letters motivated by vengeance. Many abortions however are not prosecuted because they take place abroad in countries like Great Britain, Switzerland, and Poland; although interruption of pregnancy performed in Holland, for example, where abortion is illegal, may be prosecuted in Belgium. However, those who have money or connections can procure abortions abroad with impunity as well as more readily evade the law. Between 1961 and 1969 there were about 150 prosecutions for abortion each year of which on average 125 were convicted, three quarters getting a suspended sentence and probation.

In order to reduce conflicts over abortion within and among political parties, the government set up an ethical committee in 1974. Its task is, among other things, to give advice on possible modifications of the abortion law. The work of this committee was to be completed in October 1975. To date, nothing has been heard. The committee members have been silent now for more than a year. But from a commission composed mainly of male jurists and doctors, women can hardly expect salvation.

Witness 4: Holland

In the Netherlands we have a law dating from 1886 which states that the woman and the doctor who treats her are guilty of a criminal act in the case of abortion. Much struggle and many demonstrations were necessary before it became possible, in spite of the law, for women to obtain abortions in a clinic.

Since 1970 the actions of the Dolle Mina (a Dutch Women's Liberation group) have drawn a lot of attention. Their first action was in March 1970; a group of Minas strolled into a convention of gynecologists. Once inside, they proceeded to lift their blouses to show, written on their stomachs, the slogan BAAS IN EIGEN BUIK—literally translated—BOSS OF OUR BELLY! This action aroused enormous interest in the problem. In November 1970, the book *Dolle Mina Denounces . . .* was published. In this book women told of their own deplorable experiences with abortions; the book was sent to all general practitioners and gynecologists. Accusations were directed at those who refused to help women obtain abortions, those who were working against reform, men and women who were opposed to the use of contraceptives, doctors who refused contraceptive use to minors, and parents who neglected the sex education of their children.

In November 1971 women's action groups appealed in a T.V. broadcast to all general practitioners and gynecologists to recognize women's right to abortion. In February 1972 a massive demonstration was held in Utrecht. The result of all these actions was that there are now thirteen abortion clinics in the Netherlands, where women can be helped in a medically responsible manner in spite of the law against abortion.

Even with the law against abortion, the entire abortion problem would have been solved if politicians had let well enough alone; now, unfortunately, there are three different abortion laws waiting to be considered, none of which will obtain a majority vote in parliament. Women must now keep fighting to prevent abortion laws from becoming a political power game going on above our heads, and without our having a say in the matter. Of the three proposals, the only one acceptable is that of the Labor Party. This states that abortion may take place after consultation with a doctor. The other two proposals are totally unacceptable since they restrict both the woman and the doctor. Their implementation would also mean that women from other countries would no longer, or seldom, be helped. Many Dutch women's organizations are now united in the committee—Wij Vrouwen Eisen, We Women Demand!—to carry on the struggle together.

We demand: Abortion out of the penal code; Abortion through the national health organization; the woman decides!

Witness 5: Norway

After more than 60 years of struggle, Norwegian women still have not obtained the right to decide for themselves whether they want to give birth to a child or not. At the last parliamentary elections the Social Democratic Party, now in power, and the left-wing Socialists, put abortion on demand on their respective programs. The non-socialist parties campaigned to keep the existing law and to make it even stricter. The bill that would give women the right to choose was rejected, and the law that was passed was a compromise which will not bring any improvement in the situation of women who want their pregnancies terminated.

In 1975 when the bill which was to give women freedom of choice was put before the parliament it provoked violent reactions in conservative and religious circles. A veritable campaign was launched to fight women who wanted abortions and to throw suspicion on those who were struggling to get the new law passed. Women asking for abortions were presented as criminals, and some people even drew a parallel between their action and the extermination of the sick and handicapped under Hitler. The circles that condem abortion on demand are at the same time strongly opposed to contraception and to any information on the subject being made available.

At the parliamentary elections of 1977 the non-socialist parties will have a chance of getting a majority. Powerful pressure groups will do their best to introduce stricter legislation. Every year in Norway 1,400 women have their requests for abortions turned down. Still 30–40% of them do not give birth to a child. The ones who have enough money have legal abortions abroad; the poorer woman have them illegally in Norway.

Our new abortion law is no improvement at all on the previous law. The woman has to appear before a panel of doctors which has total power to decide the outcome of her request. The new element in the law is that the woman has the right to address herself directly to the panel whereas before she had to go through a doctor. The new law also allows abortion on social grounds, but there is nothing new in this since under the old law a certain number of social cases were accepted. The crucial point is that the woman still has to leave the decision to a committee of doctors and thus runs the risk, as before, of having her request treated very differently depending on whom she deals with.

The most serious objections to the new law in Norway are as follows. Firstly, the law represents a total negation of the woman's responsibility. It takes away her right to decide whether she wants to have a child or not. Secondly, it allows for different interpretations of acceptable grounds for abortion, and consequently it allows different applications. The moral or religious attitude of the doctors will often determine whether or not the woman can have an abortion. Thirdly, the law is geographically discriminatory: the chances of a request succeeding are much greater in or around the capital than in the rest of the country. Fourthly, it discriminates on economic and social grounds. Research has shown that it is predominantly those from economically and socially underpriviledged groups who ask for abortions.

It will probably be a long time before we have abortion on demand in Norway.

Witnesses 6 and 7 : Austria

After centuries of the strictest abortion prohibition in Austria, new abortion legislation came into force on January 1, 1975. Abortion is not punishable if it is carried out within the first three months of pregnancy, provided the woman previously consults a medical doctor. However, the doctor, as well as the entire medical profession, may refuse to carry out abortions without stating the reasons.

This law, massively opposed by the Catholic Church, might appear progressive and feasible. Unfortunately, reality is quite different. I will start by telling you about the situation in the hospitals.

Only a very small percentage of hospitals carry out abortions at all (13 out of 85 in the whole of Austria, 5 of them in Vienna). In the West of Austria (Vorarlberg, Tirol, Salzburg) there is not a single hospital carrying out abortions officially. That is partly due to the fact that so many of the head doctors of the gynecological departments have from the very start prohibited abortions to be carried out in their hospitals, since they cannot reconcile it with their "consciences." Even if some doctors might be prepared to do it individually, they cannot do so against the will of the head doctor. Numerous hospitals are maintained by the Church, in which case the prohibition comes directly from them. Smaller district hospitals, which are maintained by local authorities dominated by the conservative party, prohibit abortion via their local authority councils.

But even where there is no direct influence in the form of prohibitions, many difficulties arise. The Government which has enacted the law, does not bother about its implementation. Even in federal hospitals, not one new post for doctors and nurses has been created nor one extra hospital bed has been added, although it was well-known that 100,000 to 150,000 women are forced to abort in Austria every year.

Hence, where abortions are carried out, this is done at the expense of the hospital staff who must continually work overtime. They are therefore not particularly friendly towards the patients concerned. The quality of the medical care is also affected. Only in very few hospitals do vacuum aspirators exist, which means that the main form of abortion in Austria is curettage, often without anaesthetics "otherwise the woman will be here again after two months." The necessary stay of one to two days in the hospital after the curettage is usually not possible for lack of beds. In most of the hospitals the women are told right upon reception that no second abortion will be given—they needn't come a second time. The waiting time is between three and six weeks, so that women who do not realize immediately that they are pregnant, have nearly no chance of getting an abortion in time. The costs range from 700 Austrian shillings ($38) for vacuum aspiration for out-patients, up to 2,500 Austrian shillings ($136) for curettage with anaesthetics and hospital stay. Social security does not pay anything for the operation. Women wishing to obtain abortions in hospitals situated in other provinces than their own are regularly refused. This applies in particular to Vienna, the capital.

Under the circumstances just described it is obvious that the majority of women have no other choice than to have their abortions done by private doctors, because they might otherwise run the risk of missing the three months time limit and become punishable by the law. In many cases doctors whose "conscience" forbids them to carry out abortions in hospitals are highly willing to do the same operation during their private consultation hours. It also happens quite often that doctors send women away from the hospital for having exceeded the three months period, but let them know on the sly that privately they would very well be prepared to do it. Such an operation costs at least 8000 Austrian shillings ($434).

The Chamber of Medical Doctors, an influential professional organization, openly declared their position against abortion.

Women are more and more pushed into the role of beggars, and get the feeling that an abortion is an act of mercy on the part of the doctor. That, of course, raises the prices.

The consultation centers are official centers staffed with social workers and psychologists. Here women are talked out of having an abortion, and informed about government supports and social services, which are greatly praised. However, child allowance is by no means sufficient to raise a child unburdened, apart from which there are other reasons not to want a child. The step from the consultation center to a hospital lies in the hands of the benevolence of the consulting person. Women who can express themselves more easily have a better chance of succeeding. Similarly, women from marginal social strata, whose children the state doesn't want anyway, are more likely to get permission to abort. However, in the provinces, especially in the west, the consultation centers are mainly run by Catholic Church organizations, though financed by the Government. No abortions can be obtained from such centers.

The Austrian birth rate has been sinking continuously for years and in 1973, for the first time in decades, it fell below the death rate. Neither the state nor the economy want a sinking birth rate, as taxpayers and workers are needed. Therefore, the government admits openly that the law, and above all, the consulting mechanism are expected to yield an increase in the birth rate. The Federal Chancellor also declared that no woman had a legal right to an abortion. Other members of the government have explained the necessity for women seeking an abortion to consult a doctor, by saying that women in such a situation were not capable for deciding for themselves.

♀ ♀ ♀ ♀ ♀

I would like to speak about the influence of the church on our abortion law. For over a year, we have had in Austria the so-called *Fristenl ·osung* which means that we are allowed to abort within the first three months. Although this "Fristenlösung" does not function particularly well because there are far too few beds available, and because very many doctors refuse to do abortions. The church has tried to cancel even this small relief for us. They have tried to bring an unbelievably confused, misogynist and legally absurd law into parliament and unfortunately, they have succeeded. In this law it requires that every women who aborts will be persecuted if she does not find herself in an unavoidable emergency situation. Whether her situation was such an emergency or not is to be established by a judge after every abortion is performed. If the judge does not establish that it was an emergency, she will be punished, the doctor will be punished and the nurses will be punished. If it is established that it was an emergency situation then the man is punished as the cause of it. That means that in every case, the aborting woman or the father of the aborted embryo is condemned.

This law is not in force at present. It will be dealt with in our parliament in just over a month's time.

Witness 8: England*

I am shaking like a leaf. But I would very much rather speak to you as I am doing now, than go to an English doctor for an abortion! Because, while it is generally believed that we have a liberal law, in fact the English abortion law is pernicious. It is very oppressive to women. Women have to beg for an abortion. Abortion is only legal provided two doctors are prepared to do it. So this gives doctors a marvelous opportunity to play God, which happens all the time. Women are meeting punitive paternalistic and moralistic attitudes from doctors. Some women have gone to doctors for abortions and have been turned away because they are considered to be immoral and deserving punishment. Other women have been told: "Don't be silly. One more child won't make any difference." The people who suffer the most in our country are, of course, working class women, because middle-class women can go and pay for abortions in the private sector.

Now I will tell you about my personal experience with abortion and problems with different methods of birth control.

I married in 1966 immediately after qualifying as a teacher. By that time I had been advised against the pill because of varicose veins and a family history of thrombosis. I could not use the coil because those available at the time could not be used by women who'd not had a baby. I tried the diaphragm, but I hated it, so my husband used a sheath which I sometimes combined with pessaries. I also took risks, usually during the "safe period."

When I became pregnant I'd never even heard of abortion, having been brought up in a Roman Catholic convent. So I had the child. My husband's income was quite inadequate; he was doing post-graduate studies at the time and we could not find

*The personal part of this testimony was only available at the Tribunal in so summary a form that we invited the witness to expand on it since so little personal testimony was available on this topic.

accomodation when returning to Liverpool from Bristol. So I lived in a hotel room with my baby, while my husband lived at work. Finally we were forced to take a flat beyond our income. I found a child-minder and a part-time teaching job, but in the second term I became pregnant again. I discovered later that I had no "safe period" as I have a 21 day menstrual cycle and ovulate before the end of it.

I discussed abortion with a friend. We did not know that abortion was then legal. She had had a backstreet abortion and I couldn't face that, nor could we afford it. I decided to continue my pregnancy so that the first child would have company. Our family would then be complete, and my husband felt OK about having a vasectomy.

I had a difficult second pregnancy. My veins were painful, and I felt isolated and resentful. I felt people are entitled to have a decent sex-life, but it seemed that ours was ruined. I went back to part-time teaching but I was often really exhausted with having to take care of my two children as well. The hospital where I had my second child had strongly advised me against using the coil, but offered no alternatives. So, I became pregnant again. I was advised by a feminist doctor how to approach the National Health Service. She said that since I was married with only two children and since my husband was in the professional class with good future prospects, I would need to put on a good performance when stating my case.

I first saw a junior doctor or registrar who examined me physically and whose unsympathetic and superior attitude paved the way for my good performance. I was in tears when taken to a psychiatrist who, after about three minutes discussion, advised *electrical shock treatment.* I was reduced to hysteria by this suggestion, not just for myself, but because it occured to me that many women might have actually had damaging psychiatric treatment when all they wanted was an abortion. I was taken to a medical social worker who had my husband with her and who appeared to feel sorry for this hard-done-by young man in a similar profession to hers. She clearly regarded me as inadequate, and asked irrelevant questions like, "What little things do you do for your husband?"

I was finally taken to the gynecologist who was surrounded by students. They had obviously been discussing my case. The gynecologist said they'd decided to *grant* me an abortion, but that I should be sterilized. I said that my husband was prepared to have a vasectomy. The gynecologist said my husband was too young for that. This double standard infuriated me. I felt like a used and now useless old hag. I knew through the women's liberation movement that having sterilization at the same time as an abortion increased the dangers, and had ended in death for some women. So I appeased the gynecologist by saying I would have one when I'd recovered from the abortion.

Several women in the ward where I had my abortion had had experiences of the medical profession that were just as ghastly as mine. I have never regretted the abortion. I *have* regretted both my marriage and having children.

Witness 9: England

I got a letter from a sister in London who was unable to attend the Tribunal, and which I will read to you.

> It was recently my misfortune to be a patient in a Victoria hospital in Nottinghamshire. I had a miscarriage. While I was there, I was shocked and angered by the sufferings of a 16 year-old girl who was being given an abortion. She had requested termination at an early stage of her pregnancy but the gynecological consultant at this hospital had refused to allow termination to take place before she was 18 weeks pregnant. She told me he had said: "If silly girls like you are going to play around with sex, you are going to pay for it.
>
> Abortion was induced by a catheter inserted into the uterus under general anaesthesia. Her labor lasted for 25 hours. (In fact I left the hospital before she had expelled the afterbirth.) No painkilling drugs were given her until she had been in labor for about 18 hours when an injection was given in response to other patients' pleading on her behalf. The argument given for denying her painkilling drugs was that they would slow down the uterine contractions and prolong the whole process. I have never heard this argument used against the administration of painkillers to women in childbirth, and doctors I have spoken to since about this say there is no medical foundation for this argument. They are also of the opinion that the contractions which happen at 18 weeks are as strong and as painful as those of a full-term pregnancy. I am quite sure myself that this young girl was suffering very intense pain indeed. The previous night I had myself spontaneously aborted and I could tell from her reactions what kind and degree of pain she was having.
>
> I consider the use of abortion in this primitive way—by delaying until a long, painful and dangerous process is necessary, and then denying painkillers—to be a hideous crime against women, and I would like the attention of the conference drawn to this practice. If doctors wish to disapprove of young people having sex, they should remember it takes two to make a baby but they are enpowered to punish physically only one. Severe beating would have been a far

milder form of physical punishment than what that young girl had to endure. We must through our protest try to insure that her suffering was not in vain.

Witness 10: Belgium

I want to testify about an experience I had with a Belgian doctor. I had been raped and was afraid that I was pregnant. Because I was unable to walk the next day, I asked my mother to call a doctor to prescribe the "morning after" pill, for I knew that it had to be done within 36 hours. My mother called a doctor she knew well, and he came and examined me and told me that my hymen had not been ripped and that therefore nothing could have happened. I knew for a fact that my hymen was long gone, for I had had intercourse regularly for the past two years, so the doctor had simply made a wrong diagnosis or perhaps he did not want to upset me. Then he prescribed what I thought to be the "morning after" pill, although I was rather puzzled when he told me that I should wait four days before taking it. Because I didn't feel well and could not leave the house I did what he told me and waited the four days. But nothing happened. I thought it all very strange and went to some women friends for advice. There I learned that it wasn't the "morning after" pill that he had given me, but just some medicine to bring on my period a bit earlier in case I wasn't pregnant.

Not only is abortion prohibited in Belgium, but you cannot even get the "morning after" pill when you have been raped and fear pregnancy.

Witness 11: Belgium

I am also Belgian and I have come to testify about something that happened to me personally. It happened ten years ago. I was a student with little money. I made love without contraception. I became pregnant by a man with whom I had been living for two years. This man refused to give me money. Other friends refused also; they said that I should have been more careful. Nevertheless I found a doctor who did not ask for too much money for an abortion. The first time he operated nothing happened. I went back after one week like a thief in the night, telling my parents: "I am going out, I am going to a dance." It was about ten or eleven o'clock at night. The doctor refused to give me an anesthetic. He did a curettage which was very, very painful.

I have told my story as a personal plea for a revision of the law in Belgium. We must try to get free abortion on demand. We must also strive for better contraceptives and a change in attitudes. As I started this testimony, I had a hard time talking about my abortion, even after 10 years. It took me about 8 years to get over it. I think a very important part of the pain is the fact that you're alone with your problem, that you can't talk to anyone about it because it is a taboo subject, and because you are afriad of the consequences, legal and otherwise.

Witness 12: Italy *

The struggle of Italian women for abortion erupted in the spring of 1975. The big international demonstration for free abortion on demand, which took place on the 6th of December, saw in the streets of Rome 25,000 women determined not to suffer the violence of the system any longer.

Italy has more illegal abortions than most other countries—about 3 million a year. It also has the greatest financial exploitation of women's bodies; an illegal abortion performed by a doctor in a private clinic costs up to 1½ million lira ($935). The leaders of the movement for free abortion on demand have been denounced and imprisoned. In answer to these repressions there were big demonstrations, and a strong awakening of the majority of women represents the culmination point of this struggle.

Women from the Communist Feminist Collective in Rome, like other Italian feminist groups, see in the struggle for free abortion an opportunity to mobilize women, as well as a necessary step by which to express their refusal of the dreadful exploitation of their lives and bodies. We want to forge a link between the feminist practice of the militant women, and the daily plight of millions of Italian women. That's how a videotape project, called "Rome, Abortion—Women Speak" came to life. Our purpose has been to give women from different social conditions in Italy the possibility to be heard through the video-recorder.

R. is a young Roman woman working part-time. During the recording, a strong and intimate relationship grew between her and us; this feeling intensified her evident need to talk, for the first time, about the nightmare and the "shame" that her abortion

*This testimony was obtained from a letter. These women had wanted to show their videotape at the Tribunal, however we had been told there were no facilities for showing videotapes at the Palais.

has been for her, and its consequences.

When *R.* tells us about her abortion, when she confesses the fears and inhibitions which she still has, when she talks about her constant sexual dissatisfaction, and when she reveals her state of submission, she also discloses the plight of each woman, dispossessed of her own body, submitting to the rules of a system which reduces her to a reproductive function or an object of pleasure. Her story not only denounces the horror of abortion but also reveals the impossibility to live our body, our sexuality.

We also included in our film the voices of proletarian women for whom abortion is an experience which recurs throughout their child-bearing lives and which has therefore become quite natural; also those of lower middle-class women who, as soon as they have access to the privileges of the dominating class, adopt the bourgeois values, and express themselves according to the prejudices of that class, even though these are obviously against women.

Alternate solutions to the problem of illegal abortion are being sought everywhere in Italy. Groups of women who practice self-help raise the question of the neutrality and objectivity of medical science which always acts for the dominating class and against women. Abortion, performed by women, de-mystifies the medical power over women's bodies. The Karman method* is commonly used in Italy nowadays, still illicitly, but amidst women's organizations it is growing more common.

Thanks to the big mass movement which emerged around this problem, a bill (resulting from the compromise between the Christian Democrats and the Italian Communist Party) is going through parliament. It is yet again a bill which does not allow the woman to make decisions regarding her own body, delegating this power to the constitutional authorities. We must still undertake a major struggle to fight against such a reformist and repressive attempt. Abortion does not mean women's liberation, but the struggle for abortion can become a unifying and awakening moment for all women.

Witness 13: France

I would like to make an announcement on behalf of the six women of the MLAC (*Mouvement pour la Libéralisation de l'Avortement et des Contraceptifs*—Movement for the Liberal-

*Karman and his method of abortion is being denounced by feminist self-help groups in the U.S. today.

ization of Abortion and Contraceptives) of Aix-en-Provence, who have been charged with attempted abortion. Last year, women's groups and the MLAC fought hard and forced the government to bring in a more liberal abortion law. But abortion is still illegal for minors and immigrants without papers. Also no money has been given to hospitals to enable them to perform abortions. Therefore, there are very few abortions done in hospitals. So, last November, women from Aix-en-Provence aborted a minor. Afterwards the girl was very frightened of her family's reaction and wanted to be taken to a hospital. The hospital told the parents, and the parents complained. At the present moment there are six women from the MLAC charged with attempted abortion. All of them are liable to two years imprisonment.

MLAC has called together all the women's groups to launch a collective campaign to defend these women. Yesterday, we demonstrated in Paris. There were 15,000 women. We are also drawing up petitions, and writing a *dossier noir* about the methods used for abortion, especially in hospitals. Also there are still some private clinics which charge 2,000 frances ($444) for an abortion. The fight for abortion and contraception is not yet over. We must get abortions financed by social security, abortions for minors, and for immigrants without papers. We must make factual information on contraception available in the provinces, the factories, and the schools, and we must get it broadcast by the media.

Witness 14: Israel

In Israel abortion is illegal unless the woman's life is in danger. But this law has never been enforced. Any woman who wishes to buy an abortion privately from a doctor can do so in his private clinic or in a hospital. However, with inflation, the price of abortion has become so expensive that now it is only very wealthy women who can afford it.

There is now a draft law before the *Knesset*, the Israeli parliament, to formally legalize abortion. Just before coming to the Tribunal, there was a reaction by the Israeli medical profession which I read in the newspaper. I will give you a few brief quotes from this article. "In a statement published on the 26th of February, the Israel Obstretical and Gynecological Society said that its members would refuse to perform abortions if the new law passed. 'We think the liberalization should not be absolute. This law, in effect, allows any woman who wants an abortion to get one. We feel there should be many limits to this. The border between abortion and infanticide is narrow. We don't think a woman has the right to interrupt her pregnancy without her husband's agreement. A pregnancy belongs to two people.'"

Even with regard to very young women, the doctors—who anyway would perform abortions for money anytime—said: "If a girl of 17 interrupts her pregnancy there is a possibility of permanent sterility. A very large percentage of our cases of sterility are the result of an abortion." None of these things bothered these doctors before. Only now that it is to become legal, and therefore *not expensive*, they claim to be bothered by them.

Witness 15: Switzerland

Earlier a sister from Belgium said that you could have legal abortions in Switzerland. But I would like to emphasize that it is absolutely untrue that Switzerland is a haven for abortions. In Switzerland we have a federal penal code which is interpreted differently according to the *canton* (state) and it's relatively easy to get an abortion in two or three big towns but only if you are well informed and have plenty of money. Some of us worked with an abortion group in Geneva for three years but were not able to do anything about the way the doctors are exploiting women. If we accompanied a woman seeking an abortion the prices dropped a bit, but the next women who had appointments had to pay twice as much so that the doctors could make up their losses.

Please don't believe that Switzerland is a paradise in this respect. Even if the abortion law is eventually changed by the Swiss parliament, it won't be until the 1980's. So, forget about Switzerland!

Witness 16: Canada

Ten years ago, in Canada, a Dr. Morgenthaler started speaking out against the injustice of the Canadian abortion law. After a so-called liberalized law was passed, he decided to challenge the law by opening an abortion clinic in Montreal, Quebec where the Church has the strongest domination over women. He opened up a safe, clean clinic in Montreal. He used the vacuum aspirator that he had pioneered and brought to Canada, and he charged women according to what they could pay—nothing if they had no money.

Then the law moved in. Anyone who dares to challenge laws that oppress women must be stopped. Morgenthaler was charged on twelve counts of performing abortions on women. The first count that he was jailed for was an abortion done on a Carribean woman who was deported because of this. He was put in jail even though he was acquitted by two French speaking juries in Quebec. The government appealed those acquittals and had them overturned by a higher court, finding him guilty although the people in Quebec, the women in Quebec and across the country, felt that he should be set free.

While in jail he was put naked in an unlit isolation cell and he suffered two heart attacks. He has finally been released after serving twelve months of this sentence, but he faces eleven more charges and up to eleven years in jail. His only crime has been his total support of a woman's right to have abortion safely.

We would like to ask this International Tribunal to send a statement of solidarity to this doctor and to the women's movement in Canada, because of the harassment against him. All of us who have talked about this believe that the harassment against him is a crime against Canadian women, and that if we can free him it is a huge advance in our rights in Canada. I have addresses where people can send telegrams, and I would like to know if you will approve, by a show of hands, sending a telegram to the Canadian government demanding that they drop the charges. (The telegram was approved).

♀ ♀ ♀ ♀ ♀

All women, whether they recognize it or not, suffer for the refusal by patriarchal societies to recognize our right to choose or reject motherhood. The number of women who actually die every year as a consequence is not known, but it is probably as high as the number of casualties in the most lethal, patriarchal, geo-political wars. However, the casualties of the war of men against women are hidden, and unrecognized for what they are.

CHAPTER 2

Compulsory Non-Motherhood

While many women are forced to be mothers against their will, others who want to be mothers are not permitted to do so. The testimony from Puerto Rico shows that this applies particularly to Third World women in a colonized situation, whether the colony be internal or external. It also applies to many unmarried women who are pressured or forced by parents, lovers, or sometimes the State to have abortions or give up their children. While testimony here is limited to Puerto Rico and Japan, lesbians and women in prison are also frequently victims of this crime, or vulnerable to the possibility of becoming victims. Open lesbians invariably lose custody of their children if their husbands decide they want them, and women who give birth in prison are often compelled to give them up for adoption.

FORCED STERILIZATION

Witness 1: Puerto Rico

Puerto Rico has the highest rate of sterilization in the world. The demographer Vascos Calzada demonstrated in a study in 1968 that 35% of Puerto Rican women of childbearing age had been sterilized. This compares with 5% in India and 3% in Pakistan—both countries that also have public sterilization programs. 19 clinics for sterilization in Puerto Rico are working at maximum capacity performing up to 1000 sterilizations a month. Two-thirds of the sterilized women are between 20 and 49 years old, and 92% of them are under 35 years of age. This was the result of intensive political propaganda which led people to believe that the economic crisis and unemployment was due to the increase in people.

The sterilization program is financed by the government of the U.S. through the Department of Health, Education, and Welfare, which reimburses the colonial government of Puerto Rico 90% of the cost of each sterilization. As a colony of the U.S., Puerto Rico serves as a research laboratory for the genocidal policies engaged in by the U.S. towards Third World people. The great majority of the sterilized women in the U.S. are black, Chicano or Puerto

Rican. In other places in Latin America, for instance in Columbia, 40,000 women were sterilized between 1955 and 1965; in Brazil, one million between 1961 and 1971; and in Bolivia, Indian women were sterilized without their consent.

The U.S. is also drastically reducing its help to family planning programs while increasing the funds for sterilization. According to Dr. Antonio Silva, director of the sterilization program in Puerto Rico, this is done because it is much cheaper to perform sterilization than to use another method of contraception for population control. But sterilization is an operation which carries consequences both physical and psychological, which the majority of women are ignorant of at the moment of the surgery. Many women accepted because of the hysterical propaganda about the so-called demographic explosion, but then 19.5% reported that their health suffered as a result of sterilization, and 10% that their relationships were adversely affected.

The majority of women who were sterilized did not have access to enough information about other anti-conception methods. All the while abortion remains illegal, which shows that Puerto Rican women are not intended to be able to control their reproductive capacities. There are cases of women who submitted to sterilization, not knowing that they were pregnant. Many sterilizations take place at the time women have just given birth, when it is easier to convince them and they have to decide in a hurry. The Request and Consent for Sterilization questionnaire required by law is not used in the majority of cases. Sometimes when it is used it is only available in English—a language most cannot read. Furthermore, the three-day waiting period required by law between the moment of consent and the operation, is rarely respected. Many women also accept sterilization under the impression that the operation is reversible. Sterilization advice is part of the follow-up of all hospital deliveries, i.e., 78% of births.

If other methods of birth control were available, they would be chosen. Sterilization is free; contraception and abortion cost money ($250 for an abortion), and 60% of the population live below the U.S. poverty level.

We do not condemn sterilization *per se*. We condemn it when it is manipulated or forced. In Puerto Rico, a government whose decisions are made mainly by men, has taken upon itself the right to control our bodies, by determining when we should not reproduce. While traditionally our ability to have children has been used to create myths about our inferiority in other endeavors, it is enlightening to see that when that ability is economically counter-productive, it loses all mystique and becomes a "function" that must be disposed of. It should also be noted that the Catholic Church, which is strong in Puerto Rico, does not oppose sterilization.

In conclusion, we denounce sterilization as a genocidal, racist and sexist practice, in which Puerto Rican women are manipulated in order to carry out imperialist plans against the Third World.

SINGLE MOTHER'S RIGHTS DENIED

Witness 1: Japan

Japan is a country where people place great importance and value on marriage. So if a woman does something outside the framework of marriage, it is seen as very shameful. In 1971 a single mother's plea to bring up her own child was rejected by the court. It became known as Keiko's Case.

In 1968 Keiko was a kindergarten teacher, 25 years of age. She was raped by the father of one of her pupils. After raping her, this man intimidated her into continuing the relationship. When she found herself pregnant, after much thought, she decided to have the baby. She would continue working as a kindergarten teacher, and her mother would take care of the baby while she was working. But the father of the child, who already had a wife and a child, did not want her to have the baby. So, he and his relatives tried to persuade her to procure an abortion. However she was determined to have the child and would not obey them. So they secretly planned to have the baby adopted by someone. Without knowing this, Keiko had the child, and a week later she visited the man at his home to ask him to legally recognize the child. While she was there the baby was taken away somewhere by the man's relatives. Keiko, who had made up her mind to bring up her baby by herself, asked them to give it back, but they refused, and would not let her know where it was. However, she eventually found her baby with a couple, and asked them to give it back. They replied that the baby had been adopted with Keiko's consent. It was, of course, not true that she had consented, so she brought the problem before the court, believing the court would be just.

One and a half years later, in 1971, she lost her suit. The reasons for the judgement were that Keiko was unmarried, that she kept company with the father of a pupil, and that in spite of the "fact" that the child would be in unhappy circumstances as a bastard (or so the court assumed), she had had the child without any solid plan. It was therefore considered very doubtful that she had any true love for the child.

In short, the judgement was that if a woman is unmarried, even though working, she has no qualification for motherhood, and so it is better for her child to be adopted.

Reading of this decision in the newspaper, women in the women's liberation movement were angry, and began to form groups to support Keiko. In 1975, with the help of one of these supporting groups, Keiko took back her child, already 5 years old, by force. This appeared to be the only way she could get her child back. Finally, after considerable difficulties, she succeeded in legalizing her claim to her child. However, the court ordered her to pay consolation money to the wife of the man who made her pregnant, while he was not punished at all!

Women are often defined in terms of their maternal role in patriarchal societies, and women who never have children are often seen as not being real women. Yet, if a woman refuses to attach herself to a man, her supposedly natural capacity to raise children is suddenly regarded as totally nonexistent. If women have to be whipped into line like this to insure that all fruitful wombs will be owned by some man, then the traditional patriarchal family clearly is serving only mens' interests.

CHAPTER 3

Persecution of Non-Virgins and Unmarried Mothers

Since men don't have wombs but want children which they can be sure are theirs genetically, they have tried to arrange things so that they can possess totally those people who do have wombs. However, they also enjoy sexual conquest, and hence women are used to fulfill this desire too. This has created two classes of women—those who have wombs that men would like to own for the purpose of exclusive impregnation, and those designated unworthy of this "privileged" role. This dichotomy takes different forms, but in societies which outlaw contraception and abortion, it is still based on the difference between a virgin and a non-virgin.

Although testimony is included here only from Portugal and Brazil, women in many countries are affected by this virgin-whore form of patriarchal persecution. The woman from Yemen, whose testimony is included later with others from the Third World, also gives powerful evidence on this crime.

♀ ♀ ♀ ♀ ♀

Witness 1: Portugal*

In Portugal there is no distinction between prostitutes and unmarried non-virgins, even if rape is what causes the loss of virginity. Portuguese civil law requires that a woman be a virgin at the time of marriage, and if she is not, she may be repudiated. She then will be considered a whore by law and social consensus—even if she has been raped by a man who wanted to verify that she still had "honor." This means that the situation of single mothers in Portugal is quite appalling. If an unmarried mother is able to get the father to write his name on a document acknowledging paternity, then the mother has no rights over this child

*Due to language difficulties, considerable additions were made to this testimony from material about the witness sent prior to the Tribunal.

whatsoever. But if she does not do this, she is considered a prostitute.

M. who is here at my side, only speaks Portuguese, so I will speak on her behalf. When *M.* had almost finished her nursing studies, she was raped by a doctor, Luis Azeredo, an orthopedic specialist. This doctor had called her to his office in the hospital where she was on night duty. He talked to her, finally saying that he didn't believe she was a virgin. He then raped her, and only when she bled did he realize the truth. He exercised psychological pressure on her to continue the relationship by telling her that he could have her expelled from the nursing school, and that she was lost anyway, now that she was not a virgin, and that he would tell other people about this if she did not continue having sexual relations with him. She became convinced that now she was a "bad woman."

When *M*, became pregnant, this well known doctor, who was married, said she must have an abortion. *M.* didn't want to; however, he insisted. It was a very painful experience for her; apparently the anesthetic did not work well. After this *M.* refused to continue the sexual relationship with Doctor Azeredo. He retaliated with a campaign against her, telling colleagues that she was an easy lay, etc. In this way, he managed to get rid of her, preventing her from finishing her training. The woman benefactor who had been paying for her studies didn't continue, so she was expelled from the hostel where she had been living because she had no money.

M. then obtained a job as a nursemaid. At a party, drugged without knowing it when she was drinking a beer (something that happens quite often in Portugal) *M.* had sexual relations with someone she can hardly remember. She became pregnant again.

The same woman gave her an abortion, but said that her life might be at risk if she did it a third time. Soon after, *M.* became so depressed she tried to kill herself. She was taken to the hospital. When she recovered, she had nowhere to go, so she moved into a hostel created to "rescue prostitutes." She was 21 at this time. At this place, the women and girls have to work very hard, cook, clean and do embroidery. They get very poor pay, though their embroidery is sold at a great profit. They are badly fed and treated as "bad girls." I was told when I went there that half the girls are not normal, that most are born from incest, and that those in charge of the place have given up the "rescue", since they have had no results whatsoever. No wonder! The atmosphere when I was there was as bad or worse than a prison.

M. later met a young man she liked. She thought they would marry. She became pregnant again. He went off to Angola, and came back married. Since *M.* couldn't have another abortion, she had to have the child. When she was pregnant, she had to hide from everyone because of their hostility and her feelings of shame. *M.* had a daughter who was kept at the child care center of the hostel. She breast fed her daughter for several months; subsequently she was permitted to see her only on weekends, and she had to insist very much to get to see her this often.

Because of the way *M.* has been brought up, she now feels that no man will ever accept her; she has lost "her honor." Until very recently she was convinced that the way she is treated is simply a misfortune she must accept.

Witness 2: Brazil

Feminists from Brazil sent us the recently published story of *S.* She was born in a small town in the northwest of Brazil, in a very poor family. In order to help her father bring up her ten brothers and sisters, she had to work in a public school of the locality. At the same time she was taking courses at the high school, an institution directed by priests, so as to be able to have better work possibilities in the future. Three months before the end of her studies, she found herself pregnant. The director of this establishment made the decision to expel her. A lawyer defended *S.*, but a year went by before a decree of the court demanded her readmission. The director of the school, a priest, decided to resign rather than respect the court order, so he was replaced.

S. married the father of the child, and returned to school in order to finish her studies. However, when the time came to receive her diploma, it was not given to her. Saying that the decision of the court was immoral, the Monseigneur decided to close the school. About a hundred students found themselves unable to continue their studies. But the director will not consider reopening the school unless he is sure that no diploma will be given to *S.* He declared that the school was ruled by "Canon Right," and that it did not accept conception outside of marriage.

CHAPTER 4

Crimes Perpetrated by the Medical Profession

Upperclass men are rarely viewed as routinely violent towards women. Yet testimony increasingly reveals that male members of the medical profession act out their sexist attitudes towards women in ways that are truly brutal. The testimony from Italy about the treatment of women giving birth in hospitals sounds almost incredible. Because of this startling testimony, a male Italian journalist investigated the accusations and found them to be true. This incident is more fully described in the final chapters on the impact of the tribunal.

♀ ♀ ♀ ♀ ♀

BRUTALITY TOWARDS WOMEN GIVING BIRTH

Witness 1: Italy

I want to tell you about a crime which is widespread in Italy; it's the way in which women have their babies in Italian hospitals. All European statistics confirm that the situation is very serious. I'm going to describe a concrete case which is in no way exceptional. It happened in the north of Italy in a public hospital, and it falls into the normal pattern of things. But this is just exactly what we want to attack—the acceptance by the doctors and the boards of governors of the hospitals of using violence on women in hospitals when they are giving birth. The campaign I took part in—not only as a woman who had had two children but as a feminist and a member of a wages-for-housework group—started when we found out the way a certain baby had been brought forth at birth with a weight attached to its feet while a nurse jumped on the mother's belly. After two hours of this kind of labor, the baby was born with lesions and had to be treated for a month in the pediatric ward. When the mother had screamed at being touched, since by then she was sore all over, the doctors had the nerve to scold her, saying that if she wanted to have a son she'd have to be brave and good and not complain.

It was this episode which awakened in us the desire to fight. We drew up a pamphlet and sent it to various newspapers. We also circulated the pamphlet in the hospital itself. In it we pointed out that if—instead of only telling each other the things we hear at the hairdresser or at kindergarten—we brought those things, even to a small extent, to public notice, the effect would be enormous.

The political parties met to discuss all this, the newspapers talked about it, the medical union held meetings and they all had their bit to say. But we didn't trust any of these groups and we held meetings for women where we asked for help in an organized effort. The women, non-feminists, became so incensed that they lay a complaint before the courts. One hundred and ten women from Ferrara drew the attention of the judge to the circumstances in which they had each given birth. Labor was usually very long—20 to 30 hours. As to the babies—a survey showed that of 92 babies, more than 50% were born spastic, because of the delivery methods used in the hospitals. There was not adequate medical care—in spite of a minimum staff requirement of 40 nurses, assistants and doctors there were often only 20 at the hospital. The doctors on stand-by duty were often very young, straight from the university, and often there was no one capable of doing a Caesarian section. Also there was none of the equipment necessary for checking the condition of the baby—caesarians were diagnosed by stethoscope and the heart beat was not properly checked.

The court case went ahead, supported by a whole series of testimonies sent in by women. There was, for example, the case of a woman who went into the hospital a week before her baby was due in order to avoid any mishap. On Sunday morning she was given castor oil to facilitate the birth. At 8:15 P.M. she gave birth without any medical supervision. At 9:30 P.M. they finally put in the stitches. The baby was born spastic, because they induced labor and then abandoned the woman. For 4 months after she could not control her bowel movements and now she is left with a spastic baby. Then there was the case of *E.* who went into the hospital on Thursday February 8th, 1973. That Saturday her water burst and there was no doctor around. Finally one did turn up and listened to the baby's heart beat with a stethoscope, but is was too late to do a ceasarian. She gave birth at 5:30 in the morning with someone pressing on her stomach, giving her bruises which lasted for a long time afterwards. The baby, which was spastic, was kept in the hospital for another 25 days. The mother was not told of the baby's condition. It took her months to find out that the child was spastic and necessary treatment was delayed.

There were many other testimonies. We wanted to hear about all the kinds of violence used against women in hospitals. Among forms of violence, we included the isolation of a woman who is left alone for 24 hours when she is about to give birth, and who is only allowed one visitor for an hour each day. We have a testimony which tells of a mother who wanted to stay at the hospital to help her 18-year-old daughter, but she was told that if she didn't leave, the police would be called. We have testimonies of curettage without pain-killers. One of those came, in fact, from a woman whose child was born spastic after hours of labor. We have testimonies of insults used, such as "bitch," "whore," "if you want to have a son, you must enjoy giving birth," and that kind of thing. We have testimonies from women who were beaten during labor because they were not helping enough. What was important was to have understood that we could only achieve results by organizing ourselves, and through the women's movement. After the first stage, when everyone recognized the inadequacies of the hospitals, all the officials were anxious to put their consciences at rest once more. The only ones who were not prepared to let things lie were the women because they were the ones concerned.

Women must be organized in order to show how our weakness in the hospital is another of the infinite number of slights which our weakness in the home forces us to accept every day. In the home, all our physical, emotional, intellectual and sexual energy is exploited in the service of the family. We are expected, then, to keep quiet and be subservient in the hospital too; to make it possible for the authorities to economize on equipment, to spare the doctor work. We produce the labor force. And it is the product we are making, our sons, who are treated as much more important than us. And even if a few of them turn out spastic, it doesn't matter too much—there are always so many more anyway. It is a question of outright malpractice, of not respecting people. We have realized that the sacrifice we're constantly asked to make on behalf of others does not help anyone; rather it destroys our lives and the lives of our children. Housework is the basis of our slavery. It is this campaign of wages-for-housework which looks to the real cause the vulnerability of having no money—and gives strength to all the fights wherever they may be—in the factory, in the hospital, in the home, in the street.

GENERAL MEDICAL CRIMES

Witness 1: Germany

While we are giving this statement here in Brussels, women in the Sudan, Kenya, Tanzania, Ethiopia and other parts of the world, undergo *clitoridectomy*—removal of the clitoris. In the U.S. until 1925 this cruel method was used along with circumcision, which was performed until at least 1937, to prevent women from masturbating. Castration—the removal of the uterus and the ovaries—is today as common in the Western countries as it was in the 19th Century, when doctors actually exchanged female sexual organs like trophies. Today it is a common operation on women during their menopause, and on lower class women who have abortions. Hospitals in West Berlin and Germany force women who come for an abortion to sign a paper which allows doctors to remove their uterus if it is considered necessary. Furthermore, doctors make money from the many useless operations they perform on women.

Here are some statements made by doctors: "No ovary is good enough to leave in, and no testicle is bad enough to take out." "You want a child, but your uterus is bent. We have to operate on it." "You are frigid. We can do something about that. We only need to shorten the uterine ligaments." This chauvinistic treatment of women when they give birth expresses much hostility. Episiotomy* is routine, after which women are sewn especially tight to increase the pleasure of men. Sometimes women are sewn so tight that the skin tears during intercourse and they have to be cut and sewn again. Behind these methods is nothing but hostility and contempt for women. This becomes obvious in the sexual abuses which we are subject to—especially from gynecologists—such as suggestive comments and looks, fondling, and even rape during illegal abortion.

To too many of us, the following statements are not unfamiliar. One doctor said to a woman who cried because one of her breasts had been removed on account of cancer: "Why in the world are women so upset about their drooping tits?" Another said to a woman in a hospital, five minutes before she was going to have an abortion: "Why didn't you take the pill? Now we have to clean up the shit." We have more information about these crimes in a booklet we have prepared for this Tribunal.

---

*surgical enlargement of the vulva.

I will now give you the testimony of a woman about an experience that could happen to any of us. It is happening every day. "The whole thing really began with my first menstruation. I already had excrutiating pains periodically. Visits to different gynecologists did not help. I became so fed up with what they said—for example, "You will see, once the first child is there, everything will be alright." They said that many girls suffered with such pains, as if it was the most natural thing in the world! In June 1974, I got up one morning and I had no feeling in the right side of my body. I had pains in my abdomen. At that time I had not been in Berlin long, and I didn't know any doctors. A friend gave me the address of a gynecologist and I went to see him. His diagnosis was that my uterus was bent backwards and lying on the spine. According to the doctor an operation was necessary; I was supposed to go to his private clinic the same day. I objected that this was too fast, that I felt pushed, and I asked him to give me time to think about it. Meanwhile, I needed written certification of my illness from him for my employer. To this he said: "Either I operate on you today, or you continue working until you change your mind." Since I was in such pain, and he refused to give me the written certification, I had no choice. In the evening, around 6 P.M., I went to the clinic. In the morning, at 9 A.M., he operated on me. There was no preparation. They did not take my blood pressure, determine my blood group, or anything else, even though I had mentioned I had problems with my blood circulation.

"On the third day after the operation, I woke up for the first time and to my great surprise, I had a thick bandage around my belly. I knew that a shortening of the uterine ligaments is done through the vagina! That same day the doctor happened to drop in, and he said: 'The operation went very well. But you no longer are able to have children. The tubes were inflated like hot-dogs and had to be removed.' I was so surprised that I couldn't think of anything to say, and I didn't consciously register his words until much later. I couldn't change anything anyway, so I tried to accept the new situation."

"I had new pains after one month. The doctor tried radiation treatment, but that didn't help at all. Then he tried to insinuate that I had had an abortion at some point in the past, suggesting that the pain was all my own fault!"

"I feel outraged by what happened to me for the following reasons: (1) At that time I was still a minor (20 years old). (2) The doctor performed surgery on me without asking my parents for their consent. (3) My money-greedy doctor pretended he was going to perform a minor operation. Instead, he took advantage of my helpless situation and performed major surgery on me which destroyed my ability to have children. And he did this without taking the trouble to talk to me about it beforehand."

Witness 2: Belgium

I was operated on two years ago for a fibroid tumor. I was told that I would have a hysterectomy—a removal of my uterus. The morning after my operation the surgeon told me that the operation was successful but that while doing it he also had removed my ovaries, which, considering my age, were not useful anymore anyway. He had also removed my appendix though I never suffered pain there.

This was an abuse on my person. He had no right to remove anything that was healthy even if, as he said, the ovaries were of no use anymore considering my age. Two days earlier my age was the same and he could have warned me and asked for my consent.

Witness 3: Spain

I would like to state that in this world which is called civilized, there exists a singular paradox: a woman who wishes voluntarily to abort, cannot; while on the other hand, in my personal case, I can testify that I was mutilated without my consent, and without previous knowledge. What happened was that a small lump had appeared on my breast. I went to see the doctor and he told me that it was not serious, and that he could perfectly well give me a local anaesthetic and remove the little lump. On the day of the operation I went without making any special arrangements, and without fear I submitted to the operation. When I came round, the pain was very violent. I then discovered what had been done to me. My breast had been removed. The astonishing thing was that when I asked the doctor for an explanation he only answered that it was disagreeable to be a doctor on certain occasions.

CHAPTER 5

Compulsory Heterosexuality: The Persecution of Lesbians

Patriarchies have occasionally turned a tolerant eye on male homosexuality, but they have always persecuted lesbians. The degree to which lesbians are persecuted indicates the degree to which pressure is placed on women to be heterosexual. Lesbians in some countries are becoming increasingly aware of the source of their oppression, and acting against it, as some of the following testimonies illustrate. But so far, few heterosexual women realize their lack of free choice about their sexuality, and few realize how and why compulsory heterosexuality is also a crime against them. Testimony on the persecutions of lesbians from Norway, England, Germany, Holland, France, Switzerland, Mozambique and Spain follows.

♀ ♀ ♀ ♀ ♀

Witness 1: Norway

A lesbian is a woman who feels attracted to other women. The term "lesbian" should be used for all women who feel this, whether we act on it or not. This means a great number of women are lesbians—in fact, it's hard to say who isn't.

The crimes committed against lesbians are crimes committed against all women. But the lesbians who refuse to be imperialized by men will be punished in ways that heterosexually practicing women will never be punished. My testimony will be concerned with this particular kind of punishment.

There has been no research on the oppression of lesbians in Norway. My testimony is therefore based on talks with other lesbians and on the knowledge of myself and others which I have gained through many years as a practicing lesbian. When I started to feel attracted to women at the age of 3, I felt this to be most natural and beautiful. The story of my life from the time I was 3 to the time I was 20 was the story of a growing realization that I was a pervert. I was a homosexual woman. I thought I was the only woman in the world who felt attracted to other women. Time would show how utterly wrong I was. Between the ages of 20 and 34, I increasingly realized that there are lesbians everywhere. So I returned to my intuition as a 3-year-old—that for women to love other women is most natural and beautiful. I had been wise at the age of 3. But in the process of growing up to be a so-called "real" woman, this wisdom was stolen from me. This was the first crime that was committed against me as a lesbian. My wisdom regained, I started having the illusion that society would accept my lesbianism the moment I told people about it. Time again would show how utterly wrong I was.

The present society does not accept homosexuality in women. The proof of this is that the moment we are honest and open about our lesbianism, society ingeniously finds new ways of punishing us. This punishment is more severe than the one endured during the time of concealment. I think most lesbians in Norway and everywhere else know this, and that's why most of us prefer not even to practice our lesbianism. In the Norwegian homophile organization we get letters from women from all over Norway who have lived all their lives in heterosexual marriages even though they have known all the time that they have wanted to be with women. Why don't they break out of it? In most cases, this is quite impossible. They would have to move, but they have no money, no education—they have been housewives all their lives. They have fine children. They have, they often assert, kind husbands who need them. And even when they do not have all these practical obstacles to their freedom, they don't have the mental courage to leave the foundations of their lives. So, most of these women stay where they are, in emotional isolation, and without ever getting fullfillment of their personalities. This is the plight of the vast majority of lesbians in Norway. There are only a small number of women like myself who belong to the lesbian movement in Oslo, and openly call ourselves lesbians. Most Norwegian lesbians are faithful, hardworking wives scattered all over the country, who never have the chance to act on the fact that love between women is natural and beautiful.

What, then, happens to the minority of women who do act on this fact, when we do break out of our isolation and say or show openly that we are lesbians? There are hundreds of episodes in the restaurants in Oslo when we are violated physically or verbally because we are lesbians. Men may beat us up, or threaten to beat us up, scream "lesbian cunts" at us, smash their glasses of beer in front of us—all without anyone raising a finger to protect us. More often than not it's the lesbians, not the offending males, who are forced to leave. Two lesbian friends of mine went to a heterosexual discotheque, Key House, in Oslo. When they danced together, they were brutally parted from each other by the owner and two waiters and forced to the doorway. The two lesbians refused to leave before they had gotten their entrance fees back. Then they were beaten in their faces and on their backs, and kicked, by the same three men. They immediately went to the police and told their story with blood and bruises on their faces. It was about 11 o'clock at night, and the police said it was too late to go to the restaurant. The lesbians had the name of one witness that they gave to the police. A few days later they got the message that the police had dropped the case because it was "of little importance." They had not contacted the witness. One of the lesbians went to a chiropractor who found that part of her spine had been displaced. She was an eager handball player, but she has had to give up her sport. She still has pain in her back now, one and a half years later, and the treatment of it has cost her 2,000 Norwegian kroner ($361) so far.

Another lesbian friend of mine has always said openly that she is a lesbian. When she was at school, she was taken out of the gym class to go to the school doctor. Inside the office, the doctor pulled down her pants and exclaimed "but you look quite normal!" When she went to prison because of "hash" she at first stayed locked in a cell with another woman. After they realized she was a lesbian, she was removed to an isolated cell by herself. The prison doctor told her that they could not risk all the inmates turning lesbian. He said that many women turned lesbian in prison and they always made trouble. Since the "disease" obviously was contagious, they had to take precautions. The doctor made life so unbearable for this woman that, in the end, she had to tell the women from the lesbian movement in Oslo who had been coming to visit her every day, to stop coming to see her. My friend said that about half of the women in the prison in Oslo are lesbians.

Another lesbian in Oslo was in a heterosexual marriage that didn't work, so she started taking tranquilizers and ended up at the health sanatorium for treatment and rehabilitation. At first, she did not realize what was wrong, but she soon found out because she fell in love with one of the nurses. The moment she said in family group therapy that she believed that she was a lesbian, the doctor told her she was not. He knew from "looking into her eyes," he said. She had the eyes of a woman who wanted sexual intercourse with her husband. So she was subjected to so-called "touch therapy." She was put into a comfortably heated room, naked, on a bed, and for an hour her husband was to touch her body and try to excite her sexually. The result was that *he* got sexually excited. The idea was that the touching was always to end with sexual intercourse. Afterwards, the lesbian was to tell the psychologist what she had felt. She felt stronger and stronger aversion. She threw up and sometimes ran out of the room to avoid this "treatment." The more strongly she asserted that she was a lesbian, the more violent the forced heterosexual intercourse became. This treatment went on for about six months. She escaped from the hospital, but she was brought back. Again she escaped. She has not been there since. In the end she realized that she had been subjected to forcible rape for six months.

This is what Norway offers its lesbians: isolation, refusal to help in case of need, no protection in case of violence in the streets and restaurants, isolation in prison, and forcible rape in hospitals. We have no figures and no research. We only have our own testimony as lesbians. Even if society says we do not exist, we believe that we ourselves experience the truth.

Witness 2: England

I am a member of a group called "Wages Due Lesbians" which is a group that is organizing autonomously as a group of lesbian women inside the movement for wages-for-housework. Now I want to talk about the way that lesbians have been separated from other women. Many people think that we are not women at all. We have been "ghettoized," set apart as a separate kind of people who have to be in a separate kind of place, and act in a different kind of way. But as women, we are expected to do the work of women, and when we refuse to do that work, we are attacked.

When I was first asked to speak as a lesbian at the Tribunal, I thought that I should not, because the crimes that had been committed against me had been perpetrated by other women. For example, some of the women I have worked with did not want to sit with me or to talk with me because they suspected me of being lesbian. But then I realized that this is a crime all lesbians suffer from. And secondly, I realized that it is perpetrated by those in whose interest it is that we be heterosexual and that we continue to do the work that is expected of women. For that reason they keep lesbians separate and divided from other women and confined to a ghetto of one sort or another, whether it is a lesbian bar or whether it is a ghetto inside the women's liberation movement.

So we are attacked not as passive victims, but because we ourselves are making an attack—we are refusing to be a service station for men. In the traditional family, the woman is expected to get everybody fit to work another day. She is very productive for the system in that role. We are refusing this role. We are refusing the usual domination men have over women because of their money. But we are also saying that we as lesbians have our own needs; we have a right to love each other with no holds barred. We are breaking the discipline which says that we can work with women, we can talk with women, we can spend most of our lives with women, but we must not make love with women.

Lesbianism is used as a threat against heterosexual women. Whenever women step out of line, whenever women say "no" to a man, whenever a woman refuses to smile in the street, she is called a lesbian. People use that threat to keep us in line and doing the work that is expected of women.

We lesbians have to pay a heavy price for our rebellion. First of all we face a great deal of the same work and of the same conditions as other women, but we face them in particular forms. Most women are short of money, but lesbians usually have no access to a man's wages. This has an enormous effect on our lives. For instance, I know some women in Canada who are being forced to go back into the closet and to deny that they are lesbians because the economic crisis means that they do not have enough access to money. I also know that in Italy, there are very few lesbians who have been able to "come out." It isn't an accident that there are no Italian women on this panel. It is very hard for any woman to get a paying job in Italy and therefore, it is very hard for a lesbian to come out. Secondly, we have very little time. The housework that we do is in some ways different from the housework that other women do, in that we do not have to serve a man. But when we come home from an outside job, we have to do all the work of looking after ourselves in the little time that is left to us, and when we have little money, it is even harder. Thirdly, the stresses on our lives and the stresses on our relationships due to an environment that is hostile to lesbians, means that we are continually having to patch each other up, to put each other together again. And so we find that our sexuality is still not in our hands.

Very often we have been put on the defensive, including physically. For instance, last week we had a lesbian conference of 600 women in England. We had a dance, and at the end, the few women left were attacked and beaten up by some men. We are continually under this kind of attack which forces us to defend ourselves. But we do not want to always be on the defensive. I want to describe the strategy our group in England, and also a group in Canada, and some women in the United States are developing to deal with the persecution that we are subjected to. When we are organizing for "wages-for-housework," we are on the offensive. And we want to go on the offensive together, not to be isolated from other women. We need the strength of all of us.

What then does the campaign for wages-for-housework mean specifically for lesbians? First of all, when we win the fight, it means we can change the conditions of our lives because of the time and the money at our disposal. Secondly, we know that even by *saying* "wages-for-housework," even before we win the fight we have changed people's idea of what a woman's nature is. Housework, as well as heterosexuality, is considered part of our nature. When we say "wages-for-housework," we are saying that—on the contrary—housework is a *job*, and we want money for it. Thirdly, it means that there will be millions more lesbians. There are millions who know now that they are lesbians, but who cannot come out for economic reasons. There are millions more who do not think of themselves as lesbians, but who might be lesbians if the price they would have to pay would not be so high in terms of cash and social isolation. We do not think that there is a sharp separation of lesbians from heterosexual women. In fact, it is often very difficult to define the differences; for instance with regard to fantasies, some lesbians have heterosexual fantasies, some heterosexual women have lesbian fantasies. What is crucial for us is the *possibility* for more women to come out. That does not mean that our strategy is to encourage all women to come out as lesbians. We women should have a choice about how we live our lives. But we do want the *possibility* of coming out, and we know that we can't do that alone. We know that when a woman is in a very isolated situation and decides she is lesbian, very often she ends up insane. We want to be lesbians in a movement of women that is powerful and united enough to win the money and the time, so that we are not punished for making our own choices about our lives. This means that we need a way of organizing with other women. This does not mean that we should put aside the particular interests we have as lesbians, or that our struggle as lesbians should be submerged. Much of what we need as lesbians is the same as the needs of other women.

Witnesses 3, 4, 5, 6 and 7: Germany

This testimony was prepared by women from the Lesbian Action Center in West Berlin, and the five women who wrote it will read it.

Discrimination against lesbians represents the extreme of the sexual oppression of women. Here, men's fear of the sexually independent woman shows itself most clearly. By their way of life, lesbians represent a threat to the very foundations of the patriarchal society, marriage and family. Since women are not supposed to develop their own sexuality, sexual needs which are not related to men are prohibited. Because only penetration by a man is considered sexually valid, every woman who realizes that she does not need and does not want a man for her sexual satisfaction is attacking the sexual monopoly of men and therefore their domination. This is why the lesbian is declared a deviate, and if she shows herself overtly, is discriminated against and persecuted.

In January 1973, a campaign of discrimination against lesbians made headlines in the West German newspapers. This served to manipulate the public regarding the trial of two lesbians in the autumn of 1974. Generalizing from a few cases, it was suggested that all lesbians tend towards criminality. In a series of articles published in a newspaper called the *Bild* titled "Crimes of Lesbian Women," it was said: "When two women discover that they love each other, they are often capable of doing atrocious things" (Jan. 25, 1973). And: "When women love women, it often leads to a catastrophe" (Jan. 27, 1973). And again: "When women love women it is not unusual for it to lead to a serious crime" (Feb. 2, 1973). To justify these statements a sex researcher, Professor Doctor von Häntich, was later quoted: "Their passion can lead to the most horrifying conflicts, to abandoned children and broken marriages, to all kinds of unhappiness, killing, suicide, murder" (Aug. 28, 1974).

In the fertile ground of this "witch fear," the press was able to set the stage for reports on the trial of lesbians Judi Anderson and Marion Inns in the autumn of 1974. The two women were accused of having planned the murder of Marion Inns' husband and of having paid a Dane, Peterson, to carry it out. It was supposed to be a murder trial. It became a show trial about the sexuality of women in which men are superfluous. It became a witch trial. The court, consisting of one woman and six male lay assessors, had to pass judgement on a murder whose background of pressure to be heterosexual they could not understand and therefore could not judge fairly. The judge decided that it was a murder trial, but this decision did not prevent him from allowing detailed descriptions of how long, where, and how Marion Inns and Judi Anderson had been sleeping together and what they felt when they touched each other. Their love letters were also read out loud in public.

The judge refused to be reproached for lechery. It was important for him to know that "the two of them even fell on each other in the bathroom" and that "Judi Anderson's toes tingled when Marion touched her" (*Bild,* August 1974). The judge wanted to know this "in order to hear from the descriptions whether there was any mental disturbance which would have to be included as extenuating circumstances when passing sentence." Because he had made the decision to treat the case as murder, the judge was able to continue to deny the sexual content of the trial, and practically without restriction, admit spectators, journalists, and photographers, to the trial.

Under the cloak of tolerance, spiteful voyeurism was freely allowed. Against their wishes, the accused were made to talk in public about their intimate relations. The lawyers for the defense did nothing to protect their clients against the decision to admit the public. This is unique in the practice of justice in West Germany—the public is not usually admitted in trials involving sex offenses, or in divorce cases. In addition, the defense was based on establishing diminished responsibility at the time of the crime. Marion Inns and Judi Anderson were supposed to be insane. Lesbian love had mentally confused them.

Both women were given life sentences. The severe sentence was justified by the prosecution as follows: "If we took 'extenuating circumstances' into consideration, this would give a free hand to homosexuals." The strong pressure put on people to be heterosexual cannot be expressed more clearly.

In the newspapers each detail of the trial was taken apart. Male journalists were avidly hoping to learn the sexual behaviors of lesbians, and to get some insight into such strong emotions. The whole appalling episode was seen as the result of the puritanical environment from which both women came, their bad relationships with their mothers, and that as children they had come across the wrong sort of men and had been raped. The effects of their childhood and adolescent experiences had different outcomes. Marion wanted to be a woman who lived with a man, Judi never wanted this.

Heterosexual opinion has always regarded lesbian behavior statically and outside the mainstream of society. It can only comprehend female homosexuality in terms of a masculine/feminine dichotomy. That is, heterosexuals think there are women who are scared of men and make do with a substitute man, and there are women who compete with men and become substitute men. Even during the trial in Itzehohe, a multi-part serial appeared in *Quick Magazine* of the experiences of Marion Inns, who had sold them to the paper for 20,000 marks ($7,782). The series, in which all the details of the relationship between Marion Inns and Judi Anderson were described, reflected the categorization which society forces on lesbians. Judi Anderson was described as the lesbian who had ordered the murder, and Marion Inns as the bi-sexual woman who allowed herself to be persuaded into cooperating. The basic theme was the portrayal of Marion Inns as having been seduced. As a well-balanced "completely normal woman," Marion, because of her husband's sexual failure, became obedient "to the moody, jealous, full-blooded lesbian." Judi Anderson is supposed to have dominated her formerly heterosexual friend by using sex and tenderness. Marion does the cooking, wears dresses and behaves "indecisively" like a woman. Judi drinks beer, wears pants, shirts and ties, and has only one aim: "To dominate her friend." *Quick* explains this as follows: "Nature must have provided Judi with a high male hormone level. It has been proved that women with a lot of male hormones show extraordinary sexuality, and that these women are also similar to highly active men in other ways. They want to play the dominant role." Behind this description of Judi Anderson is an undifferentiated stereotype of the male, and also the common myth of the extremely passionate behavior of lesbians. In her memoirs, Marion Inns is a woman caught in a conflict of obedience and wanting to be normal—accusing her husband of driving her into the arms of a lesbian, as the result of his emotional frigidity and impotence, and therefore into crime. This story demands implicitly at least a considerably milder sentence if not a pardon, for Marion Inns, because the one who is really guilty—the sexually abnormal one—is the lesbian Judi Anderson.

In *Bild*, dated February 21, 1976 this announcement appeared: "Marion Inns, the lesbian murderer, is marrying a waiter. They got to know each other when he bought Inns' furniture at an auction. In his bedroom now stands the sky blue double bed, in which the lesbian murderer of her husband, deceived her husband and slept with her female lover. This 45-year-old man is convinced that Marion Inns, through his love, has again become a normal woman." Heterosexual society has gotten back the woman who had been seduced away from it. There is nothing now to prevent a revision of the sentence. The press and the judiciary have succeeded; the destruction of the lesbian love relationship has been achieved. The two women now hate each other. The way their story was told has made it clear that there is only masculine or feminine sexuality. Judi Anderson, who always considered her relations with men to be like rape and therefore refused them, is the actual enemy—as a ridiculous fake man Marion has gotten rid of.

In contrast to the sensational trial in Itzehohe, here are some everyday and seemingly banal experiences of lesbians. Much more so than in this trial where the evidence of discrimination is clear, it is everyday discrimination which grinds us down and takes its toll on all of us. Within the four walls of the lesbian organization, we can withdraw from men. But at school, at work, on the street, and everywhere else where any one of us is alone, we are scared, and this fear forces us to conform. Here is the first report of the more everyday kind of discrimination we suffer.

In Spring 1975, *M.* and I went to a woman doctor who had looked after me during my marriage. She was our family doctor. I knew her as a friendly and conscientious woman who was concerned enough to have good relationships with her patients and with whom I had already spoken several times about personal difficulties. We waited for several hours in the waiting room. We held each other's hands, and it must have become obvious to the other patients that we were lesbians. At last *M.* was called, but she was only briefly examined by the doctor. She was diagnosed as suffering from a neglected case of pneumonia, but the doctor refused to give *M.* any further treatment on the grounds that she lived in a different quarter of the city. Nor would the doctor recommend another doctor for *M.* Then the doctor called me. I was eating a sweet, and she hissed at me: "Finish eating first. I can't stand patients chewing," and called another patient. When that patient did not answer, I said I had finished eating, and she hissed at me again, "You can wait!" So we left. The following day, without being asked and without any sort of comment, she sent me a medical excuse for my employer by mail.

I will now give a second report of everyday kinds of discrimination. From 1974 to 1975, I went to a vocational training school. The teacher who taught history and biology behaved in a particularily arrogant and authoritarian way, so that I always became furious and reacted aggressively towards him. For a quarter of a year we behaved towards each other with concealed aggression or openly shouted at each other. He had probably never come across a woman who rejected him so openly. He did not allow me to make any verbal contributions in class and described me as particularly aggressive and pathological. The class was on my side when he was not in the room, but during lessons they kept quiet and were scared of any argument between us. In addition, he described me as an agitator and threatened dire consequences if the class supported me. The majority of the class knew by now that I was a lesbian. This became the talk of the teachers' room. For this particular teacher, it fit exactly into his picture of me as pathological and particularly aggressive. At the next opportunity he used it as a weapon to openly discriminate against me. Biology instruction was well-suited for this. Within the framework of lessons on heredity he spoke of sexual abnormality. He finally came around to the subject of homosexuality, and then came the blow. He did not speak about homosexuality in general terms as is usual for scientists. Instead he spoke explicitly about lesbian women, whom he said, for hereditary reasons, are particularly aggressive. It was clear to me immediately that he was aiming it at me. On the faces of the other students I could also see that they were getting the message. There was dead silence, not a sound, not a pencil dropped. I trembled and began to gag and thought "Don't cry; don't give him that triumph as well." The rest of the class did not know how to take it.

My attempt to take action against him under the Schools Act failed, because the class did not back me up. I telephoned the German teacher and asked her to try to stop him from treating me like this again. I told her that I was in a homosexual organization, conscious of my situation and proud of being a lesbian. She said she would not mention it at the teachers' meeting, but in fact she did so. The counter attack came faster than I expected. This time he spoke immediately about lesbian women. He looked at me and said: "If you feel under attack as a lesbian woman, this is only your persecution complex, and points to your psycho-pathological structure." This time I took up the attack and let out my anger. In the examination, as expected, he gave me poor marks.

In order to survive this daily battle with teachers, employers, colleagues, parents, institutions, and the whole heterosexual environment, lesbians have to organize. In order to see and live our love for women positively, we need contact and discussion, permanent jobs, and flats with other lesbians. The fact that we are organizing has political overtones, and that is the point at which being lesbian becomes a concrete danger to the patriarchal society. It is a danger because by doing this, we are visibly opposing two of the basic requirements on which the patriarchal system functions—heterosexuality and isolation of women. So that more women do not see organization as a possibility of improving their situations, we have to be shot down—to begin with, with words.

The press plays the organized lesbians off against the nonorganized lesbians, but this does not at all mean that the latter are suddenly accepted. The moment that lesbians appear organized and fighting, the mechanism of discrimination becomes different. A journalist of the magazine *Neue Revue* (no. 25, 1974), wrote that he cannot see the sense of organization because homosexual women are "never criminally persecuted in Germany and the public hardly takes offense as long as they keep quiet. Only since they started speaking up have they become a laughing-stock—and often even a scandal." But alone, lesbians are powerless in this heterosexual environment. We have a choice: retreat into isolation and resignation, or join the lesbian organization which will make it possible to tackle prejudice and to fight discrimination.

The lesbian who has spent a lot of time during important years in her development dealing with the problem of neither being a feminine woman nor a man, has known identity problems which are not easily communicated. As women, lesbians are subjected to the discrimination against all women in the patriarchal society. However, the abolition of discrimination against heterosexual women does not yet mean the abolition of the specific discrimination against lesbians.

Witness 8: Holland

Persecution of homosexual women certainly still exists in the Netherlands. Not by law. According to the law, discriminatory practices are prohibited. I have just listened to the testimonies of the German and Norwegian women, and I certainly think that the Dutch women can fully agree with them. I want to cite one example of a Dutch woman who, after 13 years of marriage, abandoned her married life, and escaped the oppression of her husband—because she loved a woman.

When she left her husband she also had to leave her children. She only sees them once in a while. Her ex-husband saw to it that the contact she had with them and her former friends, was broken. He does not want their children to have any contact with her because she engages in homosexual relationships.

This woman has lost her children, her job, and her social status. She is looking for another job now, but has been refused several times because she is a divorced woman. Suppose she would dare to say who she really is: a lesbian who loves women. She is just beginning to discover who she is. Now she is forced to hide the identity she has slowly built up. Because she is not allowed to be honest when applying for a job, she is forced again to live a life she has not chosen.

There are many women who share these experiences. In the Netherlands, women are not being locked away in camps, but that does not mean that the Netherlands is a paradise for homosexuals. In the Netherlands, lesbians are discriminated against when they apply for a job, when they look for a place to live, and when they try to get custody of their children in cases of divorce. You're fired if you take part in a TV program about homosexual women; this happened just one month ago to a woman. Homosexual women are also ignored by men in the movement of the male homosexuals and ignored by women in the women's movement. It is often difficult to detect discrimination, because many women still do not dare to admit to themselves that they are homosexual. We are here with a number of women, there is support, but there are still thousands in the Netherlands who aren't here but who would like to be.

Witness 9: France*

To police doctors we are mentally sick, perverts and degenerates.

To the brainwashed police we are deviants, neurotics, sexual perverts, and retarded.

To the psychologists we are narcissists or we are clitoris-obsessed.

To the biologists we are mistakes of nature with a gene or so too many.

To the father of psychoanalysis we have repressed our heterosexual nature.

To the father of 10 children we are abnormal.

To the normal man we are pathological.

To the common man in the street, we are dirty dykes.

To the analyst we are persons without a phallus who would, however, like to have one.

To the moralists we are vicious, debauched, erotically mad women.

To the super-male we haven't been properly handled.

To the Pope we are mortal sin.

To the lawmakers of France we are a social evil.

To our parents we are a disgrace to the family.

To the Communist party we are petty bourgeois perverts.

To the leftists, we are bourgeois, apolitical individualists.

To the sexual majority of the Left, we are a sexual minority.

And there are certain women belonging to hierarchical organizations of the extreme Left who accuse us of homosexual terrorism when we try to speak of our relationships.

---

*Testimony-cum-poem read during the lesbian demonstration.

For millions of women we are sectarian lesbians—shameful, phallic women given to sexual perversion and masculinity.

In short, we are not women but monsters. This is how we are repressed. It happens all the time. It is subtle, and usually effective.

They don't send us to prison but:

—The doctors and the psychoanalysts want to take us in hand: at best to cure us, at worst to send us to psychiatric hospitals.

—Our families constantly try to marry us off.

—At work when they know we are lesbian, they keep an eye on us. They set traps for us. They make nasty allusions, and make a pretext of the slightest imperfection in our work to sack us.

—In the cinema they make a show of us and humiliate us to amuse voyeurs.

—Men want to violate us to prove that we have not been properly handled, and wish to give us children to keep us quiet.

—The Left tries to blame us in the name of the revolution and the class struggle.

We have all endured these experiences. Never to be able to talk to anyone about ourselves for fear of rejection or even persecution; to be obliged to conceal our nature; to live with the burden of solitude, the hatred from straights, or the hypocritical condescension of the tolerant people who "understand" our problems. Homosexuality is not our problem. It is heterosexual society that sees it as a problem.

Repression is also in the assertion that they don't know about homosexuality; that it doesn't exist; that it is not serious, or that it is the worst catastrophe that could happen to us; a shameful sickness; utter depravity; inconceivably horrible. Repression serves to justify their heterosexuality and their normality, strengthen their power over women, make us conceal our way of life, divide us to rule us, isolate us from each other, render us culpable, and reduce us to silence.

Why have we become the scapegoats of their sick male society? Because we are refusing to submit to the laws of phallocratic, heterosexual men. Because we say that women are not destined for men for all eternity, and that the compulsory heterosexual relationship is not natural. We have no need to be protected by them.

The family is the institution which justifies the subjugation of woman in the name of love of a man and children, with free domestic work for the master as her prime obligation. We oppose the social norms which consecrate women to men, to children, to household appliances, and to cooking pots. Our pleasure is not joint masturbation, nor is it a regression to the mother-child relationship, nor is it a caricature of the man/woman relationship.

It is a pleasure which is women's alone, which means that it is not in accordance with, or measured, labelled, or regulated by males: it is our pleasure.

But *REPRESSION IS NOT FATAL*. In our feminist struggle we have rediscovered our pride as women, our love for women, and we are attempting to gain autonomy as women. It is necessary for all women to unite, and not to be afraid of loving women. That is our strength, and that is why men fear.

And it is not just a question of sexuality. For me, to love women is not to be homosexual, it is to be Lesbian. There is a difference between the two. Homosexuality refers to sexuality, i.e. to the homo-bi-heterodifferences. It is the label which they attach to us to divide women according to their sexual preferences—while lesbianism means for me feminine polarity: cultural, psychic, emotional, sexual and creative polarity. In my view, a female culture, a culture which concerns women, and is concerned with women, can only be lesbian.

It also means joining forces with our sisters who, through the ages, have struggled against male power: Sappho, the Amazons, the Witches, Christine de Pisan, Louise Labbé, Olympe de Gouge, Mary Wollstonecraft, Flora Tristan, Emmeline Pankhurst, Louise Michel, Louise Otto Peters, Madeleine Pelletier, Hélène Brion, Nelly Roussel, Helen Lange, Virginia Woolf, Renée Vivien, Valerie Solanas, and many more. We must now discover the path of our own creativity, find a way to build our own culture, to waken from our silence. We have no models, no norms; we must create everything for ourselves. It is a difficult task, but at least we are living and existing for ourselves.

Witness 10: Switzerland

I am 18 years old, and come from Switzerland. It is very hard for me to stand up here and speak in front of such a large audience, but I want to show in my spontaneous testimony how belonging to a non-heterosexual group of people can affect and ruin a life from youth onwards, because only one model, the heterosexual model, is considered acceptable to young people in our society. Heterosexuals have the rights and opportunities to develop themselves and their identities, but not those of us who feel differently. I am still afraid of being punished or discriminated against because of my sexuality. Young heterosexuals need not have this fear. Sexually, they attain majority status at sixteen: they don't live under the stigma of being unlawful until they are twenty, like lesbians and homosexuals.

When I was eleven I began to realize that I was different from other girls. Before, I had always wanted to be a boy, and I thought it was because they had more rights and more freedom than girls. But I felt more and more clearly that I did not only reject a girl's role, but felt differently from that which was expected of me. I only understood that I was a lesbian when I was sixteen. It was like a liberation. For the first time I could accept myself as a woman. But before I got there, I had a long painful way to go, which finally ended in jail.

Everyone in my environment was helpless and hostile towards my being different. They understood as little as I did myself. My parents tried to persuade me to pull myself together and not be crazy. In school I became aggressive, isolated myself more and more, until finally I refused to go at all. I spent most of the day in bed and in my room. I was given a lot of painkillers and tranquilizers and soon I found out how well you can withdraw by using them. One way or another I got hold of more and more of the stuff and of course became more and more dependent on it. I couldn't talk about my feelings with the psychiatrists who were called in. Loving other girls didn't fit into their mental catalogue, or if it did it was only under the category of "transitional phase: puberty." My feelings of isolation intensified.

Finally when I was fourteen, I ran away. I went over the border to Munich. I wanted to go anywhere, as long as I was far away. I had hardly any money, and the little I had went for tablets. I was continuously drugged, and barely knew what was going on when I was caught two days later. I was interrogated by the police, then finally brought to the border under surveillance. My father picked me up, reproached me, and everyone wanted to know why I had run away. I scarcely knew myself.

I then went to a number of clinics, and a corrective school. I was still dependent on tablets, still isolated because there was nowhere I could express my feelings for girls or put them into practice. I was beaten and shouted at, locked up and humiliated. When I wanted to go back to school the parents of the other girls prevented it for fear their children would be seduced by me. Later on I swallowed everything and anything, and I started dealing in drugs in order to get hold of more drugs, until I ended up in the clinic again. Finally I ran away with a woman, still full of tablets and no longer capable of thinking or of judgement. We stole what we needed. Finally the woman who was with me stole a pistol and insisted that I should say that I had abducted her because I was a minor and not much could happen to me. When we were caught I was so drugged that I said everything she wanted me to.

The detention, pending the trial, was torture. I was dragged through six different jails, always in solitary confinement. I was interrogated for hours and given no explanation of my rights and opportunities. I was always alone, facing the trained, well-organized, superior male power of the authorities, and constantly having to wait, wait, wait. I had the choice of prison, corrective school or psychiatric clinic. I thought that I would get away with two or three months if I went to jail, instead of being holed up for years in a corrective school or even going to the psychiatric hospital for an unspecified length of time. I had no idea that minors do not receive clearly defined sentences like adults. So I ended up having to spend thirteen months in jail.

All you sisters have surely realized what the main problem for us young lesbians is: we are very isolated and we need contact with you. And we need your help.

Witness 11: Mozambique

I am going to read a letter from a lesbian in Mozambique who is not able to be here.

> Dear women, I have decided against sending a tape to the Tribunal because I think a tape can be very easily traced back to me, and that might mean I might not be allowed back to Mozambique. However, I think it is very important that someone should call attention to the position of lesbians in Mozambique. It exemplifies how lesbians and single women who reject men, are treated and considered in Marxist-revolutionary countries all over the world. It is urgent that we begin to question on what premises and at what price we as feminists support such liberation movements. I feel hesitant about giving my energy to support these struggles for liberation when they deny my right to existence and reject my collaboration once they gain power.
>
> I am condemned to a life of exile because I will not deny that I am a lesbian, that my primary commitments are, and will always be, to other women. In the new Mozambique, lesbianism is considered a left-over from colonialism and decadent Western civilization. Lesbians are sent to rehabilitation camps to learn through self-criticism the correct line about themselves.
>
> Another reason why I think it is important for the Tribunal to discuss the relationship of revolutionary movements to lesbianism, is because this certainly might become a deep split in the women's movement.

Are heterosexual sisters going to accept the privileges granted to them by the revolutionary brothers, or are they going to renounce that and unite with all oppressed women until the day we can create our own space where we will be free to love each other? If I am forced to denounce my love for women, if I therefore denounce myself, I could go back to Mozambique and join forces in the exciting and hard struggles of rebuilding a nation, including the struggle for the emancipation of Mozambiquan women. As it is, I either risk the rehabilitation camps, or remain in exile.

Another point which I would like the Tribunal to note is that in the present Mozambique, all women suspected of prostitution are sent to rehabilitation camps. But the men who procure prostitutes are not sent there. Single mothers are officially insulted, but single fathers are not mentioned.

I am sorry that I myself cannot be present at this Tribunal, but I fervently hope that this letter might call attention to the position of lesbians in the Third World and in the revolutionary countries, as well as everywhere else.

Witness 12: Spain

As a lesbian, I personally suffered all the respressions that have been talked about today, during the years I lived and worked in Spain. The reactions to my lesbianism ranged from mockery to near-violence from the police in Segovia. The letters I wrote to a woman were stolen and translated with the intention of using them against her in a trial for separation from her husband, so as to take her daughter away from her for being lesbian.

Because of the intense repression of lesbians in Spain, no one dared to speak about it. I hope Spanish feminists will not discriminate against lesbians, for without us, their feminist groups will have less strength.

CHAPTER 6

Crimes Within the Patriarchal Family

The patriarchal family institutionalizes domination by husbands over wives. In many parts of the world, girls and women are still married without their consent, and/or forced to stay married for the rest of their lives—the latter particularly in Catholic countries. But even where women appear not to be victims of forced marriage, most seem willing to jump into marriages in which they are forced into a subordinate role—so successful is the brainwashing and so effective the punishment of those who remain outside the institution. This conditioning is reminiscent of the not-so-ancient Indian custom, *Suttee* where the wife of a Brahmin who died jumped willingly into his funeral pyre. But then again, if she didn't jump willingly, she was pushed by those nearest and dearest to her.

Many of the testimonies about crimes within the patriarchal family appear under other categories. Here, testimony tends to focus on the law. Women from Belgium, Ireland, Israel, France, and Canada spoke, and a second French woman testified about the sexist parental law in Tunisia.

♀ ♀ ♀ ♀ ♀

Witnesses 1 and 2: Belgium

I am a journalist and I come here to launch an appeal for action from you, because I believe that only the International Tribunal on Crimes Against Women can arouse the Belgian press. There is at this moment in Belgium, a family crime which is being perpetrated. Violette, a girl of 15, is today entering her 40th day of hunger strike in a Belgian hospital, and apart from the paper I write for, and one other left-wing publication, nobody at all is mentioning it. I am here with her elder sister who can give you all the details about her state of health and the reasons why she is on a hunger strike.

I have myself telephoned several magazines and Belgian dailies. I have spoken to journalists whom I know personally to ask them to write about it in their papers. They have replied, "We can't publish it because it is a question of morality." This amounts then, to a conspiracy of silence. This young girl was in love with a man of 41. Her father took action against the man, who is now in prison. But the problem in my opinion doesn't really lie here. It's not about a girl of 15 going on hunger strike so that she can perhaps live with a man much older than herself. It's about a girl on hunger strike in her struggle against paternal oppression. She has a family background which is very difficult and repressive in a little town in the Ardennes. Her elder sister who is here today also ran away from home two years ago. I'm going to let her speak now. This is Suzanne.

Suzanne: I simply want to tell you that family conditions, especially in poorly developed regions outside the towns, are very hard. For example, I couldn't go to the cinema even when I was 17 years old, and I wasn't the only one who couldn't. I had to put up with a lot of affronts to my dignity.

I'd like to give you some details about Violette's health: she's in her 40th day of a hunger strike. A doctor has been to see her. He's confirmed that she suffers from quite serious fainting attacks and loss of the senses of sight and touch.

It's a total strike, so she doesn't take any food at all, she simply drinks a little water and that's all. She's depressed and they have to give her valium injections.

According to Belgian law, someone who revolts within the family, and especially girls since they don't have the right to revolt, are liable to be shut up for several years in a house of correction until they are 21 years old. This situation is terrible, and I beg you to do something about it. We are going to try to organize some positive action. We shall send petitions to the father, to the judge of the minors' court, and to anyone who is in a position of power.

Chantal: Violette will soon be put on drip feeding. In a week she may simply pass away. And all because nobody does anything about it. There is no reaction in the majority of papers because of bourgeois morality which sees only that a 15-year-old girl and a man of 41 are involved. Myself, I see it as a family crime, one that hasn't been talked about much today. We've talked about the problem of women in the home, economic crimes, questions of divorce, etc. There are also 15-year-old girls who have problems with their parents, and that is important too. I would like to do something positive, like pass around a petition, or perhaps issue an official communiqué in the name of the Tribunal of Women to make the radio and television of Belgium take up this concrete case.

The communiqué could say that the Tribunal of Women meeting in Belgium at this moment, is against the situation that has led to Violette's hunger strike. It is not a question of condemning the parents, it's a question of effecting a dailogue between father and daughter, so that Violette puts an end to her hunger strike, instead of risking death within a week.

Witness 3: Ireland

The principle of the woman as a chattel is established in many sections of the Irish law, but nowhere is it more clearly revealed than in a process defined as "criminal conversation." This law is based on the old commonlaw concept that the husband's interest in his wife is a quasi-proprietary one. The law is regarded by Irish women as offensive and degrading. Under this legislation, a husband may sue any man who has an adulterous affair with his wife, the wife's consent in this matter being totally irrelevant. In January of 1976, an Irish high court jury awarded the sum of 14,000 pounds ($28,000) to a husband under this legal provision. This amount can be regarded as the current price of an Irish wife. In deciding the damages, the jury assesses the value of the wife, taking into account her fortune, her assistance to her husband's business, her capacity as a housekeeper, and her general ability in the house. Secondly, the court assesses the proper compensation for the blow to the husband's marital honor, his loss of "sexual relations," and the embarrassment and injury to his sense of property and family pride. Damages to him depend on the purity and general character of his wife. Proceedings are heard in open court by judge and jury. Until January 1976, no women were allowed on juries. And the unsavory aspects of such cases were widely and salaciously published.

Despite pressures from women's organizations in Ireland to have this law repealed, our government refuses. Meanwhile several such cases a year are heard, many resulting in substantial awards being made to husbands. Such husbands would, under a more just legal system, have been divorced by their wives, but Ireland has no provision for divorce. It is forbidden by our constitution and strongly opposed by the Catholic church. A wife's legal domicile in Ireland is that of her husband. If her husband deserts her and goes to a country where divorce is permissible, he can file for divorce in that country although his wife might still be living in Ireland. There is little she can do on the state allowances then available to her. On the other hand, if a wife leaves and files for divorce in another country, this will not be recognized in Ireland.

Witness 4: Israel

The source of the paternalistic attitude towards women in Israel is rooted in, and strengthened by, orthodox religious law. Marriage, divorce, and related subjects, come under the jurisdiction of the religious courts, depending on one's religion—and one must have a religious identification. For the majority of Israel's population this means orthodox Jewish religious law, whether or not the citizen is religious or orthodox.

In the Rabbinical courts, man and woman do not have equal standing. This is based on the concept of woman as man's property, and therefore worthless in her own right. In the marriage ceremony he consecrates her, while she remains passive. In divorce, he gives her the divorce, she receives it. If a man is unwilling or unable to give his wife a divorce, she cannot be released.

According to Jewish law a man may marry a second wife while still married to the first. While it is true that bigamy is against the law in Israel, it is worth noting that the legislators included a paragraph allowing a man to marry a second wife if he receives a permit from the rabbinical court. Such a permit is granted if a woman is unable to receive the divorce (insane, disappeared, etc.), or if she is unwilling, despite court directive. Such was the case of the couple *B.* and *J.*, who after years of wrangling on a property settlement, were directed by the Rabbinical court to divorce under the terms set by it. When the woman refused, her husband was granted a permit to marry again. This, in effect, is a divorce forced on the woman—an act that cannot be done to a man. He may be imprisoned for not granting his wife a divorce as directed. This has happened, though rarely, but she cannot be released from the marriage until he agrees. There is a case of a man serving a long prison term for another felony who refuses to give his wife a divorce out of spite, and there is nothing that can be done. If a husband is insane or disappears or has failed to return from battle but no remains are found, his wife is forever tied to him.

The meaning of "forever tied to him" is much stronger than one might suspect. If a woman is married to a man, whether or not they are living together, she is still his property, and she may not form a liaison with any other man. If she does, she is in danger of losing all her rights to her part of the property, and even the custody of her children. If children result from her relationship with another man, they are considered bastards and may never marry within the community (or without, since there is no interfaith marriage). And if she finally gets her divorce, she may not marry her lover. This was brought out in a recent case in Beersheba, where the woman had been separated from her husband for a long time, had formed a relationship with another man, and when she became pregnant, they decided to marry. When, in ignorance, she asked the rabbinical court to rush the divorce through since she was pregnant, they obliged, but also added to her bill of divorcement the fact that she was not allowed to marry the man named as her lover.

Not so a man. He may live apart from his wife, form a relationship with any single woman of his choosing, have children with her, and eventually marry her when he is divorced. Even if they never marry, the children are legal and are entitled to the same rights as his other children. The woman, who is considered a commonlaw wife, also has maintenance and property rights, but should he tire of her too, she must accept the divorce according to the terms he offers, since they were not legally married.

Because of their unequal position many women often resort to buying their divorces from their recalcitrant husbands, who fully realize their better position. Such was the case with *Mrs. S.* who gave her husband the entire apartment in order to be released; and *Mrs. K.* from Ramat Gan who gave her in-and-out-again mental patient husband 15,000 Israeli pounds ($2,033) during one of his lucid periods in order to get divorced. Their position is better than one woman who is forever tied to a known sex deviate who refuses to grant her a divorce, or another who is deaf as a result of battering by a husband who prefers to beat her rather than divorce her.

Women's position is further lowered by the fact that she may be declared rebellious by the rabbinical courts and therefore lose her maintenance, property and other rights. A woman may not leave the joint domicile without a rabbinical permit lest she be declared rebellious if her husband says, and the rabbis believe, that she did not sew buttons for him, cook, keep house, have sexual relations, and a long list of other wifely duties. This happened in the case of a Tel Aviv couple. After 26 years of unhappy marriage the wife applied for a property settlement as the first step to a divorce. In finding against the wife's claim to joint property, the judge (male) noted that for a housewife to claim joint property she must prove cooperation. Her husband had stated that his wife "had never sewn a button, so the children came to me for this," and that "As for running the kitchen, I was jealous when I saw how the neighbors ate; as a homemaker my wife was terrible." The judge concluded that the wife had not cooperated. She therefore did not get joint property rights and in addition, had to pay the 3,500 Israeli pounds ($474) court costs. The recently promulgated law on joint property, which is supposed to relieve such situations, requires a prior agreement by the couple, something young newlyweds rarely do. In any event it is only enforced on couples married since 1974.

This concept of woman as man's property means that he is the true head of the household. Even if the house was purchased by her, he may refuse entry to her friends and family. If she works outside the home their income is listed in a joint tax file, which he may view in its entirety, and which she may not, being allowed only to see her listing. This totally secular regulation springs from the religious concept that all produced of a wife's hands belongs to her husband.

Yet another debilitating situation for a woman is that she is passed to her brother-in-law if her husband dies without issue. Release from this levirate marriage involves all the same problems as divorce. The childless widow (meaning no living child) is "married" to her brother-in-law until he releases her. Many a brother-in-law uses this to extort money or property. Take the case of *G.* whose husband fell in battle before they had any children. When a few years later she wished to remarry, her brother-in-law demanded her apartment in exchange for release. Instead, she and her intended married abroad, only to discover upon return that while the brother-in-law might now give the release, their marriage was prohibited, and that even though she was expecting, her husband was ordered to divorce her. While he couldn't be forced to, it nevertheless put *G.* in a very strange position vis-à-vis her new husband. The rabbinical courts usually advise the widow to accede to her brother-in-law's demands.

Sometimes the brother-in-law can't give release because he can't be found or he is still a minor, which in religious terms means under 13 years. Such a situation happened to *L.* whose young husband also fell in battle, leaving his wife and a 3-year-old brother. Four years later *L.* wished to remarry and found she couldn't get a release until the brother-in-law, now just 7 years old, reached his 13th year.

These paternalistic/patriarchal attitudes that the women of Israel live under are quite obvious. They have little or no help from the police who see quarrels between couples as family matters, or rabbinical courts, where no woman can be a judge and where women are not considered valid witnesses. There remains a long road to equality in law and custom for Israel's women.

Witness 5: France

I have come from Paris especially to bring you some evidence about the situation of women in the process of divorce. I would like to draw your attention to the fact that the question of the payment of alimony and child-support is left entirely to the husband's good will. In France, a law has been passed permitting the woman to appeal to the Collector of Taxes, to proceed against a husband who is in default with his payments, and the costs of this proceeding should also be borne by the husband. While the papers talk about this as if it is a victory for feminism, people don't know that the statute hasn't yet been voted in by the government. Right now my husband owes me two months alimony, and he has simply told me that he has no legal obligation to pay. He can very easily get away with this because I cannot bring a criminal charge against him. This I would have to do through the civil courts, which is a very costly business and not always successful.

Divorce by mutual consent has been made much easier, but a woman with children often doesn't have anything to live on for long months at a time. I am telling you this from my own experiences, having been forced to get a divorce twice in my life. The first time was after 13 years of marriage. My husband abandoned me and our three-year-old son without ever paying what the court had ordered for our support. The second time, my husband asked me for a divorce after 20 years of marriage and working together. This placed me in a terrible position, both financially and personally. I was awarded alimony which was only a symbolic sum and totally inadequate. Through the intervention of his lawyer, my husband refused to pay two months of my support, 900 francs ($200) altogether; he said he was holding it until I returned my engagement ring, given me 20 years before. The same performance had already taken place with his first wife, and his brothers' three wives. The woman for him is a slave in the home. She must do all the housework and has to go out to work too, leaving the disposal of the money she earns to her husband's wishes. If he doesn't feel he is the undisputed boss, he will develop a complex of frustration, and castration anxiety. Men do not treat us like real companions, and the law supports this. It is so unfair. Men have got to change their attitudes towards women.

Witness 6: Tunisia

I work with a group called the Union for the Defense of Human Dignity, the fundamental aim of which is to support individual cases of oppression. International solidarity is absolutely essential for the success of its actions. It is for this reason that we want to create an international network of solidarity and we are asking those of you who are interested to give us your names and addresses.

Today we are asking you to help us expose the position of women in Moslem countries. Two years ago, a mother of five, married to a Tunisian, obtained a divorce in France giving her custody of her five children. A year ago, her husband seized the five children and took them to Tunisia. In order to get them back she has to obtain legal authorization in Tunisia. Generally, Tunisian law or Koranic law attributes ownership of children exclusively to men, and only the father can exercise parental authority. Tunisian phallocratic law grants no power to the mother. This woman's trial will take place on March 30 in Tunis. First, we are asking all women in Paris to come and demonstrate with us at the Tunisian Embassy on Thursday March 18, at 3:30 p.m. Secondly, we ask that women everywhere write protest letters expressing their disgust for this patriarchal mentality.

Witness 7: Canada*

I would like to tell you about a case that came before the courts in the Province of Saskatchewan last year. It received a lot of press coverage because it underlined the inequities of Canadian marriage and property laws. *I.* was a farm wife who gave 35 years of her life building up the farm owned by her husband. She invested all of her own inheritance money in the farm and administered the business for months at a time while her husband was not at the farm. When the couple divorced, none of her work on the farm was recognized as anything other than that expected of a housewife, and she was awarded only a monthly allowance of $200, while her husband kept the farm, said to be worth over $200,000.

Another thing I'd like to share with you is the way the Canadian government has used the funding and withdrawal of funds for day-care centers to control the movement of women in and out

*This testimony was obtained from a letter to the Tribunal.

of the labor force since before World War II. During the war, money was poured into day care in order to get women working in the war industry. After the war it was all withdrawn and women were forced to drop out of the labor market almost completely. The same thing happened, although not as dramatically, in 1952, and it has happened again in the 1960's and 1970's. In the mid and late 60's the economy was in very good shape, lots of jobs were available, and the government provided day-care funds to the provinces to administer. Now that things have tightened up and jobs are scarce, there are no more funds for day care again.

CHAPTER 7

Economic Crimes

The pattern and form of economic crimes against women in different countries is basically the same everywhere; there are only differences in degree. These similarities are very apparent in the testimonies that follow—apparent to the point of tediousness! Yet so often economic oppression and women's oppression are seen as two separate issues. Thus, the documentation of the ways in which patriarchal societies force women to seek economic security through men, thereby being forced into relatively powerless positions vis-à-vis men, is very valuable. Testimonies follow from England, Switzerland, Spain, Belgium, Holland, Norway, Iceland and Australia.

Witness 1: England

We have come to talk to you about a campaign that is part of the women's movement in England, a struggle to get financial and legal independence and full citizenship for women. It is specifically trying to attack the ways in which the State, through its particular policies in relation to social security, taxation, and family law, succeeds in forcing women into a situation where they are dependent upon men. For example, we are concerned that a woman who wants to leave her husband, perhaps because he has been assaulting her, is often unable to do this because the local council, from whom they have their housing, has registered the house in his name. This is standard policy. Women who want to leave their husbands have nowhere to live and it is impossible for a married woman in England to be regarded as homeless in her own right. She will always be instructed to go back to her husband, because it is automatically assumed that that is where her home is.

Tax allowances which are paid out for children go automatically to the husband. If it happens that the husband and wife are separated and the wife is working, and she is taking care of the children, she can't have the tax allowance on her earnings. It will automatically go to her husband's earnings.

Now, in England, we have just recently had two sets of legislation on equal opportunities in the workplace, and on antidiscrimination legislation. The state has instructed various agencies such as employers and schools to cease discriminating by sex. But in precisely those areas where the state has control, in other words in social security, taxation, citizenship, and family law, it has done absolutely nothing. So, in fact the state has made a really empty gesture with this legislation, since it has chosen to do nothing in the areas where it has some control, and is leaving it to women to try and force employers and so forth not to discriminate. In other words, they have made it very difficult to enforce the enforcement procedures, placing the burden of proof on the individual woman who is the complainant. By decree they could act to equalize pensions or to alter the systems of social security or taxation. They have chosen not to do any of these things. It seems very unlikely that we are going to get any more legislation because this recent legislation has been introduced in such a blaze of publicity, they will argue there is no need for any further action for perhaps 10 years. In fact it has been very efficiently planned.

Another woman from England has come here to describe the way in which she has been forced back into being dependent upon a man after having achieved a certain amount of legal independence in her own right.

Witness 2: England

I am a divorced woman with 4 children, depending solely on social security, which I have done for 5 years. Eighteen months ago I got friendly with a divorced man with 2 children. I didn't rely on him financially; moreover he had to support his ex-wife and children. Six weeks ago a social security investigator came to my house and said that he'd found out from neighbors that I had a man living with me, which wasn't true. He only stayed a few nights a week. He, in fact, had his own place. The social security investigator kept insisting that this man was living with me and asked me to produce my social security payment book. Because I did not know my rights, I gave him the book. I asked about future payments and he replied that, as I had a boyfriend, I was no longer entitled to social security payments.

So I went to the Claimant's Union and I was told that my boyfriend didn't have to support me or the children. So I have appealed to a Social Security Tribunal. During this time I've only been given just under 10 pounds ($20) for the care of the children. I didn't have enough money for food, so I had to steal, and I was caught. I was given a conditional discharge by the magistrate, then I was caught again and given a deferred sentence. I shoplifted, not only for food, but because it was the only way to make the social worker take any notice. Still nobody has done anything to help.

Recently, my friend lost his job and the investigator says that the only way that we can get any money is for him to claim state benefit for me, which of course we can't do because I am not living with him, and because I was an independent woman raising 4 children. I am still waiting for my appeal to go to court. The court is trying to get me off social security and back to depending on a man, which I don't want. If ever we have an argument, I can say, "What's it to you? You don't keep me. You don't pay for the food or the kids!" This was the reason I didn't ask my husband for maintenance when we divorced.

Witness 3: Switzerland

The laying-off of workers has been going on in Switzerland since last year, and it has been staggered so that public opinion wouldn't oppose it. More than 190,000 have been fired. The first to be affected were women, although the statistics don't show it. First married women, then unmarried ones, then foreigners, and lastly men. The director of a factory declared: "We are firing 60 people, of whom 50 are women. This isn't unusual because they and their husbands are making double wages." Not a word to the effect that 60% of women who go out to work do so to bring their husband's low wages up to the minimum level necessary for their family to survive.

There are several ways of laying-off women. Most of the time they are very subtle. Pregnant women have no protection under Swiss law, at least in the first seven months. Another technique is the closing down of the factory crèche,* so that women are forced to give up working to look after their children. Other methods are the withholding of work permits to immigrants so that they have to go back to their own countries; the suppression of piece work done at home; the argument that women have to take time off to look after children, especially when they are sick; and the imposition of restrictions on women because they have to follow when their husbands are transferred. Women are not backed up by the unions, who share the general attitude that the place of women is

*childcare facilities

WOMEN WHO TESTIFIED

1. Irish witness on the unavailability of contraception 2. Portuguese witnesses on the persecution of non-virgins 3. German witnesses waiting to testify on medical crimes 4. Norwegian witness on the persecution of lesbians 5. Belgian witnesses on rape in France 6. Witness on rape in USA and Denmark

Eva Besnyo

Witnesses on.the Double Oppression of Third World women: An Australian aboriginal (left), a Black American (center), and a Native American (right). The Black South African did not wish to be photographed.

Eva Besnyo

The same panel during a moment of mirth.

Nancy Budd

Irish witness on forced incarceration in a mental hospital (on the right) with Nuala Fennell, a well-known Irish feminist.

U.S. witness on femicide

Nancy Budd

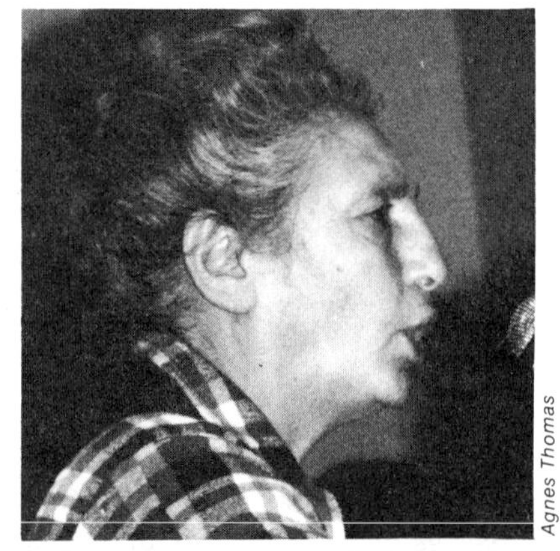

Dutch witness on wife battering

Agnes Thomas

U.S. witness on the neglect of elderly women

Nancy Budd

British witness on wages-for-housework

Nancy Budd

Helen Rymann

The banner on women prisoners. Another panel is seated because the political prisoners permitted no photographs

SOME OF THE PARTICIPANTS

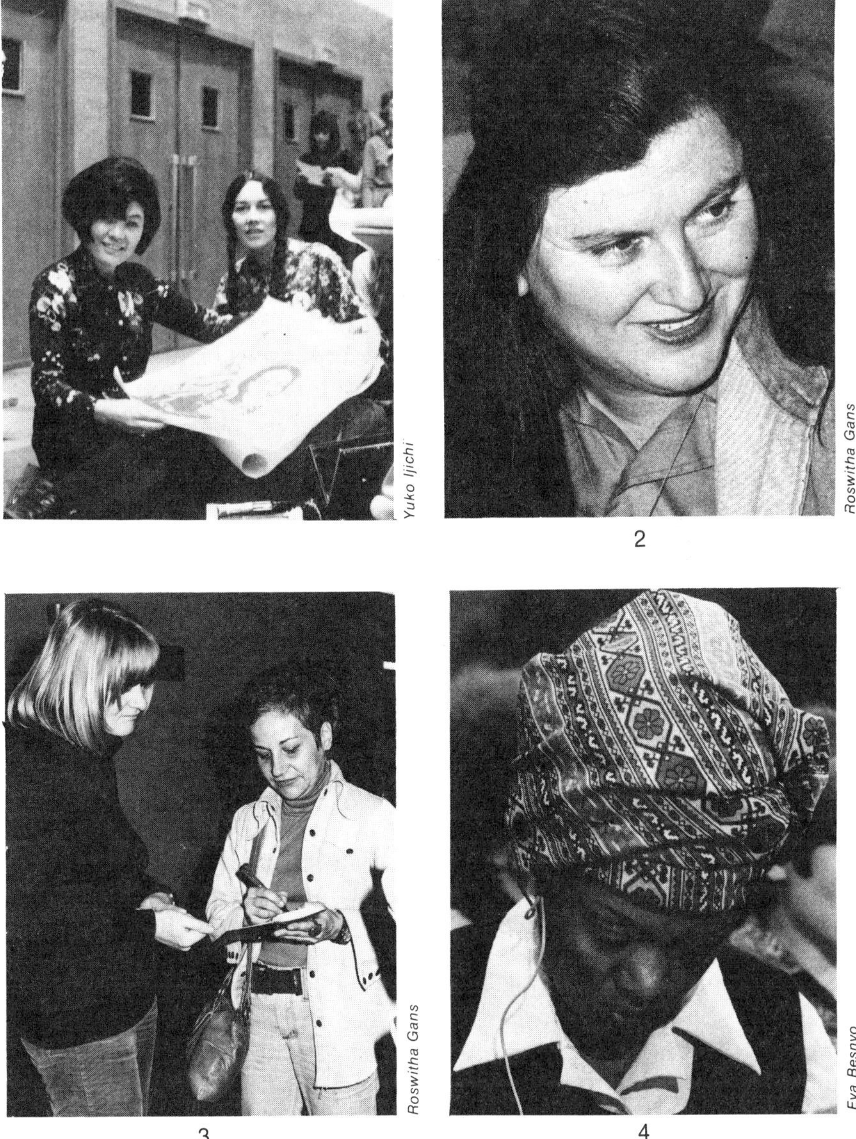

1. Yuko Ijichi from Japan with Yvonne Wanrow, a Native American on trial for killing in self-defense 2. Shelley Fernandez, a Chicana Board member of NOW,(National Organization of Women), who was active in the workshop on women battering 3. Marcia Freedman, a member of Parliament in Israel, who read the Israeli resolution, talking to Alice Schwarzer, a well-known West German feminist 4. Catharine Day-Jermany, who testified on the disproportionate number of women living in poverty in the U.S., working on her testimony

in the home and that their wages are simply a second income; that it is the man who must have the job and be the breadwinner.

The conditions to be fulfilled before receiving unemployment benefits are very hard. Part-time work under 20 hours a week doesn't qualify one, for example. Those who carry on work at home (mainly women) or who have a craft can't get any protection at all against unemployment.

Our feminist group in Switzerland is working on problems of unemployed women: the problem of money, since the woman is again entirely dependent on her husband; isolation; and the stigmatization of women in the role of housewife. We are also trying to support the women who are members of an unemployment committee in their struggles to defend their interests.

Witness 4: Switzerland

I was laid off work about nine months ago, after which I became a member of a committee of unemployed workers. In general, women feel the cold breath of unemployment first, given the hierarchical structure of the present system. They hardly feel that they have any right to unemployment benefits. Usually, the only ones who are signed up for benefits are the women who are alone: single women, widows, divorcees, and the women who have independent professions, or who have a difficult family background. And most women don't join an unemployment committee, even though they talk a lot about it among themselves. They are really under a lot of pressure from their husbands not to. Speaking from my own experience, what I got from joining an action committee was a better understanding of the capitalist system and those who control us, and the assurance necessary to take part more usefully in a society which up till now, has ignored women. The fact of being able, for the first time, to set out my ideas with confidence and clearness without being ridiculed by men, of being able to explain the problems of all women, was for me very liberating. It has freed me to take part in demands and actions for social equality.

I am very happy to be able to state that, contrary to what we have always been told, the masses can be made to understand that it is false to say that women are lacking in capability. Women grasp problems as well as men do, if not better, as they are in closer contact with social problems. Moreover, the moment that you join an unemployment committee, or something similar, outside the cycle of the consumer society, your eyes are opened to the power of the capitalist system where most of the gadgets are only designed to trap women into the cycle of conspicuous consumption so that they forget what life is about. Life is worth living, but not just to please a husband or one's colleagues. Women fill in the gap in their lives by good works which are well regarded by our society. But isn't it in political and feminist groups that we should take our place?

To all women I say that you should try to develop yourselves not only in family life but also in collective activity. The day a woman joins a group like this, she will understand just how women have been downtrodden, and she will see the necessity of extending the struggle so that all women can be liberated.

Witness 5: Spain

The following words of José Antonio express what became the official ideology of the Spanish state in 1939 regarding women. He said: "We are not feminists. We do not understand that the way to respect a woman consists in removing her from her magnificent destiny and leaving her with masculine duties . . . It has always made me sad to see women in men's roles, hard pressed and confused in a rivalry which takes them among the morbid complacency of their masculine rivals, and in which they stand to lose all."

From the end of the civil war, professions which had been open to women were forbidden them. Since then there has been a marked tendency to equate women working with children working, to regard it as a necessary evil, and to abolish it if possible. This position is held by the State and advanced under the so-called "protective" laws. For example: night work for women and children is forbidden, and efforts are made to "liberate" women from working in factories. This has the effect of legally limiting women to work in domestic service and housework—for years the fate of masses of Spanish women. In addition, married women are limited in their working capacity, as they need the permission of their husbands to sign a work contract and to receive pay for their work.

Women earn only 62.7% of what men earn, and higher qualifications are required of women for the same work. Furthermore, the productivity of women is assumed to be 20% less than that of men. As for social security, married women contribute the same amount as men, but they don't get pensions if their husbands die, only when he is incapable of work.

In 1974 an amendment to the Spanish constitution about the political rights of women was finally approved. This amendment had been open for adoption since 1952. It determines that women shall have the right to vote in all elections under equal conditions with men, and that women are eligible for positions in public collective organizations, and that they have the right to occupy public appointments and exercise all the public functions established by national legislation. But the amendment also states that these rights are not intended to prejudice the dispositions in present Spanish legislation determining the condition of the heads of family, normally the father. And Articles II and III state that no prejudice should be done to the fact that some jobs, by their nature, can only be properly performed by men or by women, which is in accordance with Spanish law.

The 22-year delay in approval of this amendment, and the limitations of the legislation just mentioned, are proof of the inequality in the rights of Spanish women and men. This is further evidenced by the fact that in May 1975, women only held the following positions within the administration of the State: Director General: one woman—99 men. In local administration there are no women presidents of departments. Provincial representatives: 7 women—52 men. Mayors: 52 women—8,650 cities. Soliciting Attorneys: 8 women—552 men. In international organizations in which Spain is represented, there are no women. In the unions, women are only at the bottom; in administration of professional colleges there are no women.

Witness 6: Belgium

Belgium is one of the many countries where many legal resolutions have been adopted which adhere to the principle that men and women should be treated equally in employment situations. But Belgium is also one of the many countries where the real situation is very different from the declared legal principles. At the moment more than 30% of all women work outside the home in Belgium. At this moment 10% of those working women are unemployed. That is a very high number, and there are more unemployed women, in actual numbers, than unemployed men. One of the reasons for this is that women usually find themselves in a special employment market, namely the so called "secondary employment market," where women hold jobs which are poorly paid, little appreciated, unstable, and in which promotion possibilities are nil.

The wage problem is closely related to this unequal employment situation. There is a 32% difference between the earnings of women and those of men in Belgium. Of the 32% wage difference, 19% is purely based on discrimination i.e., purely due to the fact that the work that women do is considered inferior to the work that men do. The rest is based on the lack of seniority and the fact that women are less qualified. The employment situation for women in Belgium is further complicated by the fact that women are burdened by family obligations. Women are, in the first place, expected to fulfill their roles within the family, especially for the upbringing of the children. It is a known fact that society does far too little to make it possible for women to develop their talents outside the home, and too little to make men aware of their responsibilities in the home. So the problem of the double load that women have to carry is very real here.

It has also been proven that there are far too few provisions made within the community to indeed make it possible for women to work outside the home. There is only room for one sixth of the children of women who work outside the home in daycare centers. The second problem is that many women give up their professional lives when they have children and during the period that the children are very small. Re-entering the job market after having been away from it for many years presents a real problem, especially for those in the 35-40-45 age bracket, because many of them find themselves divorced at that age and obliged to earn a living. The difficulty in adapting to the lack of education are some of the real problems these women face.

Another problem relates to social security. There are two aspects to it. On the one hand there is a regulation for women who stay at home and who do have some form of social security, even though it is related to their husband's employment. Their social security is based on the fact that they are the wives of men who are employed, or the girlfriends of these men—that is to say, the unpaid housekeepers. This whole social security regulation reflects the opinion of our society that a woman is in the first place a housekeeper, dependent on her husband. On the other hand, there is a problem of social security for employed women where even though women pay the same premium as employed men, their benefits are less. Finally, it is important to point out that in Belgium, women are very poorly represented in decision-making positions of important organizations such as unions, boards of directors, wage and price committees.

Witness 7: Holland

Women in the Netherlands belong to the uneducated or poorly educated, the unpaid or underpaid labor force. They are so far behind in their development that it will take at least two generations to catch up. The labor law in the Netherlands dates back to 1919. To this day women are kept from working on Sundays as well as from working the night-shift. Until 1973 there were many such restrictive regulations for women and children in the labor force. For example, one regulation stated that women with a family to look after were not allowed to work Saturday afternoons.

What is the significance and what are the consequences of the labor law, not only in the field of employment, but also on the educational opportunities for women and girls? Women and girls are forced to do the so-called "women's work." Uncomplicated work, monotonous work, work without promotional possibilities, underpaid work. Few women have decision-making positions. There are no women employed in well-paying technical professions. In the metal industry, in the chemical industry, in aviation, in public transport, women occupy quite a different position from men, especially married women. And the social security laws also discriminate against women. According to the Old Age Act of 1957, the man is the breadwinner and a married woman has no independent right to benefits. To collect unemployment insurance benefits, a man does not have to show that he is the breadwinner. However, a married woman must do so. If she cannot prove that she is the breadwinner, she will not receive the benefits.

In the Netherlands, most part-time workers are women. In cases of unemployment, part-time workers usually receive only two months benefits instead of the normal six months. Taxation laws discriminate against women as well. Taxable income after deductions is lower for a man than for a woman. A married woman who is also a breadwinner has a right to fewer tax deductions than a man who is a breadwinner.

The liberation of women is *impossible* as long as women are discriminated against in socially productive employment and are pushed into private household work.

Witness 8: Norway

As in most other countries, women in Norway are regarded as spare working power. This goes especially for married women—

of whom there are about 600,000 in Norway. Most of these women want paid work outside their homes, but very little has been done to provide employment and satisfactory conditions, e.g. chilcare for them. As a housewife, whether you partake in farming, or raise children, or just cook for your husband, you have no rights, but are completely reliant upon your husband's good will, abilities and possibilities.

Norway is a rich country. According to labor statistics, only a small percentage of the people lack work. But large groups of unemployed people—among them the housewives—do not meet the requirements for unemployment insurance, and are thus not included in the statistics.

Among the women who are employed, married and unmarried, too many have only part-time jobs. Lack of full-time work, as well as full responsibility for home and children are the main causes for this. And in full-time employment, women's wages are on the average considerably below those of the men, despite the ruling principle of equal pay for work of equal worth. Furthermore, very little concern is shown for women's biological functions. Pregnancy, bearing children, and monthly pains do not concern the employers at all, and are treated as disturbing the regularity of the work place. All this leads us to conclude that a formal equality between men and women as we have in Norway today will not change the situation of women. Women need to be liberated from their social and economically oppressed situation.

With the recent discovery of oil in the North Sea, Norway has become even richer. A need for more working power has followed. As a consequence of this, the government has cast its eyes upon the reserve army of women workers. We are now promised better conditions, nursery schools, shorter working hours for parents with young children, etc. Women are verbally encouraged to get better education and enter into traditional men's jobs, but material conditions are not much changed.

A closer look at the government's promises shows that they have not based their policies on women's natural and constitutional right to paid work, but upon the needs of the industry. Maybe something like 5,000 positions will be available for women, if we are lucky. But the work will not be found where women live today. Rather it will be centered in and around rapidly growing urban areas where social problems are already too great for society to tackle. And when women have to work far away from their homes, the burden on a housewife again increases.

The number of new positions available to women in the oil age is of course much too low to fill even the present need for paid work. In addition, many women are currently losing their jobs. Due to a general rise in wages and increasing competition—a consequence of oil money—several plants and concerns employing women have had to stop or reduce their stock drastically.

At the present speed at which the oil industry is being developed, there will be a need to invest outside the country. We know that investments in developing countries most often leads to greater exploitation of the people in these countries. Even when applied as development aid, money from industrial countries tends to affect the position of Third World sisters for the worse—relatively and absolutely.

Witness 9: Iceland*

As in other Scandinavian countries, the situation of women is better than in many other countries. For example, the law stipulates that there should be equality in work. However, in reality women get the lowest paid jobs, and they are the first to lose their jobs in times of unemployment. And, as in other countries, women who work outside the home have a double work load. The State contributes to this by not providing enough daycare facilities. Women with children sometimes have difficulty finding employment, and women in general are regarded as unreliable workers because they have children.

Witness 10: Australia

I want to talk about the unemployment of women in Australia. There are a lot of women who have lost their jobs in Australia in the last few years. One serious inequity is that married women don't get unemployment benefits. This often means that women are imprisoned in their homes. Because their husband cannot afford to give them money for childcare and in some cases because they don't want to, most women we have talked to cannot even go out to look for a job again.

This testimony was prepared by a woman who had been working in steelworks in an industrial city in New South Wales. Several years ago the women's liberation movement in Australia had

*This is a summary of the testimony that was to be given, extracted from a letter because the 3 women from Iceland were not able to come at the last minute.

a campaign to get women into the steelworks. Recently, this effort has been taking a very bad turn. Because of the economic recession, the steelworks have been closed down, and many women lost their jobs. The employers shifted many women and men to various other parts of the plant, but the areas where the women were shifted were the hardest and the worst places to work. The union, which is strong and in support of the men, doesn't help the women at all. Mostly there are migrant women working there, particularly Italian women. The women claim that they have been deliberately put there to force them to leave work. The men in the area can gain other employment but there are no other jobs for women. The employers stepped up the pace of the work so that many women cannot stand it any longer, and some of them actually collapse. The women are terrified to give information because they are afraid to lose their jobs. A woman who had already lost her job because she collapsed, was the one who told the story of what was happening in the factories. Just after Christmas, 1975, she collapsed in an area which was very dangerous to work in, where there were signs saying "deadly fumes." Now, she hasn't got a job. Since then she has tried to get compensation. Compensation is given to men because the union fought for that, but the union did not fight for her at all. So she is left with no unemployment benefits, no job, and no compensation.

CHAPTER 8

Dual Oppression by Family and Economy

The testimonies in the previous two sections indicate clearly that the patriarchal family and the existing economic structures are both built on the exploitation of women (the existing economy is also built, of course, on the exploitation of other groups of people). The entire existing economic and social structure would have to be transformed if women were in a position to refuse to play the domestic role.

The last three testimonies of this section express the view that women should be *paid* for domestic labor. Others believe that the role itself has to be eradicated. Testimony follows from Austria, Japan, Northern Ireland, Italy and Canada.

Witness 1: Austria

The role expectations of Austrian women are deeply rooted in tradition and convention. Women still want to marry, and believe the man should be better educated and should receive a higher salary. They believe also that, for them, emotions are more important than for men, and they do not consider themselves creative and productive.

But in fact 39 percent of the workforce in Austria is women, and 50 percent of these women have at least one child below 15 years of age to take care of. However, even among these women, the majority do not believe that mothers should work outside the home. This means that the majority of women by no means work because they want to, but because it is an absolute financial necessity. Hence, the textile industry is an area primarily staffed by women and very badly paid (82 percent of the women earn less than 2,000 Austrian shillings ($163) a month). More than 80 percent of the workers work mainly for financial reasons. If we combine the role image of Austrian women with the absolute financial necessity to work outside the home, we clearly realize the permanent situation of conflict in which these women must live.

This traditional role image is taught in Austrian schools from the very first grade onwards (in curricula and textbooks), and is intensified by the mass media and in advertising.

The acute contradiction between the expected female role and reality has three main practical effects. (1) Married women who work outside the home have a double workload since the household and the children are seen as their responsibility as well, and men help hardly at all. (2) It serves as an ideological rationalization for the extremely low pay received by women since women's work is considered "an additional income." (3) It causes a variety of psychosomatic and psychic complaints, such as stress illnesses, neuroses, and drug addiction.

The role forced upon women is also responsible for the fact that women are restricted to a few professions, usually those with low pay (services and office work). For example in the clothing industry more than 80 percent of the workforce is women, 75 percent of whom are working in the three lowest wage groups. In the metal industry which employs about 55,000 women, two thirds of all the semi-skilled women are occupied in the lowest of all semi-skilled groups, and the higher wage groups are reserved for men only. In addition, women who have received a full training in a different profession receive the wages of a semi-skilled worker, while men who have learned a different profession are classified as skilled workers. In the low voltage electricity industry, women are classified as semi-skilled workers in the lowest wage group. Their work requires extreme accoustical and optical concentration, and the women working for piece wages are under permanent time pressure. In the entire metal industry there is no example where men in the same wage group were required to work under similar pressure. In many firms the highest categories automatically are classified as male.

It is hardest of all for mothers working outside the home. Although the legislation for pregnant women at work is relatively progressive, they still have considerable gaps. The one-year maternity leave to which every salary- or wage-earning woman is entitled, is highly problematic. Firstly, a married woman can hardly live on 2,200 Austrian shillings ($119) a month, or 3,300 Austrian shillings ($179) for unmarried women. Secondly, this year can only be taken by women and never by fathers. This, of course, has its effects on the income and job advancement opportunities of women.

Once a women goes back to work after the maternity leave, her double workload begins right away. The number of crèches is minimal, that of childcare centers utterly insufficient. There are virtually no all-day schools in Austria. Most women must bear the entire burden of housework and education of their children in addition to their work in the factory or in the office. The total working hours generally amount to 12 to 13 daily, and quite frequently up to 16 hours.

Part-time work, praised as a good way out of this dilemma, cannot be considered a solution. It reinforces the notion that it is the woman who is responsible for household and children. It also facilitates dicrimination against women on the job, for example, by offering no job advancement possibilities. Still, 30 percent of Austrian women work part-time.

Witness 2: Japan

I have been married for over 15 years. I married the man I wanted to, against the wishes of my parents. At that time I did not believe that I would have to be supported by my husband, like the majority of Japanese women. I never wanted to follow public opinion which even today claims that married women should be supported by their husbands. In Japan firms usually make girls promise to leave their jobs when they get married, or when they become 25 years old, even sometimes demanding this in writing. Most Japanese women have to be content with temporary jobs, or part-time employment.

Sometime after I was married, my husband said to me: "You can't go out to work because you have to do the housework and look after our children." Besides, I had been looking for a crèche where I could leave the children, but I didn't find one. For all these reasons, I gave up the idea of working outside the home and for 15 years I have done all the housekeeping myself, and shared the care of the children with my husband. Even though my husband isn't bad or authoritarian, it's always his wishes which take priority over mine. It's exactly the relationship which exists between master and servant. Without realizing what was happening to me, I put it all down to my own inferiority. I lost my self-confidence and my vivacity. One day, two years ago, I said to my husband "I'm going out to work, and to have a profession." This seemed to astound my husband. He asked me "Are you going to turn into a man like me?" This question of my husband's shows that, to him, we are not in the least equal. I wish to declare here that women as well as men must go out to work in order that men and women can have equality in their marriage.

Witness 3: Northern Ireland

The woman is not given any wage for all the work she does in the home. I started doing housework when I was ten to eleven years old, as my daughters are doing now. I have never received a fee for my work either from the State or from my husband. I am a jack-of-all-trades. More so since my husband left me, as I now have to do all the jobs in the home that he did, like painting and general repairs to the house, and I have the full responsibility for rent, rates, electricity, clothing for the children, without an occasional extra pound from my husband. Although I am now living below the State assistance level, the State refuses to pay me for my work.

But this same State rules the home from the day that you get a flat or a home. When a woman is due to have a baby, the State says which hospital she has to go to. In a lot of cases the doctor induces labor so that the baby is born in the State's time and not in its natural time. When your child is four and half years old, the State tells you the child must go to school. They decide what sort of an education she must have, whether she has a high enough I.Q. for grammar or secondary school, at what age she should leave. Then they try to put her into a job *they* want her to do, and not what she wants to do. If the child is a slow learner, there is no hope for her. She will be given any odd job, and if she refuses she is then classed as a troublemaker. While the children are growing up, and while the State is dictating what is right in the home, the woman who obeys the State orders does not receive one penny in wages. But if through ill health or anything else she does not come up to standard, then again the State steps in and takes the woman to court.

The reason a lot of women are in ill health and suffering depression is because they have money problems in the home. If the State was doing what is right, and paying a woman her rightful wage, she would have far fewer health problems.

I applied for work at the employment exchange. The State trained me as a leather stitcher, and there were only two factories that would employ me. I had to turn these jobs down, because they were in the heart of a Protestant loyalist area. I had been threatened with my life if I was seen there again. When I explained this to the Social Security officer, she made me sign a form to say I had refused two jobs, and then I was told I would not get any benefits at all.

This happened to me three years ago. I reapplied just before Christmas for unemployment benefits. After four weeks of fighting for it, they granted me five pounds ($10) a week for myself, but nothing for my three children. If I was being paid for housework, I would not need to go out to work, and my family and I would not be living under the poor conditions we are at this moment.

When women unite and win wages-for-housework they will then realize how they have been exploited by the governments of their countries and also they will be able to be independent of men, which in turn will make them realize that they need no longer be doormats to male bullying and dominance.

Witness 4: Italy

I work in a clock factory in Italy with 900 employees, 400 of whom are women.

Nobody doubts that when a doctor or nurse is looking after patients they are working. Some people are even beginning to realize that when we are at home looking after our loved ones, we are also working; it is a part of domestic work. However, usually it is not defined as work, or seen in the same terms as jobs outside the home. Housework is part of that obscure, taken-for-granted, feminine mission of dedication to the family and the home, requiring patience, sweetness, sacrifice. Since housework is not paid for, it has no value in terms of exchange. Women are exploited from the day of our birth until the day we die. This process of exploitation has serious effects on the physical and mental health of women. Women in the labor force are exploited twice over; they have double work, double physical fatigue, and hence much greater vulnerability to physical illness. However, they haven't the time to cure themselves.

One hundred and eighty of the women in our factory had a pap test. When the tumor center sent the results, many of us (25%) discovered we had cervicitis, vaginitis, erosion of the neck of the womb, parasites, inflammation, etc. Not that we had believed ourselves perfectly healthy before this. Once we finish our work in the factory, our domestic work begins, so we lack the time to pay attention to our exhaustion, discharges, rising temperatures, pains and various discomforts. When can we permit ourselves to be ill? Never, unless we have cancer, tuberculosis, or have to undergo an operation. It is necessary that our life be in danger and the work that we do in the home and in the factory must also be in danger before we can take the time to attend our health needs. As a result of the pap test, many of us were told to go and visit a gynecologist. Such a visit amounted to four lost days of paid employment; a half day for the visit to our own doctor, another half day to go to the Social Security to fix the appointment with a specialist, another half day for the visit to our own doctor to get the necessary prescription. And then the whole process over again at the end of the treatment to get the results.

Every woman from now on must refuse to do unpaid domestic work because it weakens and enslaves her. Getting money for housework, that is where the first rise in power and solidarity among women must begin. The weakness stemming from unpaid housework has repercussions at all social levels, not only on health, but in the family, in society and even at the political level. It is verified by our experience in the factory—men do not want to recognize our autonomy, our struggle, especially the refusal of free domestic work and the demand to have this paid.

Witness 5: Italy

I am on the Committee for Wages-for-Housework in Mestre, Italy. I will tell you about a woman who was in a psychiatric hospital in Padova. She is 64 years old, unmarried, from a rural family, with not much education. Upon the death of her parents, it was seen as natural that she go to live with her brother to do his housework, in order to guarantee at least her physical survival. However, when she refused to do housework for him, she was hospitalized. Her brother referred to her as useless. She would not do housework or take care of the children, and she did not even want to work in the fields. So she was put in a psychiatric hospital. For 20 years she preferred to accept the rules and structures of the hospital, than to do unpaid labor for her brother. But at the age of 62 she became more active and started to eat more and to work, and she was therefore pronounced recovered and discharged. But this only lasted one week, after which she returned to the hospital saying that she was made to work too hard at her brother's house, that the children did not leave her alone, that the work in the fields hurt her hands, and that the work at the hospital was better. From then on, her brother lost interest in her.

The experience of this woman is not an isolated story. Women have always had to pay with isolation if they refused to work for free. Society has created institutions for dealing with our refusal. We have the choice to return to work for free, each one of us in our own house, or to be treated as sick. The woman about whom I told you was considered cured the moment she communicated her desire to return to housework. This is how they have neutralized the revolutionary vein of her deviance. This must never be our reality again. We do not want our rebellions turned against us. We do not want our normality measured by our productivity. The more we submit and accept the disgusting conditions in which we are reduced to live and work, the more science and the masculine power consider us in good mental health. This woman who refused to submit was powerfully eliminated. We must never struggle alone again. We must demand wages-for-housework so that we will not be constrained to choose between unpaid housework and madness.

Witness 6: Canada

I will read a letter from Canada that has come to the Tribunal:

> It is impossible for us to separate ourselves by countries, because one of the greatest crimes against women is the way in which we have been divided by the status and income of the man we marry, by whether or not we work full-time in the home, by whether or not we are with men, by whether or not we have children, by whether or not we are natives or immigrants, and by language, race and nation. In our view the crime against us internationally, from which all the other crimes against us flow, is our life centered around servicing men, children, and other women in order to produce and reproduce the working class. For this work, we are never paid a wage. The crime of work and wagelessness brands us for life as the weaker sex and delivers us powerless to employers, government, planners, and legislators, doctors, and the police, prisons and mental institutions, as well as individual men, for a lifetime of servitude and imprisonment. Our campaign for wages-for-housework is a campaign for power—the power to refuse this destiny of unpaid work which we carry out in every country, wherever we find ourselves.

CHAPTER 9

Double Oppression of Third World Women

As the testimony in this section so powerfully conveys, Third World women always have a double burden, and often a triple one, since they are so overrepresented among the poor. The women from South Africa and Australia indicate strongly that racism is by far the most vicious oppression they have to deal with, and they certainly prove their point. However it does not follow that Third World women should ignore sexism. Just because being lynched is worse than being raped, doesn't mean that if one is vulnerable to both, one should do nothing to try to stop rape.

For Arab women the issue is different. Here the extreme sexism they have to deal with is staggering. Testimony follows from an Australian Aboriginal, a Black South African, a Native American, a Vietnamese woman living in France, and an Arab woman.

Witness 1: Australia-Aboriginal Woman

There has been a conscious governmental policy of silence on internal racial matters in Australia. This has been coupled with an explicit policy against the immigration of people of non-European racial stock in Australia—commonly known as the "White Australian Policy." Even this name suggests that Australia has no black population. Aboriginals, although the largest population, are not the only Black group in Australia. As a result of the colonial expansion of the western capitalist system, Aboriginals have had their land expropriated by successive waves of farming, timber, and mining interests. This has been accompanied by the introduction of diseases and a conscious policy of extermination. So successful was this extermination policy that Australia can boast of being one of the few nations that has implemented genocide—against the Tasmanian Aboriginals.

By colonialism, racism and sexism, Aboriginal women's status has been reduced to the lowest level in the hierarchy of Australian society, and her traditional status in Aboriginal society has been destroyed. Lack of understanding and attitudes of superiority and ethnocentricity led to the imposition of the white western model of male/female relations, which was inappropriate for traditional Aboriginal society. In the traditional Aboriginal society women were the basic producers of food. Women were economically independent. A woman's daily activities were not under the control of her father or husband but were collectively organized with other women. The introduction of a cash-based European economy meant that the intrinsic value that women had as food producers was destroyed. Women became a liability and not an asset since their major role had become redundant. On the basis of the stereotype that in hunter-gatherer societies "males go out to hunt while the women stay home to tend the children," as well as due to the division of labor in European society, any work that was available was given to the men by Europeans. Only occasional work was offered to women as domestics.

The role of Aboriginal women as educators of their children has also been affected by the white educational system, which teaches children the values of white society and subverts them away from the beliefs and values of their traditional society. For this, the Aboriginal women are blamed by the men, because traditionally women have been in control of raising the children.

When one compares the position of Black women today with that of white women in Australian society, whether it be legally, educationally, in the home, the workplace, in prisons, or in regard to their eligibility for state welfare, we find that Black women are very severely disadvantaged. Racism is so entrenched that it is the primary cause of the oppression of Black women, economically, legally and in all other spheres. The oppression of Black women vis-à-vis sexism is secondary. For instance, while white women have been exploited as housewives, Black women have faced the double oppression of virtual slave labor on the sheep and cattle stations and in the sugar cane fields in return for their "keep," in addition to trying to fulfil their family needs. An illuminating example of Australian policy concerning women and Blacks is that white women were granted franchise at the federal government level in 1902, yet it was not until 1967 that Blacks, male and female, were given the franchise by a national referendum.

Concerning the welfare system, even when Aboriginal women were finally able to benefit legally from pensions, they were denied welfare for widowhood, etc., because they were not seen as "civilized," whereas white women were denied welfare on the basis of their lack of "respectability." It is exactly this analogy of the uncivilized Black woman and the unrespectable white woman in the eyes of the chauvinist racist white man that is the basis of the horrific treatment of Black women in Australia. Black women are raped, but very rarely are the rapists brought to trial, often because it is the police themselves who are the rapists. Black women are sterilized by force, especially in the Northern Territory, because they are seen as unfit mothers. On cattle stations it is common practice to give Black women their weekly rations of food and tobacco only if they give their sexual favors.

The average living conditions of Black people in Australia are among the worst in the world. Unemployment among Blacks is officially 40%, but it is as high as 90% in some country areas. Of course these figures do not include Black married women who are not eligible for unemployment benefits because they are married and therefore are excluded from the official statistics. Housing consists everywhere of tin humpies and old car bodies, and sanitary conditions are abominable. Black people are forced by society to live in "camps," as the unofficial reserves are called, and in the brutal words of one wit, "Australia's policy isn't *apartheid.* We don't need it!" The exception is the state of Queensland where a regime of apartheid is enforced under the Aborigines Act, 1971, and the Torres Strait Islanders Act of 1971.

Aboriginal reserves and camps are typically located some distances from towns, on worthless land that is often flood-prone and infested with mosquitoes and flies. Infection and malnutrition among adults is high but among the children it is catastrophic. Infant mortality rates in parts of the Northern Territory are the highest in the world, and in Sydney, the largest city in Australia, the Black infant mortality rate is 2½ times as high as the white rate. It is in this atmosphere of dehumanizing degradation that Black women are forced to admit that they are bad mothers, even by their own standards. Not so long ago in the balanced but plentiful tribal life, they could give their children everything they needed and wanted. But in the depressed conditions of racist Australia they can no longer meet their own standards of motherhood. From the moment they conceive, their own poor health conditions affect the health and growth pattern of the child in their womb.

It is in this context of oppression that the demands of the women's movement for equal pay, free abortion on demand, etc., are irrelevant to Black women. It is not the male chauvinist who is the oppressor but the entire white society. For example, child molestation is abhorred fairly universally, but when the child is a young Aboriginal girl of 9 or 10, a common comment is "Well, you know that they mature much earlier than whites."

Liberation for Aboriginal women cannot be achieved primarily by liberation from their men; first and foremost there must be liberation from an alien social system.

Witness 2: South Africa—Black Woman

According to the South African government's classification, there are three different non-white groups. But most people now are beginning to think in terms of two groupings: the franchised group, and the disenfranchised group. The Colored people, the Indian people, and the Black people in South Africa do not have the vote. The Colored people and the Black males used to have it, but it was taken away from them. The Black woman is at the bottom of the six-layered heap. You get white men, white women, Colored men, Colored women, Black men and finally Black women. As far as things such as wages and job opportunities go, it goes like that too. The system effectively prevents the Black woman from any meaningful participation and involvement in the political and economic arena.

Every Black South African must carry a "pass" in which her or his qualifications are listed. Passes indicate what area a Black person is permitted to be in. The Black woman is regarded by law as a perpetual minor. In their passes they are therefore described in terms of their relationship to men—as the daughter of your father, or as the wife of your husband. When a Black woman is married to someone who qualifies to live in a particular area, she is permitted to rent a council house. (No Black is ever allowed to own immovable property in the urban areas. I can never own a house, or the land on which the house stands.) If my husband dies, then if my son qualifies to be in that area, I might be allowed to go on occupying that house as his mother. But if my son happens to be 10 years old, bad luck. I have to leave.

The system of education in South Africa has been designed to retard the Blacks. Even in Parliament it has been admitted that it is designed to make the Black child see herself as the labor force of the country. This educational system makes sure then that the Black people in South Africa never aspire to certain types of jobs. For example, only a certain percentage are allowed each year to train as nurses. There are areas such as Cape Town where a Black cannot train as a nurse. And in the urban areas there are no boarding schools and teacher training colleges for Blacks because these are permanent structures and the Blacks cannot have permanent structures in the urban areas. This means that if I want to train to be a teacher, I have to travel three days by train to the rural areas to take up this training. Consequently, about 80% of the Black women of South Africa are absorbed into the domestic service, and about 60% of these women are "live-in maids." They stay with the family that they are working for. Perhaps the verb "stay" is a bit misleading, because the white family you'll be working for will be living in a mansion. At 6 or 7 or 8 o'clock in the evening when you finish washing the dishes, you leave their house to go into your own little hut in the back of the house. So you don't really live in; you live detached from the house in a hut which is not as big as the garage.

Wages are very low for Black women, but the State disability grants and pensions are even more unbelievably low. For instance, you are expected when you grow old or when you become disabled, to exist on 13 Rand ($7) every other month.

As support or maintenance for your children, if your husband should desert or divorce you, it is just not worthwhile for Black women to go and stand in the long queues to be humiliated by the white people, because there is no law to enforce the payment.

In the urban area there are large numbers of what are called in South Africa "bachelors." They are the migrant laborers who are very much married, but who are forced to leave their wives and children in their homeland, and come and work in the urban areas. These so-called bachelor quarters pose a problem for the Black woman in the urban situation. As a mother you know that your 10, 12, or 14-years-old daughter can very easily be enticed into the bachelor quarters where thousands of men who are forced to live in celibate conditions, live near by families. So you get rape of children and women, and you also get prostitution. Women who have no alternative because of job reservation,* poor education, and lack of opportunity, sometimes lose themselves and cross to the bachelor quarters so that they can have somebody to sleep with and to give them food for a night, or clothes, somebody who perhaps after sleeping with them doesn't even give them water! The government refuses to recognize the fact that these men are *not* bachelors.

For a Black woman in South Africa your life is never really yours to determine. From the moment you are born everything is prescribed by others. Now that I live in Western Cape, for in-

*In South Africa the best jobs are reserved for whites, by law, and the worst ones for Blacks.

stance, I can't just decide one day that I have had enough of the Western Cape and I will go and live in Johannesburg. I qualify to be in the Western Cape because I have been living there for more than 15 years, and I am confined to that area. I cannot go and live in another area even 30 miles away. I must live there forever until I die.

The fact that I am a divorced woman means that I can never legally be allowed to rent a house. Fortunately for me I live with my mother who has a house. I am only allowed to do certain types of jobs, and also I am only allowed to earn a certain amount of money, and also I am only permitted to live in one particular township.

My children's school is prescribed, the language in which they will be taught in that school is prescribed, the subjects they shall be taught are prescribed, where they shall go to the university is prescribed. *Everything* is prescribed for Black women in South Africa.

Witness 3: U.S.A.—Native American Woman

My name is Yvonne Wanrow. I am a Native American. I was born and raised on an Indian reservation. I left there to get an education and I completed high school. I married young, but got divorced right away. I have three children, aged 12, 5 and 22 months, whom I have had to raise by myself. I live now in the state of Washington on the Colville Indian reservation with my mother, sister, two nieces, my children, and two other family members. Thirty-two years ago I was born into a defensive position. I was born to be oppressed, and I am fighting for my life.

Three and half years ago, I was arrested and charged with murder and assault. I was put in jail. I was brought before an all-white jury at the time of the Wounded Knee occupation in South Dakota, a time when all Native Americans were seen as militants and extremists. I was convicted by this all white jury on Mother's Day, May 13, 1973, and sentenced to two twenty-year terms, and one five-year term for the use of a gun. Why? Because I had killed a man in defense of my child, my babysitter's child and myself. William Wesler was a 62-year-old white man, six foot two inches tall. He was known to the police as a child molester and rapist. He wasn't particular: he molested both boys and girls. He had previously raped the seven-year-old daughter of my babysitter, and given her venereal disease. He had also attacked my son. He lured him into his home, locked the door, and picked up a knife. But my son was able to escape with only a lump on his arm. The next night when I was at my babysitter's home with my children, my babysitter and her daughter, Wesler and another man broke into the house at 5 in the morning.

I had a broken leg at the time, and when Wesler headed towards one of the children, I screamed for help. Wesler, who was drunk out of his mind, turned, lurching toward me. So I shot him. I immediately called the police to report what had happened. They arrested me and put me in jail. I feel all I was guilty of was being a mother who loves her children.

At my trial the judge refused to allow evidence on Wesler's history as a child molester and rapist. He did not allow the babysitter's daughter, whom Wesler had raped, to testify because it was "irrelevant," and she was too young to be believed. It was said by the probation officer at my sentencing that I must be prone to violence because I had purchased a gun. But I had purchased the gun for self-protection, because my life had been threatened by white people, and I was living alone in a neighborhood known to the police as a troublesome area. I was told that I could pursue my career in art in prison and that I could teach other inmates art, and that I could counsel other Native American women in prison. And the probation officer said that as I come from a large family, there certainly would be no problem as to who would care for my children during my incarceration. He also implied he was an authority on Indians because he had spent two years on my Indian reservation. They really didn't care what happened to me. The judge said, "Hurry up. Let's get this over with. Let's wrap it up by the weekend!"

My tone of voice was used to convict me; they said I was calm because I was not screaming on the telephone when I reported what had happened to the police. And the prosecuter used my calmness in the courtroom against me, telling the jury: "Look at her, how coldblooded she is. How calmly she sits there!"

When they put down in their books, "the state of Washington vs. Yvonne Wanrow," they declared war on me as a person, and as a woman, and as an Indian woman, and as a mother. Since the Indians started to ask for their rights, there has been an undeclared war on Indians. My people are being killed every day, little children are being shot, their mothers are being shot in the back, in the head. And they are using the Bureau of Indian Affairs to train Indians to kill Indians. I am a political prisoner because the prosecutor is a political climber. He wants to have a higher position some day, and its easy for him to get there by putting minority people in prison. It's easy to put minority people in prison because those who do not have money to hire an attorney, have to take a public defender, men who are paid by the State to defend poor people—and *they* talk you into pleading guilty.

I appealed my convictions and won the appeal, but the feeling of happiness was shortlived. The prosecutor is now appealing that decision. The case rests now in the hands of nine white men in the State Supreme Court in Olympia, Washington. They are going to decide over the next few months whether or not I got a fair trial, or whether or not I deserve another trial. So, I wait, as I have been waiting for years, with the threat of being separated from my children, with the threat of a lifetime in prison. They want me to hand over the next 25 years of my life to satisfy a system that is dominated by men. By white men. But I decided not to sit back anymore and quietly watch the judge plan my destiny. I decided to make a stand because I had nothing to lose anymore. And I am asking you to stand with me, whether it be in spirit, or whether it be physically, by writing letters or doing whatever you can think of to help me raise money, to fight my case. I have been able to organize some defense committees in the States. I have one in Canada too. I would like to have one or more overseas. If there are any of you who are willing to help me establish some defense committees, please contact me later. If the men in the State Supreme Court know that the world is watching, they will be very careful in reaching their decision in the next few months. If I win a new trial, we will fight for a dismissal. If I lose, we'll fight for a change in sentence. This can go on for another two years. But at least I am able to remain out on bond, to be with my family. Thank you for your kind attention.*

Witness 4: U.S.A.—Black Woman

My name is C., mother of three, and victim of a sexist welfare system.

I would like to share my experiences of the oppression suffered by many sisters in poverty within the United States. I hope that my statements will help raise the consciousness of all women here and strengthen us in the development of an international sisterhood so powerful that all crimes against women will end now and forever.

Poverty means more than the lack of a job or the lack of

*As of September 1, 1976, Yvonne is still waiting to hear the outcome of the appeal.

money. Poverty means powerlessness—the lack of control over our own lives and over the institutions which have a daily impact on us. Women are more vulnerable to poverty than most realize. For a woman who has been out of the labor force (raising children) and for the woman whose husband leaves her, welfare may be the only solution in the U.S. With welfare comes all its "supportive" institutions, ethics and controls. Welfare is a back-door marriage, with an inadequate, male-controlled, government subsidy.

Before discussing my personal plight of poverty and the welfare system, I would like to talk about some general aspects of welfare and poverty in the U.S.

Many women throughout the world do not consider the problem of poverty in the United States a serious one. For those of us who must live in the "Land of Plenty" with *nothing*, our plight is no less than the crimes against our sisters in other countries. Our children go to bed hungry when our country pays the farmers *not to grow* the food we need. We are sick, when the U.S. scientists have the cures for most of our problems. In the rural areas of the U.S. many families are without electricity, bathrooms, or fresh running water. Education is not available to all of our children on an equal basis. Poor women do not have access to decent, safe and adequate housing.

Inflation is particularly a problem for the lowest-income group because the prices of necessities have risen faster than the prices of luxuries. Women and minorities are more likely to be poor than any other groups; poor people spend a larger portion of income on necessities and therefore feel the impact of the economic crisis especially keenly.

Women and minorities who try to obtain income increases in line with inflation are in a poor bargaining position. Working women do not usually earn wages that include cost-of-living adjustments, and outside the workforce, a high percentage of women and minorities are on fixed incomes.

Welfare is a dirty word and a badge of inferiority in the United States. Aid to Families with Dependent Children (AFDC) is the program which most single women on welfare—and their children—are victims of. The basic eligibility requirements of the program reflect the attitudes of men towards women who, due to choice or circumstances, must survive without reliance on the financial support of a husband.

In order to receive AFDC benefits for herself and the children a woman must be needy. Each state sets its own standard of need to measure the poorness of the women. In addition, the father of the children must be deceased, physically or mentally incapacitated, or gone from the home. She must certify this under the threat of imprisonment for perjury every month in order to be eligible. In addition, she must register for work, subject her child/children to numerous blood tests to establish the identity of the father (if it is questioned), sign a criminal complaint against him, and sign away all the current and/or future rights to support for herself and her children.

Being Black and living in a low-income neighborhood limited my ability to be mobile in my choice of education and environment. It was easy for me to make the wrong choice in a husband, at the age of 15. I immediately began my family. With the lack of educational opportunities afforded to my husband, he also had little choice, and consequently, a low paying job. His income would have been sufficient, but because of his need to prove himself a man, he had to spend "his money" on "his car" and "his clothes," and his family went without. That went on until I decided I couldn't take it any more.

I had one small child and another on the way. I tried to get child support, but that proved impossible because the county district attorney claimed he could not find my husband. So, I decided to get married again, only this time it was to the Welfare Department! At least I didn't have to sleep with the department, although I felt I was getting screwed all the time, every day. The Welfare Department gave me only $103 per month. My housing cost was $80. So, I only had $18 per month for food, clothing, electricity and all the other things that I needed.

The social worker came to my house one day and decided to inspect my cupboard, and my dresser and my closets. She took my drawers and dumped all the stuff out saying that she had to make sure I didn't have any man's things there. Another time, because of my severe arthritis it was necessary for me to have a gardener cut my grass. They happened to see the gardener cutting my grass one day, so I got a notice the next month saying: "We had to cut your check because you are living with a man! And the man was living at home with his mother, his father, his sisters, his brothers, and his six kids, but they were saying he lived with me just because he was cutting my grass.

After my daughter was born, I decided that this was not the life for me. I contacted my husband, gave him our son, which was very hard to do, and gave my daughter to my mother. I went back to school, got a job, and went through a number of changes to get myself together. I was lucky, and I had the motivation to try to beat the system. I haven't yet, because as long as the economic status of women in the United States and the world is based on the benevolence of men, we will never beat the system. I am here today, to join hands with my sisters to continue to struggle against the crimes and oppression faced by women of the world.

Witness 5: France—Vietnamese Woman

My name is *M.* I am a Vietnamese living in Paris. During the whole period of the Vietnamese war, I was an active militant against this war.

I will tell you my personal history, an experience lived between a man and a woman during a period in which war devastated my country, and in which Vietnamese women who refused to submit to the law of the oppressor were tortured, raped, and killed.

I was married to a Frenchman, Jacques Doyon, who defined himself as a radical left intellectual. This characterization meant to me in that period, someone who is against war. All the people from the West holding this position were to me persons rejecting domination and oppression, the domination of nation by nation, of human group by human group, or of one individual by another. If this man called himself a leftist, I assumed it was because the suffering of the oppressed echoed in his ears and his eyes could not stand the tortured bodies and souls anymore. It must be because he was looking for another kind of relationship with others, trying to cancel from his life relationships of injustice and cruelty, institutionalized or not. And I assumed it must mean that he intended to try to live this.

In December 1969, Jacques Doyon left his position with the newspaper *Le Figaro* to write a book on Vietnam, signing a contract with Fayard Publishers. I worked with him on this book on deserters from the French army during the first war in Vietnam, and the position of the PCF (French Communist Party) on this issue. I participated with all the interviews with the deserters. They are for the most married to Vietnamese women. The presence of an Asian woman neutralized the mistrust of these women and reassured them. My belonging to the Vietnamese world in struggle, served the same goal. Upon their arrival in France, these women experienced general bewilderment, racism, and the humiliation of the systematic rejection by the French community of these "colonials," rejection which pushed some of these women into a psychiatric clinic upon request of their husband's family.

Doyon also asked me to contact politicians from the PCF and "democratic" organizations. I was brought to lie and to invent false stories in order to get information. My Vietnamese female identity was used to open each and every door. Furthermore I typed. I typed a lot, and retyped texts again and again. In addition, I did the housework, the cooking and the washing. I talked about my liberation without knowing that I was this male's slave, being exploited on two different levels: intellectually, by having ideas that belonged to me stolen from me, and manually, by being used as a housekeeper.

After two years the job was finished. Doyon signed the book and had the bad taste to dedicate the book to me: *To M. and to the land of her ancestors. It is a fine land and very fertile so that it is easy for characters like Jacques Doyon to exploit it.*

He is not the only one to exploit in this fashion. It is an exercise practiced by people from the right as well as from the left, by those with power who have few ideas and so take the ideas from people who are oppressed and without defense, just because they have the money.

Witness 6: Middle East—Arab Woman

I have been asked to speak about the oppression of Arab women. My sisters from Egypt and Saudi Arabia were invited to attend the Tribunal, but once again the unheard voices of Arab women were stifled; they were forbidden to come here to tell you of the oppressive and barbaric treatment suffered by Arab women.

I am from Yemenite Arabic descent, but I was born in England. My grandfather and father were of peasant background. In some parts of the Arab world, ancient customs still exist in those countries which are economically backward and primitive. The old traditions are adhered to most strongly among the peasantry. The Arab peasant woman works in the fields alongside her husband. She then has to work in the home tending to her husband's and family needs. If any problems arise within the home, the wife is never consulted. Problems are discussed among men only, as the Arab man plays a very dominant role in all spheres of Arabic culture.

The birth of a female child is not welcomed in Arabic culture. My father was disgusted with my mother for not giving birth to a male child. In some parts of Southern Yemen, girls of ten years old are sold into marriage. The girls have no say in the matter as the marriage is arranged between families. I personally have heard of cases where girls of ten have been married off to 60-year-old men. My mother was approached on numerous occasions by Arab men who offered sums of money to buy my sister and myself. At that time we were only small children and the offers were for marriage!

Polygamy is still widely practiced in Saudi Arabia and other parts of the Arab world. A man can have 4 wives and if he wishes to end the marriage, he only has to utter the sentence "I divorce thee" three times. The marriage is then legally annulled. The Arab woman has no rights whatsoever in divorce. She is totally dependent upon her husband.

If an Arab woman commits adultery, either her husband, her father or even her own brother will kill her, because she has brought disgrace upon both her husband's family and her own family. The killing of the woman is called "the honor debt." Her dead body will restore honor to the family name.

The Arab woman has no rights to property. When her husband dies the property automatically goes to the son of the family or the husband's brother.

There are no such things as welfare clinics, maternity hospitals or medical treatment for the Arab woman. Medical treatment is only available to those who have money. Customs also play a large role in the question of medical care. If a peasant woman is ill she will not be allowed to see a doctor if the doctor is a male, as she is not allowed to undress or remove her veil before a man.

The university-educated westernized Arab woman, although oppressed, is of course far better off than the nomadic or peasant woman living in the desert or in the rural areas of Arab countries. Some people think that Algeria is a progressive country, but this is not the case as far as women are concerned. I will give you a brief example of a marriage which takes place in an Algerian village. The bride who has never met her husband before the wedding day, has the harrowing experience of ritual rape on her wedding night. She is taken into the bridal suite while both the family of the bride and the family of the groom stand outside. The local villagers gather outside the house, beating drums and singing songs for the honor of the families. The bride who is usually in her teens, is petrified, for if it is not proved that she is a virgin on this night, she will be killed by her father or brothers. The proof of her virginity will be a sheet stained with her blood which the groom will hold up for all to see. Proof that the girl is a virgin will cause great celebration. The mothers of both families will hug each other in joy over this evidence of virginal honor.

While I talk to you at this conference, the Arab people of

Dhofar in the Arabian Gulf are fighting against a feudal ruler who is being propped up by the British and American governments to ensure the safety of their oil interests. Dhofar women are playing a very prominent role in the revolution. In the liberated part of Dhofar a women's center has been set up to fight against the old Arabic traditions of forced marriage, polygamy, and other oppressions which Arab women suffer.

CHAPTER 10

Double Oppression of Immigrant Women

Immigrant women are among the most oppressed in Europe, whether or not they are from Third World countries. Sometimes they are even seen as "Colored" when they don't see themselves that way, for example, Portuguese and Spanish people. Their terrible powerlessness as women, as foreigners, as poor, and sometimes as Third World people, has made it very much more difficult for them to become politicized and organized.

Testimony follows from an Indian woman living in Britain, and a Spanish woman living in Switzerland.

Witness 1: England

As an Asian woman, I would like to tell you about the thousands of Asians and West Indian women in Britain and the kinds of double oppression they face.

When you enter Britain at Heathrow Airport, you see a vast army of middle-aged Asian women sweeping the floor, clearing the dustbins, clearing the tables. If you stay in Britain you find out that these women are the symbol of the kind of oppression of Asian and West Indian women that occurs in Britain. These women are unorganized, they are underpaid, they are underskilled. They have no chance of attaining greater skills. British employers have acquired what they consider a docile, quiet, subservient and low-paid workforce. The textile industries, the light engineering industries, the plastic industries of Britain hire considerable female labor, including Black female labor which is doubly exploited. The trade unions are white, and they are male chauvinist, and they are not concerned with organizing these women. In fact, when these women have taken matters into their own hands and come out on strike, the trade unions have been quite antagonistic to them, and quite indifferent to their interests. Nevertheless, I have never found women's groups in Britain coming to the factory gate and saying to the women "You are on strike. What can we do for you?" Never. Why?

The women's movement is white, and perhaps has not considered the case of Third World women. Also women in the movement come from a class that does not directly come into contact with the majority of Third World women, that is, manual workers, factory workers, members of the British working class. But without the help of the unions or the women's movement, Third World women in Britain have shown a degree of militancy and organization over the past 18 years that nobody expected. They have stood up and said: "We are not going to work in these conditions. We want dignity. We want respect. We want more money. And we will organize ourselves." In factory after factory they have fought for union recognition. These women have shown that not only are they capable of challenging the kind of oppression they face in their workplaces, but they are also capable of leading the men in those same workplaces. In Imperial Typewriters in Leicester, for example, where white and Third World labor was viciously exploited, 27 Third World women led a walkout and they took the male folk with them. In a small textile factory in Wolverhampton, the women fought for three months for union recognition and the right to elect their own representatives. They fought for the dignity of working women. In Battersea, in a television factory where the union signed a document with the management to sell out the entire working force and shut down the factory, 80 Asian women walked into that factory, occupied it, locked themselves in and fought for their right to work.

In fighting oppression in the factory, the women have to stand up before their husbands and say "Look, I am on strike. I can't look after the children. I am not free. I have to go on the picketline." And when she says that, she is fighting for her liberation within the home. When she says, "I have to go on strike for higher wages," she is saying to her husband and to her employer: "Money and my livelihood are important to me. It is not just a question of needing pinmoney." So you see there is a direct relationship between fighting oppression at home and fighting oppression in the workplace which cannot be ignored.

The Immigration Act in England, as in many of your countries, discriminates against Third World women. For example, it does not recognize Asian women as married to their husbands if they are married in their own countries. That is a bloody insult! And it also stops them from entering the country. Other women have the right to be with their husbands who are working in Britain. But forty thousand Pakistani women are waiting to be united with their families.

Immigrant women are the most oppressed women in Europe. It is easy to feel strongly about the oppression of Black people in South Africa. But you in Europe need to face the racism on your own doorstep. When racism and sexism are combined, it results in much greater oppression and there are millions of immigrant and Third World women all over Europe.

Witness 2: Switzerland

A small group of women, a Spanish woman, myself and another sister, have been doing a study of the situation of immigrant women in Switzerland. Immigrants come from countries that traditionally furnish cheap labor, for example Italy, Spain, Yugoslavia, Turkey. They are the least skilled and the worst paid of the proletariat. Without disregarding the discrimination which all foreign workers suffer, we want to underline the fact that immigrant women are victims of a double discrimination, as foreign workers in a xenophobic structure, and as women in a patriarchal structure. On the economic level, immigrant women bear on their shoulders the greedy exploitation of monopoly capitalism that results in the constant acceleration of the rhythm of work in the factories to the detriment of the health and nervous equilibrium of the women workers. In the event that they cannot physically cope with the increased pace of the work, women are demoted to even worse-paid tasks. It is very clear that the foreign women workers are given the most strenuous, dangerous and degrading jobs in Switzerland, jobs that Swiss women would never accept.

Let us now look at how the immigrant family is devastated by this situation. Even with a work permit, the immigrant worker is only allowed to have his family come to Switzerland after 15 months. When the woman finally can join her husband in Switzerland, she is confronted with very difficult problems. For example, the housing situation is very difficult for foreigners. They usually live in barracks, or in unsanitary houses that Swiss people would refuse to occupy. As much as 20% of the immigrant's pay is deducted for health insurance etc., which forces his wife to accept whatever work she can get no matter how low the wage.

While working, the immigrant woman is confronted with many insoluable problems: lack of crèches and kindergartens, most of the crèches being private and prohibitively expensive. There is a black market of nurseries where children are kept without official control in a small room in the care of an incompetent person. The immigrant women also suffer from an abnormal separation and alienation from their children who grow up in a social and cultural environment different from theirs. Some immigrant women, for economic reasons, are obliged to leave their children in their native countries in the care of a grandmother. For parents who are not allowed to bring their children under a certain age to Switzerland, another solution is to settle them at the other side of the frontier and to see them at the end of each week. The psychological, moral, and economic consequences of this can easily be guessed.

The lack of facilities makes the life of the immigrant difficult. Switzerland accepts immigrant women as a labor force, but refuses to accomodate them as mothers. Switzerland is a country with one of the highest weekly work hours: 45 hours in industry, 46 in trade, and 50 and more in hospitals, to which the housework hours must be added for women. We have here in Italian, German, English and French, a booklet titled "The Immigrant Women's Manifesto."

Witness 3: Switzerland

I am a Spanish women who emigrated in 1962. When I was 21 I came to Switzerland. Here my life became very difficult. I arrived in a country where I didn't speak the language, but after two days in the country I began working in a watch factory. Two months later I was told that I had to do piece work. I was supposed to do 3,000 pieces a day. If I did less than this amount, they would pay me only for the work I had done. In order to do 3,000 pieces a day, I had to work at a forced pace and in so doing I became like a machine.

In 1963, I got married. After three days of vacation I continued working. At this time I became doubly exploited. I worked 9 hours at the factory and 5 hours at home. In 1964 my first daughter was born. During the 9 months of my pregnancy I continued to work at the same pace. In fact, I worked right up to the last moment. The day began at 5:30, and at 9:30 that night I entered the hospital. When my daugher was 3 months old I returned to the factory. Since there were no creches I had to have my child cared for by a Swiss family. I had to pay 15% of my earnings to them.

We lived in a house that had no conveniences. Before we moved in, it had been used as a stable. There were rats and, of course, no bathroom facilities. You might ask, "How could you live like that?" The reason was that signs for apartments to rent said, "Swiss only: foreigner refrain from applying." Because of the bad conditions of my house I was forced to take my daugher to Spain.

Here in Switzerland, women have no social services, let alone foreign women. Our daughter was in Spain two years. During this time I changed my house and job. I now worked in an electronics factory, doing the same work as men, but was paid 50% less than men. I remained at this factory for 3 years. When I asked for a raise, they told me no, that I was a woman and couldn't earn as much as a man. In 1968 I left the factory, because they would not give me the raise I requested.

Returning to the watch factory, I was forced to do piece work again. In 1962 they wanted 3,000 pieces a day, but in 1968 I was told that I had to produce 7,000 pieces. To produce 3,000 pieces I had had to work without breaks; to produce 7,000 pieces I worked without even being able to go to the bathroom. This is what happens in a capitalist system; they exploit you more and more. In the factory I worked 45 hours a week as well as spending 10 hours in traveling time because the factory is situated 15 kilometers from the house. The factory schedule is as follows: leave home at 6:30, work until 12:15, begin again at 1:00 and work until 6:00, which makes 9 working hours and 2 going and coming. At 6:00 when I return home, I must do the housework. So in total I work 16 hours a day which amounts to 96 hours a week. For 13 years I've realized how truly exploitive this is.

Because of this situation, I can't take care of my children well (I have two, 1 and 6 years old). While I work, the oldest stays at home until it's time for school, and the youngest I take to a nursery school, where I have to pay 400 Swiss Francs ($155). In order to earn that I have to work 9 days.

In Switzerland today, the owners now discriminate against women more than ever. In almost all factories, women's wages have been cut more than 2 francs (.77 cents) an hour, and changing work often means encountering worse conditions for immigrant women. In general, immigrant women are nearly all in a state of extreme nervous tension, due to the excess of work. I am one of the immigrant women who came to Switzerland healthy, but I am now in a nervous state as a result of the working conditions.

CHAPTER 11

Double Oppression of Women from Religious Minorities

Patriarchal societies treat women according to their relationship with men. If a woman is married to, or mother of, or lover of, a man who is a political or religious militant, she is immediately suspect. Women are seen as mere appendages of men who can be assumed to share their religious and political views. Hence, they are persecuted for whatever their men are persecuted for. Testimony from Northern Ireland follows.

Witness: Northern Ireland

I come from Northern Ireland and although Northern Ireland is always on the news media, our women's point of view is never heard. I come from Belfast which is occupied by the English State. They have their soldiers there to stop the people from trying to free their own country. I come from one of the segregated areas which is Catholic. This area is sealed off by iron gates at the end of the streets, and we, the women from the minority areas, have suffered a lot through state control. First, because it is hard to get hold of any money. When you apply for a job in Northern Ireland you have to state which school you went to, so all the firms can know right away what your religion is.

Eight years ago my husband became redundant at work. He applied for about ten jobs for which he was well qualified, but was turned down because of his religion. So he went to Scotland to work. The State paid his fare there, since then I have not seen him. He sent me some support for my three children aged 13, 9 and 8, but what I get from him now is well below National Assistance level. Although the State knows this, they will not give me a penny towards the support of my family. I have even applied for free school dinners for my children, but I have been turned down because the government judges my needs not by what I get from my husband but by what he earns. The point is that I have no rights by law. I am not the only housewife in our area like this. I know of others who have 5 to 6 children, and the State gives them a bare subsistance. When these people apply once a year for a clothing grant for the children, which they are entitled to, they are turned down. The State sees women as cogs in the wheels of their machines, cogs that are not even worth oiling. This is how the State works in the homes of Belfast.

When the British soldiers reach one of the homes of women whose husbands and sons have been interned or sentenced for political reasons, or the homes of their sympathizers, they degrade and insult the women. Many a time a woman has woken up to find soldiers standing at the foot of her bed. The raiding patrol just bursts into the house saying "This is a raid. We are going to search your house. Get out of bed!" When the woman asks them to leave the room, they just laugh. Often she may not get her dressing gown, but has to wrap one of the blankets around herself, and get out of bed. If there is a military police woman with them, and if the woman or any of the children want to go to the toilet, the military policewoman goes with them. If the woman tries to hit the soldiers for being so insulting, she will be beaten up. This is the only time that the State treats women as equal to men—under interrogation, interning, and sentencing.

CHAPTER 12

Violence Against Women

There is a widespread notion that women, being the weaker, gentler sex, are gently treated by men. This is undoubtedly sometimes true. It is also true that not all men are physically violent towards women. But, as the following testimonies show, the idea that men treat women with kid gloves is often a total myth. Nor do women meet with violence only when they "step out of line." Men use violence to maintain, advance, or protest a setback in their power relations vis-à-vis women. And, because they can often get away with it, they sometimes act out the anger and frustration they feel towards others or themselves or life in general in violence towards women. This is a simple case of abusing power.

RAPE

Besides presenting the following introduction to the crime of rape, French witnesses offer four testimonies. These are followed by the combined testimony of two Belgian women who were raped in France. Testimonies from Denmark, Portugal, Holland and Norway follow.

> Torture has been denouced as an action against the principles of the Declaration of the Rights of Man and the Charter of Nuremberg. And what about the Rights of Women?
>
> The definition of torture is as follows: bodily and psychological torment perpetrated against the will of the victim with the aim of annihilation of her personhood by breaking her resistance. Rape is the term applied in the case of a woman who refuses sexual relations imposed on her by force. Legally, rape is recognized as a crime with physical aspects only; namely the penetration of the vagina by the penis against the will of the victim. In effect, however, the real crime is the annihilation by the man of the woman as a human being. It means breaking her resistance by means of sex.
>
> Rape is a class crime—of men as a group against women as a group. Every woman is a potential victim of rape: little girls, adolescents, single women, married women, middle-aged women—and even dead women. Society countenances rape and becomes an accomplice to it, so that it lends support to a situation of permanent insecurity on the part of all women. The woman who refuses the

status that is imposed by patriarchal ideology is morally raped every day by a series of structures and institutions that deny her integrity and her identity as a woman.

Women live in terror of rape from the most tender age. An incredible number of children are victims of sexual aggression even in their own families or from relatives. The climate of terror thus formed continues into adulthood and pushes women to look for "protection" just where it cannot be secured: from men. On the other hand, from childhood on, every woman, as a potential rape victim, is made to feel guilty and is accused of provocation. Thus it is that the guilty men can throw the blame back on the women victims.

The consequences are that in France rape is a crime that is talked about very little. It is a crime women are ashamed to report. Only one out of 20 women who are raped, dares to report the crime (1,538 in 1974), and even fewer cases come before the courts. Often a report of rape is changed to a case of maltreatment and assault, as in several cases about which you will hear testimony today. Among the men accused of rape few are sentenced, or the sentences passed are not severe, and are often not fully served.

Rape is the only crime where the victim is treated as the accused, because it is a crime which society prefers to deny rather than punish. Rape is a taboo subject. This applies equally to the rape of minors by members of their families, uncles, step-fathers and fathers—a situation more common that most people realize. Through rape, a man seeks to subjugate and humiliate the woman, and if possible to make her participate in her own subjugation and her own humiliation. These are the same goals sought by the structures of the patriarchal society: the nuclear family, economic exploitation, class hierarchy, authoritarian religion, militarism, control of our reproductive functions, the sexist system of education, prostitution, pornography, and sexual permissiveness disguised as liberation. As long as these structures persist, we will continue to be raped.

In order that we stop being victims, we ourselves must take up the struggle against rape. Individually and collectively we can break the silence and make it no longer a taboo subject, or something shameful which weighs us down. We must report the men who rape us, bring charges despite the shame, the disgust, and the wish to forget. We must pursue our legal actions right to the end. We must demand not only the application of the existing laws, but also the revision of the laws on rape. When we are raped, we must demand women doctors, women lawyers, women police. We must be mutually supportive, morally, materially and in all ways.

Witness 1: France

One Monday evening I went back to my house around 9:00. I live on the 4th floor. At the third floor I ran into some young guys sitting on the steps. They followed me, horsing around, and when I opened my door, one of them came in with me. He told me they were waiting for my neighbor who hadn't come in yet and he asked me if they could wait in my studio. I said O.K. They put a note on my neighbor's door and came into my place. Later, my neighbor, having found the note, came in too. Shortly, a couple joined us. Then some people went out to get a record player and something to drink, and they brought back alcohol. It seemed like a normal enough evening with talking and dancing. They told me they were students. There seemed to be no reason to mistrust them.

Two of the guys tried to flirt with me. They cornered me and tried to kiss me. They tried to argue with me saying: "Why don't you want to? I'm not a chauvinist, don't you like me? Anyway, you are a liberated woman, aren't you?" I told them, "No, I don't want to!" At one point I was really fed up and I went down to the street. One of the guys came after me to persuade me to come back up, saying they would settle down. So I went back upstairs.

I went into the bathroom to wash my hands. My bathroom is tiny, two people can hardly stand in it together. One of the guys came in and cornered me there, blocking the door. He took down his pants and tried to take down mine. There was a struggle; I fought and managed to get out. Then, very upset, I broke down. My neighbor said, "Listen. If he bothers you that much, you can go to my place." The two of us went down. At her place, she suggested I sit down on the bed. Then I realized that the guy had followed us in. He told her to leave, which she did, and I found myself alone with him. He tried again to persuade me by talking, for the length of a sentence. Then all at once he started to knock me around. I started to cry. He half strangled me and managed to get my clothes off and raped me. Afterwards, he told me: "Now I have won 15 francs!" ($3.33).

The others came into the studio, then I was alone with a second guy, who also raped me. Then he left to give his place to another. Between the second and the third rape, I tried to find my clothes to escape, but the others had taken them. After my third rape I managed to get out, naked, on the landing. I went up to my place, but they followed me, and pushed me on the bed. I started to shout. A neighbor heard and cried through the walls, "If you don't stop, I'll call the police!" I shouted, "Do it! Do it!" and the guys got scared and left.

Rape is, first of all, the negation of being. And after the rape, the rape goes on. One is raped morally in the name of justice. The interrogation, the repeating of the minutest details, is very upsetting. The raped woman is forced to prove that she has been raped, and these proofs are then turned back against her. The fact of having lesions in the vagina is only considered the result of normal sex—"a little brutal," but "completely normal." "A woman cannot be raped" said my judge. My complaint of rape was never even registered at the police station. Only the complaints of theft, assault and battery were recorded. I was examined by a doctor who was angry at having to do it, and who did not examine me correctly. He noticed the blows and wrote only "trace of rape." Because I was in pain, I went to see my gynecologist who found lesions, though it was some time after the rape. I was not conscious of any physical pain during the rape. What I felt most strongly was the look in his eyes which completely negated my existence as a human being. I was no longer a person. I was only an object, his object.

The law does not understand why a raped woman does not show a superhuman resistance and an Olympian calm, both during the rape and afterwards. During the interrogation, we do not have the right to crack up. For the police, if a woman cracks up, it is because she is lying and not because she has lived through a traumatic situation. Personally, I often felt like letting the whole thing go just so as not to have to be made to relive the experience with all the talk. The law merely registers a complaint about a purely physical act. But for me rape does not consist of a physical act, but in the intention of the rapist. It is an act in which the effect of the rape continues after the purely physical act is finished. And the law does not want to solve the problem. That's why I accuse all courts of rape!

We haven't the courage to face the police and the examining magistrates by ourselves. That's why I make an appeal for solidarity among women. On my own, I would never have been able to lodge a complaint and go through with it among all those males—male police, male doctors, and male judges.

Witness 2: France

I was raped by my father's best friend when I was 14. My father had died only a little time before this. This situation was really traumatic for me, not solely because of the rape, but mainly because it was the outcome of the rejection I felt by my parents and the lack of love which existed in our family. Afterwards, I was made to feel dreadfully guilty. This man blamed me. The next morning he told me I was a bitch, a whore, a little slut etc., etc.

And when I tried to talk about it, when I tried to say what had happened to me, people threw the same accusations at me. They said, if it was true, if that really had happened to me, it was obviously I who started it. So, in fact, either I was the guilty one, or else they completely refused to acknowledge the situation. Since I felt so completely put down at that time, I felt I had no choice but physical death or internal death. For years I suffered terribly because of this experience. I was 18 before I managed to speak about it again. It is thanks to feminism, and the struggle, and to women, that I could do this.

Witness 3: France

A number of testimonies have been prepared on rape. But it's not just a question of giving evidence, it's a matter of what's going on at this time which concerns us French women and, I think, the other women here. I am referring to certain films which have been released this year, films which are called pornographic, 'porn de luxe.' In these films it is suggested that if you are a liberated woman you enjoy being beaten. Among others there is the "Story of O." The testimony which I am going to read to you seemed to us particularly significant, inasmuch as we, a group of women who went to see this abominable film together, saw that the individual who raped the woman followed the plot of the film exactly.

The French Committee of the International Tribunal wishes particularly to denounce the daily aggressions by men against women in the street and in public places. *M*, who was not afraid of the street, tells us how she met some people there whom she thought would be friends but who acted violently towards her:

> I was in a bar in Montparnasse where I occasionally went by myself. It was a bar where one meets people easily. I sat down not far from an attractive, friendly couple who were talking, and we began to talk together. After a few moments, the woman and I went downstairs to the ladies' room together, continuing to chat. I told her about myself—that I am a simple girl without problems, from a middle class background. She seemed to me to be a complicated "artistic" type of woman, maybe a painter, and I told her how glamorous she seemed to me.
>
> We went back upstairs and the conversation continued on different and interesting subjects. They spoke of "reinventing the world" and said they hoped to see me again. At the moment of leaving, I offered them a drink at my place, mentioning that I lived with friends who might be sleeping, but that if we were quiet it would be all right.

"No. Listen," they said, "it would make more sense to have a drink at our place." I accepted, and we stopped by the store to buy some drinks. Since I don't have a car, they promised to drive me back to my place afterwards.

They lived in a comfortable apartment in a very respectable neighborhood. When we arrived there, they poured me a drink. The man made a few casual advances towards me that I brushed off. I felt uneasy. I explained to them that I was not at all interested in sexual "scenes." But he kept lifting the skirt of his friend. Then he lifted mine, and I said loudly that this behavior didn't interest me at all. He then kissed the other woman and sat down on the desk, brandishing a book. Suddenly, with a deliberate will to shock me, he slapped me, knocked my head against the wall many times, tore my dress, and hit me again.

I took my stuff and ran out of the apartment, crying for help on the landing. I looked for the stairs but right away he caught me. He grabbed me by the neck, squeezing it so hard that the woman said, "Stop! You're going to kill her!" He threw me back into the apartment, locking the door. He slapped me again, beat me with his belt, kicked me with his shoes, and said that I was his slave and that I had to obey him, and that I would understand later. He made me suck the woman in front, then behind, then he slapped me. "Do better than that" he said, "You really don't know anything about how to do it." He made me suck him, too, and slapped me continuously. "But you don't know anything" he said, "She is going to mount you now." The woman said, "No. That's disgusting!"

He called a friend on the telephone, and passed the receiver to me. A woman was on the other end. I asked her what I had to do. She told me to hit him a few times. When I protested, he abused me twice as much. I asked him, "When will you let me go?" As always he answered, "When I decide to." Next he made me talk on the telephone with a certain Paul, whom he invited to come share in the evening. He told him that I had tried to escape, saying it was very bizarre. "That's the first time that has happened!" he said. The other man responded, "Hold on. I'm coming with my chains," and he laughed. I was scared! I asked the woman, "How can you accept this?" She replied, "You will understand tomorrow!" I asked, "Are you going to save me?" They had me completely stupified, knocking my head and tearing out tufts of hair. I couldn't defend myself! When I resisted, they started to strangle me. "Why me?" I asked them, "Why don't you do this among yourselves?" Answer: "Our choice has fallen on you."

The man took a cigarette. I asked him for one. In response he burned some of my pubic hair. I was so scared. Scared of being mutilated. When he said, "What can we put in you?" I shouted that I preferred him to an object, and he said, "I only make love with people I love." And then he said to the other woman, "I don't want her anymore." He insisted that I say obscene words. I cried, "Shit, Whore." But that didn't make them happy. I started crying, completely exhausted and having lost all courage. They made me read a book by Bataille, a description of a sexual act, and I had to masturbate while they had sex.

They made me lie on the floor to sleep. I asked for a blanket, which made them laugh. I was cold, but I arranged myself as best I could. While they drowsed, I looked for the key, but I couldn't find it, and they kept an eye on me. At eight o'clock the next morning, I asked them to let me go. They did so and the man even kissed me goodbye!

At first I didn't even think about making a formal complaint. How could I prove that the story was true? It wasn't exactly a rape that had happened to me, but for me it was ten times worse. It was slavery. Debasement. Humiliation. Later, my brother-in-law persuaded me not to go to the police. He thought that it was better to forget the whole thing. Also, I was afraid of reprisals. But a number of my friends convinced me to make a complaint. Thanks to them I was able to speak, to deliver myself of this thing. Without them, I would have been repeating this story over and over again in my head for years. A doctor verified the fact that I had received blows, and reported it to the police.

The man was called before the police. He said: "I don't understand why you make such a big thing out of such a harmless affair." He admitted the facts of the case, but said it was just a game for him. He didn't think it would traumatize me so much. He didn't seem to realize what he had done, or what he had risked.

The police said that it wasn't an actual rape, as legally defined. If I had been raped, it would have been much more serious, they said.

Witnesses 4 and 5: France

C : In the night of August 21, 1974, around one o'clock in the morning, we were sleeping in a small tent near Marseilles in France, when we suddenly were awakened by a bright light being shone on us. Three men appeared and asked to share our tent, under the pretext that they couldn't get back to Marseilles. We refused. They laughed. A discussion followed, during which it gradually became clear what their intentions were: two single girls on holiday could surely do with some male company. One of them tried to get in. We hit him with a hammer. Blows were exchanged. We yelled "Help!" as loud as we could, although almost speechless with fear. Statements made to the police confirmed that nearby campers heard us, but they said they thought it was just young people larking around. We were told we should have shouted "Fire" to get people out of their tents!

These three men had come to "avenge" their slighted manhood after one of them had made an unsuccessful pass at us two days before. They admitted they wanted revenge. They proclaimed it proudly as though it were something natural, something that was owing them, even an honor that we should accept. A nightmare that lasted hours followed during which they threatened to kill us, cut us up, and throw us into the sea. They hit us everytime we tried to defend ourselves.

Exhausted, at the end of our tether, paralysed with fear, threatened with death, having tried to reason with them, we finally "gave in," as they call it. In spite of our struggle, the blows, the threats, that single moment when we failed to offer "the same degree of resistance throughout the assault," as specified by French law, was interpreted by the magistrate—a woman!—as consent on our part. None of the rest counted. Hence, the charge of rape was reduced to that of assault and battery. This is a common procedure in rape cases. It is up to the woman to give material proof of the events of which she has been the victim, the best evidence of rape being death or vaginal laceration!

For rape to have occurred the following conditions have to be satisfied:

1. to have cried "Help!" at least once.
2. to have offered the same degree of resistance during the whole assault.
3. to be found in a defenseless state (e.g. with hands and feet bound).
4. to have had a witness.

The fact of being alive is in itself proof of consent. Blows, insults, violent handling of other parts of the body, threats of death, none of that is accepted as proof of rape. But rape is what we experienced, rape which is so much more than forced penetration by a man's sexual organ.

Immediately after we were raped we went to the police station. "Do you want to lodge a complaint?" we were asked. "Yes!" we said. The process of justice was slowly put into motion. It was six o'clock in the morning. We were told to go to the hospital. At the hospital they barely listened to us, and we were shunted from department to department. Finally, we refused to go any further and collapsed on a seat. After an hour and a half they found a bed for us. The consultant arrived with his students, and showed them how to make a report: "You have to be very careful with the law" he advised, "they can make trouble for you later." Finding that we weren't virgins he said that what we had been through wasn't all that serious.

Fortunately, three women doctors appeared. They took a vaginal smear within five hours of our being raped. If you wait any longer the presence of sperm cannot be detected. The laboratory tests confirmed the presence of sperm, but that was still not enough proof. The period of one of us came earlier because of the shock, and the other had been made pregnant and had to have an abortion, but these facts were also not enough.

The next day we appeared before the magistrate—an appalling woman, cold, cutting and aggressive. The questions she asked were typical of the sort of trap laid for women. For example, "Do you want to live?" she asked, "Do you value your life?" We were silent, "Come on, I'm in a hurry, I have no time to waste. Yes or no?" She demanded. "Yes, I want to live. I value my life," we both said. She took this simple assertion as evidence of consent. To her it meant that we would rather submit to physical outrage than expose our lives to risk. Furthermore the fact that we were homosexual was interpreted by the court as a provocation, and as yet another insult to the manhood of the three men.

In the waiting room before we appeared in court, the father of one of the men tried to buy us off. He offered us money to keep us quiet. He said his son needed country air and that he suffered from nerves. This same son was to request, in front of the magistrate, the legal assistance of Mister Floriot, one of France's 3 most famous lawyers, and a "friend of the family," he said, trying to intimidate us even more.

T : In September 1975, one year after we were raped, the reduction of the charge of rape to one of assault and battery meant that we appeared in front of a court of summary jurisdiction. We claimed that the court was not competent to try us. Our women lawyers refused to plead, since the fact that we had been raped was not recognized. Three weeks later, the court, presided over by a woman, declared itself not competent, and referred our case to an Assize Court. This was a great victory, as this sort of thing hardly ever happens. The three men, who couldn't even agree between themselves about whether we had consented or not at a given point, then lodged an appeal. This was heard a month ago, in February, at Aix-en-Provence, France, and we won yet again. The appeal court recognized that we had been raped, and therefore sent the three men to the Assize Court where that trial will finally be conducted in some months time.

These victories are thanks to the solidarity of women from many countries in Europe and elsewhere who have sent telegrams, organized petitions, and been present in court at all our trials up to now. Without these women, without their support, we could never have distanced ourselves from this rape enough to be able to talk to you about it now.

What can we learn from our experience? First, that the woman is considered responsible for the assault she suffers, merely by being a woman. And we have come to realize that it is *ordinary, habitual,* and *normal,* at certain times and in certain streets, to get raped. Public places belong to men, not to women, especially if they are alone and unattached. Rape is a *daily* event, it happens in all spheres of a woman's life, at work, at the office, in the street, while out walking, in the woods, on a journey.

Furthermore, rapists are *ordinary* men. The three men who raped us are aged 24, 25 and 30. The eldest one has 5 children. Two of them are French and one is Italian. They are the kind of men you find everywhere. Men want to prove their virility, which they confuse with the use of force and domination by force.

People have criticized us for bringing a complaint against these three people because they are working class and not middle class. They forget that one of us is working class too. They bring everything down to the class struggle.

For the forthcoming trial, which we see as a "political" trial, we need enormous support from you in all your countries. We need a lot of financial help, as the two of us can't bear by ourselves the financial burden of a trial in the Assize Court where a large number of witnesses are necessary. We need a lot of solidarity in the form of telegrams, personal letters, and personal appearances in court.

This trial is the first in a long line which is getting longer every day. Thanks to our common struggle, you and us together, we will make this into a show trial and bring women's solidarity out into the open. We are fighting for our principles, for a change in the law, and for a change in people's minds too. Our aim is to get as much publicity as possible for our case, to get these three men's names published in the papers. This trial is an opportunity to point the finger at men's attitudes to women, at their desire for a relation of force and power over women which leads to rape.

We are not concerned with demanding stricter penalties for rape. That is not our aim. Men invented prison, let them take responsibility for it. Every rape should be reported in the press with the names of the men who committed it. We must also demand maximum damages, and with the money, create organized groups that can offer a refuge for battered women or rape victims, and help them with their court cases from start to finish. We feel that these two concrete solutions—posting the names of the rapists and the crimes committed on public buildings and at their places of work, and demanding as much money as possible—are two things that will embarrass men very much and might bring them to reflect on their pseudo-virility, and their pseudo-potency—since prison is unlikely to effect these attitudes at all.

We are not just fighting for justice, we are fighting for our existence! We are making an *urgent* appeal for the solidarity of each one of you in your different countries, a solidarity that will rise above any political, social and philosophical differences between us. We want your help for our trial in the Assize Court which will probably take place in September.

Witness 6: Denmark

I am a rape victim. I have been attacked twice. The first time was in 1974 when I was stabbed with a kitchen knife in a room at the University I was studying at in Boston, U.S.A. The second time was in Denmark. The first time I was assaulted at 5:30 in the afternoon by a man I had never seen before. He walked into the room that I was in, alone, turned off the lights, and demanded that I take off my clothes. I tried to stall him, hoping that somebody would come by, but nobody did. So, I began to scream. He then stabbed me in the neck. After I was stabbed I stopped resisting and I was forced to have oral and vaginal sex with him. When I was taken to the hospital, I had lost so much blood that they had to do open-heart surgery on me to keep me alive. I was at the hospital for a couple of weeks, and recuperating several more.

The second incident happened last September in Denmark. I was walking home alone at night on a well lit main road to a friend's place where I was staying. Just as I was about to enter the building where my friend was living, the man ran up behind me and grabbed me, pulling me away from the doorway. I managed to push my way into the hallway of the building and began to struggle with him till I realized he had a knife. I stopped struggling quite so hard then, and he dragged me outside the door and across the corridor towards some bushes, in a dark area. I kept saying I didn't understand him, because he was talking to me in Danish. And finally, something clicked in my head, and I started repeating over and over again: "You *cannot* do this to me again. I was almost killed. I have been raped before. You *cannot* do this to me again." I don't know if he understood any English, or whether he was affected by my intensity, but after several minutes he finally let me go. I ran into the building and my friends called the police. But in both of these experiences, the man was never caught. On the second occasion another woman was raped the same night.

After the second incident, even though I was not raped, it was close enough, and it brought back all my feelings about the first rape experience. I was in shock for over a week. I couldn't function normally or do anything at all. I thought all the work that I had done to get over my first experience was completely undone, completely wiped out. I developed a fear that I had not felt after the first incident, because I had had so much support and help after it. I felt a real fear that I would never get over it. That I would just be psychologically and emotionally destroyed by what had happened to me.

So I decided to try to find professional help, but that was not an easy thing to do in Denmark because I wanted a woman, and I also wanted someone who was sensitized to the issue of rape. I asked a lot of people, but no one seemed to know. Fortunately, someone finally got me in touch with a group of women who had been studying rape for over a year at the Criminology Institute in Copenhagen. Through them I was able to find a woman counselor, who helped me get over that trauma. I also had a lot of legal questions, about what would happen if the man was caught and I would go to court. None of my friends seemed to be able to answer them. Furthermore, most people I came in contact with in Denmark were filled with myths and misunderstandings about rape, such as that most women actually bring rape on themselves; that it's better to give in and not struggle, not only because you will get away better physically, but also psychologically.

I have gone through both of these debilitating experiences, these attacks on my personhood, which rape really is, and yet I am standing here, and I am able to talk to you about this. One of the things that has made this possible is the help I have gotten from other women. I believe, from my personal experience, that rape victims will suffer less if they have outlets for their rage, so that they do not internalize the shame that the society will try to tell us should be ours, instead of the man's who attacks us. And the only people who are going to help us are other women. Fortunately, there is now a group in Copenhagen which is trying to form a counseling service for rape victims and women who have been violently attacked. Not only do we hope to help other rape victims so that they don't have to go through the struggle I went through trying to find help, but also we hope that through the publicity we have gotten and will be getting, we will be able to attack many attitudes about rape.

My group in Copenhagen needs advice and information from other women who are at the Tribunal on setting up an answering service for rape victims.

Witness 7: Portugal*

Mario Taborda, a well-known Oporto child psychiatrist, raped his 15-year-old patient, Laura, in his consulting room. This case will shortly be tried before the Supreme Court due to the perseverance of Laura's mother and lawyer, who have prevented this case from being covered up as the four previous ones were. It has been fought in the lower court now for 3 years; meanwhile Taborda continues to practice and hold his 3 government appointments.

Laura started seeing Dr. Taborda after being disturbed when she saw a drowned person at the beach. After the first consultation Dr. Taborda expressed the opinion that Laura should see him once a month starting February 1971. In September 1972 Dr. Taborda told Laura that she would have to continue treatment for some time, but that he knew an association which gave financial assistance to people needing it, and he said he would put in a word for her. However, in order to do that he would have to do a special examination. This is how Laura described this special examination:

> When I got there he told me to take my pants off. I was very afraid but took them off. I thought I was getting an injection so I asked him not to hurt. Then I realized it wasn't an injection. I felt something as hard as iron being introduced into my anus. I had the sensation of wanting to empty my bowels. He told me he was using vaseline. I tried to look to see what was happening, but he kept pushing my head down. Then he tried to introduce into my vagina some sort of instrument that seemed to me to be the same one he'd used behind. He asked if it was hurting, and I replied it was. And then suddenly he held me and introduced his penis, but not all of it because it hurt, and I got up suddenly making it impossible to continue.
>
> On that occasion he gave me the first check for 500 escudos ($18), and he started treating me in a more familiar way using *tu*, and driving me home.

Laura's mother thought the check was from the "association" mentioned by Dr. Taborda, and she was very grateful that he was

*Due to language difficulties, considerable additions were made to this testimony from material about the witness sent prior to the Tribunal.

trying to help them in such a kindly way. She thanked him for his kindness, asking how she could reward him for all he was doing. He replied that he liked red flowers, so if she ever wished to give him anything, that would be a lovely gift. So every Monday or Tuesday Laura started taking him flowers. He requested she come early in the evening after the nurse had already left. On these days he started having regular sexual relations with her in his consulting room. He also made her consent to introducing his penis in her mouth, and he also used his mouth on her. He always blocked the keyhole as one of his employees was usually there. Then during the week he would see her as a patient. He often gave her money which was supposed to be for the flowers and other checks from the "association."

Laura was afraid to tell her mother. In Portugal, a loss of virginity outside of marriage is seen in an extremely serious light. A man can, by law, repudiate a woman who is not a virgin at marriage. However, Laura told one of her girl friends about what had happened. Her mother overheard her speaking to her friend on the phone, and asked Laura what was going on. Laura refused to tell her, and her mother said she was going to take Laura to see a woman doctor. Laura told Dr. Taborda, who insisted that she not tell her mother about their relationship as it would only hurt her unnecessarily. He added that Laura would also get into terrible trouble if she did, but, he said, Laura would end up being in trouble alone because there was no proof of anything, and all he had to do was to say that nothing had happened. He suggested that she should not be afraid of going to the gynecologist. She should say that what had happened was due to tampax and playing with herself.

But Laura's mother extracted the truth from her the next day by beating her. She then accompanied Laura to her next session, confronted Doctor Taborda who said, "But surely you must have known. She brought me flowers," and, "Dear lady, you must realize the state your daughter is in. It is none of my business. You should have been more careful."

Brito da Silva, the lawyer Laura's mother contacted, was not willing to accept the case at first, since he knew Taborda. He only accepted it later when Taborda's perjury and bribe attempts came to light. (In order to defend himself, Taborda had brought a case against Laura.)

It is common in Portugal for men in the medical profession to abuse women. We have other testimonies, not as well documented as this one, but of which we are absolutely sure. Also, doctors are almost never willing to say that a woman has been raped. Even if she was a virgin and there is evidence that she is no longer, they just say that her hymen is "complacent," which means that the woman didn't tear and that there are no signs. But the truth is that there are very few such cases.

With regard to rape in marriage, the law in Portugal states that marital relations have to be maintained. The expression, "He used me," is the usual way rape in marriage is expressed in Portugal, particularly by women of lower economic means. But it happens to women in all conditions. The husband seems able to use his wife's body in any way he wishes—to force her to have an abortion she does not want, to have her sterilized, to lock her up, or to beat her. Beating is so frequent that once I saw a man who was beating his wife at a circus, and the policeman only asked him to beat her where he would not disturb the people watching!

Witness 8: Holland

In Holland rape is a hidden problem. The police admit that rape exists, but when a woman comes to them to report a rape, the reaction is often that she has provoked it. Very often she is not treated seriously. That's why the group "Vrouwen tegen verkrachting" (Women against rape) started in Amsterdam in November '75. Some of us had been to the U.S. to get ideas of how to start a rape crisis center. In the first month we opened our center, we got 150 phone calls from women who had been raped or assaulted. It was a lot more than we expected.

Most rape and assault in Holland is not reported to the police. This is because the victims are often too ashamed about their experiences to talk about them. They feel guilty for not having prevented it. "Why did I go out so late in the night? Why did I ask him to drink a cup of coffee with me?" they ask themselves, as if a woman isn't free to do things like that without being raped. And if she tells someone of her experience, she will often hear the same prejudices. She will frequently meet with scorn, ridicule and blame by her family and friends. When she goes to the police, they often investigate her complaints. They ask questions that have nothing to do with the rape—such as about her sexual life, and if she enjoyed the rape.

When a woman has been raped or assaulted, she will often be very afraid afterwards. She is afraid to walk in the streets, or to stay at home, if it has happened there. It influences her relationship with her husband and other men. It influences her sexual life. We have received phone calls from women who have been raped fifteen or even fifty years ago, and who tell us that they still have problems with it. Many also say that this is the first time in their lives that they can tell someone about it. Women often don't talk about rape because many are raped by acquaintances in their own house. Most people don't realize this. Most people think rape always happens with strange men who jump out of the dark corner of the street. This also occurs, but on many occasions the rapist is an uncle, a friend, or a father. In these situations the victim of a rape often can't prove anything. They need to have witnesses, and it is clear that a man who wants to rape a woman never invites witnesses. A woman called us who had been raped by a man with whom she had a date at her home. He wanted to have sexual intercourse but she didn't agree with his proposal. He started to beat her and locked the door so that she couldn't get out of her house. They fought for one hour and she managed to escape. She ran into the street and met a police car. She told the police what had happened and showed them the wounds on her face. They didn't believe her and told her to go back home!

Many people think that the man who rapes a woman is so excited by her attractiveness that he cannot stop himself. Research in America shows on the contrary that most of these men actually plan to rape a woman. The victim is not simply the woman who is most attractive to him. She can be a very young girl or an older woman or someone who seems weak. That's why we consider rape and assaults as aggressive crimes against women, more than as sexual crimes.

Witness 9: Norway

We know that much violence is being inflicted on women in Norway. We know it from talks with our sisters, and we know it from the material collected by the Women's Free Legal Assistance Group in the two years they have been working. But there are hardly any special research findings on women as victims of violence, and the actual frequency of such violence has not been the subject of systematic study. The following record is in essence the result of what I myself found when I looked into the cases of forcible rape investigated by the police, and the cases that were brought before the courts in Norway in the course of 1972. I based my research findings on police reports and legal documents. My aim was to find out the attitudes raped women meet when confronted by the police and the court.

In theory, the statute on forcible rape in the Norweigian penal code includes cases of husbands raping their wives and of prostitues being rape victims. But in actuality in Norway there has been only one case where a man has been sentenced for raping his wife, and in my sample there are no such cases.

About one hundred forcible rapes are reported to the police in Norway every year. Between 40 and 60 of these cases are dropped because of lack of evidence. A formal charge is made in about 20 of the cases and the rest are dropped because the rapists are not caught.

According to our pneal code, forcible rape is one of the most serious breaches of the law there is, and the police have the duty to investigate all the cases they know of, even if they are not reported to them. But the seriousness with which the police treat these cases varies a great deal.

When a man goes to the police in Norway and reports that his bicycle has been stolen, it is true that the police are not inclined to raise hell in order to find the bike. On the other hand, there is little chance that the man will be suspected of never having owned one! Well, when a woman goes to the police and reports that she has been raped, experience shows that she will be met with great skepticism. First of all the police will question whether the woman was really raped, and then they often ask many irrelevant questions such as whether she has had previous sexual experience; is she promiscuous or provocative? The police seem to have the idea that forcible rape only involves a male maniac who is always a stranger throwing himself upon an innocent woman on her way home through the park at night. The cases that do not fit this pattern will be met with suspicion at the police station.

It is quite clear that the chances the woman will be believed decrease considerably if she had any previous knowledge of the man, and especially if she had a close relationship with him. The chances of being believed is 5 times greater if the rape took place out of doors than if it occurred indoors. The chances of being believed also decrease as the period of time before reporting the incident increases. That is, the less the case resembles a classic rape, the less chance is there that the woman will be believed when she tells her story.

The police cherish the prevailing idea that there is only a certain kind of woman that can possibly be raped. This is clear if one considers the intensity with which the police investigation is conducted. From my figures, it is obvious that the decision to drop a case because of lack of evidence is not necessarily a result of investigation. In many cases the police have actually not started an investigation at all, and they have not questioned any witnesses, probably for the sole reason that the woman was not—in the eyes of the police—a "probable" victim of rape.

In the rare cases which are brought before the court, totally irrelevant factors may still be taken into consideration in arriving at the verdict of guilty or not guilty. Even if the accused is sentenced, various factors about the victim may contribute to making the punishment more lenient. If the woman went to the defendent's home to drink coffee of her own free will, for example, this will serve as a mitigating factor, even if the man admits that he has raped her. If the defendant says that the woman is promiscuous, this will make for a more lenient punishment.

People in Scandinavia have a reputation for being free and tolerant. According to criminologists, Scandinavian police are considered the least corrupt in the Western world. Nevertheless, if a woman has trespassed just a few steps outside the limited sphere of her accepted premises, she will be met by suspicion if she accuses anyone of raping her, or she will be downright disbelieved. If Scandinavian women really behaved as the liberated women people in many other countries think we are, we could not count on being respected and treated with dignity.

♀ ♀ ♀ ♀ ♀

While not all men rape women, Susan Brownmiller points out in *Against Our Will* that all men in essence benefit by those who do. In these testimonies we have heard how individual women have been terrorized by their experiences, and how, but for the newly available solidarity of women on this issue, these women would have fared much worse. When we consider all these testimonies together, rape emerges clearly as a terrorist tactic used by some men, but serving to perpetuate the power of all men over women.

WOMAN BATTERING

Assault of women, or "woman battering" as it is now commonly called, both within marriage and outside of it, has much in common with rape. The fear of men that both rape and battering instill in women has similar political consequences. Both are often accompanied by an agonizing fear of death, and both sometimes result in womanslaughter—or femicide.

Most of the testimony on this crime comes from Great Britain, which has been in the vanguard of the movement to deal with the problem. A Scotswoman, two English women, and a Dutch woman testify about this crime.

Witness 1: Scotland

I am an ordinary working-class woman, and I am a member of Edinburgh Women's Aid. I am grateful to this movement for their support which enabled me to be at this Tribunal.

My story as a battered wife is not exceptional. I have met many women much more seriously assaulted, both physically and mentally than I was. But we all have one thing in common—we know we had to leave our violent and cruel husbands. But where can women with children, running away from home, go? No one wants to help. The police in Scotland will only charge men with assault if the woman has a witness to the incident. Without a witness, men are only charged with breach of the peace and released the following day, only to go home and beat their wives again for calling the police and having them charged. Social workers are overworked and have no time to try and solve each individual women's problems, so many departments in Edinburgh actually refer women to Women's Aid. Most women have parents and sisters, but does any woman want her family to know she is living in hell, that she is starving because her husband won't give her money, and her children haven't decent clothes to wear to school? Battered women also feel that they must get right away from their families because this is the first place their husbands will look for them. Also, family pressure will usually force them back to their husbands' homes.

I was married for 14 years and have four children. The oldest is 13, the youngest is 7. For 9 years my marriage was happy although money was short, and I had to work part-time to have an adequate income. In 1971, my husband had an affair with a woman he worked with. When I told him he must choose between us, he slapped me about the face and dragged me upstairs by my hair. It was the first time he had been violent towards me. He changed his job shortly after that, and became a hotel manager for a company. After he finished his training, we gave up our rented house and moved to a hotel sixty miles away.

Early in 1973, my husband started drinking and taking time off from his work. As result I had more and more to do. He went away for weekends with friends, and I was left running the hotel, managing the part-time staff, and looking after my children. When he returned from these weekends off, he unjustly accused me of having affairs with members of our staff. We quarrelled often on this issue, and I accused him of neglecting the children by being away so much, and that I was also having to neglect them because I had so much work to do.

When I refused to serve in the bar he gave me a terrible beating. He knocked me on the floor and kicked me brutally about the body, feet and head. You can imagine the mess I was in without me going into details. He warned me if I went for help he would do the same again, or worse. A week later, I was able to go to a doctor who told me I should report the beating to the police, as my nose and cheekbones were broken. I was too frightened to tell anyone in case he gave me another beating, or in case he lost his job, because that meant we would lose our home, and accommodation is very hard to find in Scotland.

We moved to another hotel soon after that, and he behaved himself for a few months until one night he suddenly attacked me, and tried to strangle me. There was no reason for this attack, and he had not been drinking on this occasion. One of the staff pulled him away from me, or I would have been badly hurt. This person reported the incident to our supervisor with the result that we were told to leave, and my husband was fired from his job. So, we lost our home. We moved again to another job and were given a house nearby. This time I refused to work at the hotel with him as the children were ill and needed me home. The quarrels started again, this time over money. He refused to give me money to buy food, or clothes, or pay electric bills, or the rent of the house. He only gave me a few pounds for a whole week, and when I asked for more, he beat me and made the children go to bed. He told me he did not care for me or the children, that I could go if I wanted, but that I must not take the children. I believe he said that to make me stay, as I love my children dearly, and would not be parted from them. The following morning I got an eviction notice for non-payment of rent. I swallowed 8 sleeping pills but when I realized what I had done, I made myself sick. I vowed then I would find a way to leave home and take the children with me. But where could I go?

I had read an article in a newspaper about a refuge for battered wives. I phoned Edinburgh Women's Aid and I was told to come right away, they had room for me. On July 18, 1974, I left my husband and was made to feel very welcome by the Women's Aid workers. The kindness shown by these workers, the help given to me and my children, was tremendous, and I thank God my children settled down well in a new school. My son suffers from asthma, and has a very bad chest condition, so the doctor gave me a certificate which allowed me to get a local council house within 8 weeks. This house which I live in now with my children, is only a few minutes walk away from the refuge where I first stayed, and I visit almost every day to try and help the women living there.

I was granted a divorce for cruelty in November 1975, and was given full custody of the children. I was also granted an order of maintenance of 16 pounds a week ($32) for the children, but to date, my husband has never paid a penny. The authorities are trying through legal means to enforce this order, but it takes up to three months to reach court. But many women are not that lucky. Some of them are in a terrible mental state. Some are so badly beaten they cannot cope with their children.

In the year from January 1975 to January 1976, 29 women and 42 children have passed through this refuge. Most of them have since settled in new homes with their children. They still attend fortnightly meetings for discussions, advice, and to air their problems. They usually find solutions from someone in the same position. Edinburgh Women's Aid now has three refuges in Edinburgh, and these are always full. We hope that many more cities and countries find a way of opening such refuges for women who are cruelly and brutally treated by their husbands, so that women can find shelter for themselves and their children.

Witness 2: England

My name is *P.* and I come from London, and I am also a former battered wife. Our marriage lasted 12 and half years, 11 of those being fairly happy. We had our ups and downs, but no violence was directed towards me. During those times when my husband got into a temper, he would smash and break things, kick the door and so on. In 1972, because of contraceptive problems, I had to be sterilized. That's when the problem of battery started. The first incident took place about four months after I was sterilized. I had gone to a dance with my husband. During the course of the night a man asked me to dance. I didn't dance with him, I went and sat down. But my husband then accused me of having found a boyfriend and got very, very drunk. After the dance was over, he took me out to the carpark, said I had found a boyfriend, and started to beat and punch me in front of all my friends and everybody else.

That was all for about six months, until in 1973 he began to have an affair with another woman. He stayed away for four nights, then came back and told me, "I found another woman and

I want to go and live with her!" I was quite shocked at this because although he had had affairs in the past, he had never told me about them, and if I found out about them, he would stop them. But this time he said he wanted to go away and live with her. So I agreed. As soon as I agreed I was accused of not loving him anymore, and not wanting him. What could I do? I didn't know if he wanted me or her. He would sleep one night with her and one night with me. This began to have a very bad effect on my health. I lost weight, I could not sleep, the children were really unhappy. Eventually I told him I could no longer stand it. I had to have a decision as to whether he was going to stay with me, or to move out with this other women. He said he couldn't make up his mind.

One evening, when he was away, a woman friend rang me up and asked me to go out for a drink with her. I had two drinks, came back to the house, and started to undress to go to bed. All of a sudden the street door was bashed in by my husband. All I had on were my underclothes. He came into the bedroom, called me a whore, asked me the man I had been with that eveing, and started to rip off my clothes. When he had ripped all my clothes off, he started to kick me, punch me, stub cigarettes out on me, until I couldn't stand up. I was then dragged downstairs by my hair, and beaten in the kitchen with his fists, with a knife, and with a chair across my back. My head was banged on a brickwall for a solid hour. And all he kept saying was, "You are a whore. You are a whore. Who is the man you have been with?" I kept telling him I hadn't been out with a man, and that I had simply been out for a drink. He had very high heeled Cuban boots at the time, and stamped on my feet and toes until my nails had all come off, and they were bleeding. Eventually after about three hours of continuous beating, the police arrived. Although the door was open, they didn't enter, they politely knocked. My husband answered the door and told them that I had been out for the evening and left the children on their own. The police didn't ask me whether this was true. By this time I was lying in a pool of blood. My face was so swollen that the top of my head met my eyes. My front teeth had been knocked out and nearly gone down my throat and choked me. I had been cut underneath the arm when I tried to defend myself. A chair had been broken over my back, my toes crushed, and all they said was, "Do you want to prosecute him?"

I couldn't speak properly because I was so badly injured, but I tried to tell them I was frightened and wanted to go to the hospital. They refused to take me to the hospital. They just said, "If you don't want to prosecute him, then we can't help." So they went away and left me with that man. He insisted that I get dressed. I couldn't dress myself because my arm felt broken and I knew he had damaged my ribs. I was cut and I couldn't move. So he dressed me, got my two children, one of five and one of nine, into the car, and took me to his girlfriend to show what he had done to me because he thought I had been unfaithful. He told her that she would get exactly the same treatment if he found out that she had been unfaithful to him. He asked her then if after seeing me she still wanted him. She replied, yes, she had had worse than that from her first husband. I said she must be mad. He got up and kicked me in the mouth. Then they made coffee and left me lying on the floor.

Eventually, after he had told her this cock-and-bull story, he decided to take me to the hospital, but warned me to say I had been attacked on the street. When we got to the hospital, *he* told them this. The doctor then asked me if it was true, and I said no, that he had done it. When I said this my husband came over and spat in my face and called me a bastard. The reason I had told the doctor was I thought they would then try to protect me by at least keeping me in the hospital. But oh no! that didn't happen. I had six broken ribs, a cut under the arm, all these lacerations on my face, the whole side of me had turned completely black, and they sent me home with that man, in a car!

We eventually got back to the house. I insisted that he get my children; he had told his girlfriend to keep them because I was an unfit mother. He eventually brought the children back, then left me with them to look after me for four days. Nobody came to help me. No one wanted to know. The social worker just came in to say, "Come to me when you feel depressed!" The National Society for the Prevention of Cruelty to Children didn't consider my husband violent towards the children because he hadn't hit them. They didn't see that he had inflicted violence upon them by forcing them to see what he had done to me. So, they couldn't help me. I went through 10 agencies before I eventually found one woman who knew about a refuge. I had been informed by the social services that because I had a nice house, my husband was fairly well off, it wouldn't do for me! *Anything* would have done for me at that time. I wouldn't have cared where I had gone. So, I arrived at a refuge which had only one stove, with one ring working, and a grill, and 12 families and 25 children. And we lived in these conditions, no windows, no heating, nowhere for our kids to play, no clothes, no money.

I thought that once I got into one of these refuges my troubles would be over. But my husband found out where I was living and came there. We had just got some money to put in some windows, and he smashed every window in that place. I was fortunate to be visiting a friend that day who hid me. The Council promised to rehouse me, which they did. They located fifteen of us in an ordinary three bedroom house: myself, a West Indian friend with 4 children, and another woman and her children. There was no gas, no electricity, no running water. We eventually sorted ourselves out, and decorated the place. The other women were moved out and there were only two of us sharing it.

By the time I got to the place, I had had an injunction placed on my husband. However, he had asked that he have access to my children. I asked the court not to grant it because I knew he would put pressure on them to tell him where I was living. On one occasion, that's exactly what happened. He had put a lot of pressure on my son, at that time only nine years old. He had actually become violent towards him, hitting him across the eyes on one of his visits, asking where I lived. In the end, my son told him. My husband then took my eldest daughter away from me. The injunction didn't help, and the police didn't help. They said, "You have a High Court injunction. Go back to *them*." The lawyer I had said, "It is not serious enough to take into court. Let's get you divorced. That would solve all your problems." That didn't solve my problems! But I eventually did get my child back. One night he came and said, "You can have her back." Then he began to hit me in the mouth until there was such a hole you could see my teeth through it!

Again, I couldn't get any help, although I had told the police there was a possibility he might come. They said that until he did something, they couldn't help. So I was in that house all night, trying to get rid of this man. Eventually I succeeded and fled to another refuge, where I again lived for three months. I was found again by my husband. With nobody about to help, nobody about to take him to court, I just had to move on. My husband doesn't see the children now, but when I go back to England I have to face another court case, because he has taken me to court to see those children. And I know if I don't win, and he gets access to them, I will be on the run again.

Witness 3: England

My name is Y. I have been married six years, and my husband started to beat me three months after we got married. I was very surprised. I had never heard anything like this. I was very naive and believed that partners in marriage were equal. When I mentioned to a friend that I had been hit, she didn't believe me. She said I was lying, and that this sort of thing only happened in the Middle Ages. So I never mentioned it to anyone again. I thought there was something very wrong with me or else it wouldn't happen.

It happened only occasionally over the next two years, but then he got very bad. My husband had decided we were to live with his brother, and I had to look after both of them, wash their clothes, cook their food, and work fulltime. I said, "No, I'll stay in my flat." If he wanted to see me he could come and visit me, but I wasn't going to move. He beat me that night, and I started hemorraging. I went to the doctor the next day, and found out that I was three months pregnant, and was threatened with a miscarriage. I was admitted into the hospital. I was allowed to go home after five weeks, but the doctor said if I wanted to keep this pregnancy I wasn't to have sexual intercourse. My husband made me come back with a certificate after each examination from the doctor to prove that it was correct that I was not to sleep with him. But he still didn't believe it. He said I was lying, and he began to hit me again even though I was pregnant. I was ashamed to tell anyone. I had told them in the hospital that I had fallen down the stairs.

When my daughter was born, it got worse! I eventually went to Germany where my mother lived. My husband gave up my flat, which I couldn't get back, although it was in my name. I tried to get help in Germany. I went to the social services there, and they told me my British-born child was non-existent, so I couldn't claim social security. According to them, I didn't have a child and so could work. But I couldn't get a job because I had a child, and I had no one to look after her. I couldn't pay for a flat or for a child-minder, because I couldn't get a job. I went in circles until finally I found a job in a restaurant as a waitress.

My child and I got our room and board at the restaurant where I worked from 9 o'clock in the morning until 10 o'clock at night. I was allowed 15 minutes at lunch time to feed my 8-month-old daughter. I was allowed 20 minutes in the evening to feed her and put her to bed. The rest of the time she spent in the playpen crying. They didn't pay insurance for me, and I worked for only 8½% of my takings! After four weeks I had had enough, and walked out. I was homeless. I was jobless. I was penniless. And no one wanted to know about it.

My husband wrote to me at my mother's address and said he was very sorry, and that he wanted me to come back. If I didn't come back he was going to oppose my having custody of the child since he said he wanted her. So I went to consult my solicitor and he said that no German court would give me custody of a British child if I was without a home, because then the German government would have to accept the existence of that child and pay me Social Security. So I went back to my husband. The home my husband offered was one room with a bed, a sink and a cooker. His landlord threw us out, so I was homeless again.

Although my mother gave us the money to buy a house, I needed my husband's signature to buy it! He wouldn't let me go out—I couldn't go to evening classes, I couldn't get a job. He told me that my place was in the home. I eventually convinced him that I wanted a job, and I started working as a waitress in the evenings. He deducted every penny I earned from my housekeeping money. I couldn't go back to Germany after what I had been through there, but I didn't know where else to go.

My husband had a girlfriend who he kept going to see. I was isolated in North England, I had no friends and I wasn't allowed to meet anyone. One night he came back at 2 A.M. We had an argument, and he started hitting me. He jumped on top of me. He laid into me with his fists, with his knees, with his feet. I was bruised all over. My child woke up and came to sit with me. He carried on hitting me, and split her lip too. Afterwards I started passing blood in my urine.

I went to the doctor the next day. I wanted to go into the hospital with my child. The doctor gave me a lecture for two hours saying that I was breaking my marriage vows if I wanted a divorce. The hospital doctor patted me on the shoulder and said that such things occasionally happened. I asked to have my child with me in the hospital, and the medical social worker said, "Your husband is such a nice man, and he's ever so sorry," and that the child was alright with him. I stayed in hospital for 10 days, and then they said I could go home. I said I didn't want to go home. I held on to the bed and said, "I'm not going back there!" And they said, "Well, there's no where else for you to go."

Luckily, my husband left me three weeks after that because of his girlfriend. If she hadn't been there, he'd probably still be beating me. So I have her to thank for that.

I'm now working in a house for battered women in York. There are hundreds and thousands of us. It is mostly because of our children that we can't get out of our situations. That, and the fact that we can't find anywhere to live with them, makes it so hard—because we are economically dependent on those men. I found the women's movement and I found a lot of confidence through it.

Witness 4: Holland

When I went to live with my friend five years ago, he was known to be rather aggressive. However, when we began living together he became a lot more relaxed. He also told my family and my acquaintances how he had changed. So I had no trepidations about us living together. And for four years it went very well. He accepted my three children by my first marriage, and I arranged for his children, whom he hadn't seen for four years, to come and see him again. When we were assigned a new house and his children came to live with us, the situation seemed ideal. The house was in his name, and because of that, he felt rather powerful. But it was during that period that he began to beat me. It was also during this time that he got in touch again with his first wife, and that he began to see her regularly. His 18-year-old daughter completely sided with him and encouraged a possible new beginning between her father and her mother.

If I got the occasional slap before this time, now I was really being mistreated. I was kicked and beaten and thrown out of bed. Sometimes he tried to kick me out of the house, late at night, because it was his house he said, and I had no right to be there. I had many a black eye and bruises. I did not go to the doctor. I was much too ashamed to go. After all, you don't talk about mistreatment. You think that you are one of the few in this situation. The neighbors knew and talked about it with each other, but nobody wanted to interfere. Nobody thought to call the police when they heard that I was being beaten and thrown about, or when I was thrown into the street. I only saw the curtain move. No one did a thing to help.

The end came when he broke a beerglass in my face. I had to put myself in a doctor's care. The doctor wanted me to register a complaint against my friend, but when he offered to have the police come to the house, I didn't dare to do it. I knew that my friend would then become dangerous. That night although he didn't beat me, he kept threatening me. He said that the only thing he was sorry about was that he had missed me with the beerglass, and that I hadn't become blind. Then at 4:30 in the morning he told me to go, and I was so afraid that I went. By telephone I got in touch with the organization *"Blijf van m'n Lijf"* (Keep your hands off my body), and I still live there.

That Saturday I went back to pick up the children. I was unsuccessful because my friend didn't want to let me have them, and he began to beat me again. When I called the police, he blamed me for having run away, although it was obvious that I had been mistreated. My friend had been to the police himself that morning to clear his name and to tell them all sorts of strange stories about me. For instance, he told them that I went to bed with strange men and neglected my children. That's why the police refused to help me. Later I did get custody of my children via the Society for the Prevention of Cruelty to Children. But I first had to prove that the stories my friend told were not true. In any case, I have come to the conclusion that as a battered woman you are totally alone, that you cannot expect help from anyone. Without an organization like *Blijf van m'n Lijf*, there is no safe refuge for women like us.

Witness 5: Holland

Woman battering isn't uncommon in Holland. We can't offer you statistics because no one bothers to find out the facts about this crime. In the Dutch judicial system it is a crime with a high penalty, but usually it never gets prosecuted. No research has been carried out about violent husbands in Holland as of now. There are some institutions in Holland where women can find shelter for a short period of time (up to three months). But these institutions aren't very clear regarding the reasons why women want to live there. They mention "marital problems," which can mean a lot of things. Woman battering doesn't exist as such in the terminology of welfare institutions. When a woman has been battered by her husband, then they say there exists a "relational problem" or "a disturbance in the communication between the marital partners." The "solution" sought is "bringing the marital partners together again." A woman told us about her "relation-therapy:" "When I told my therapist that I was afraid of my husband because he tried to strangle me last night, the therapist answered: *Mrs. X*, just put yourself in your husband's place. How difficult it must be for him that you are afraid of him!"

In October 1974 *Blijf van m'n Lijf* opened a refuge for battered women and their children. The address is secret. "Blijf van m'n Lijf" helps women on their own account, not in terms of their relationships or the marriages they fled from. It doesn't deal with men at all. There are two goals to be realized: to offer a safe shelter for battered women and their children, and to publicize the problem of woman battering. Since the refuge opened its doors, about 300 women accompanied by 600 children have come to the refuge. Also other institutions have noticed that more women have come to them with specific complaints of being battered. It turns out to be a widespread problem here. Even so, we think we have seen only a very small percentage of the women who are actually being battered. As of now, we have found that battering is not limited to certain socio-economic classes.

Battering takes many forms: pounding the woman on the head, with or without a stick; dragging her by her hair; hitting her in the stomach, on the back, or on the loins; making the woman have a miscarriage by kicking her in the stomach; breaking her nose or ribs with kicks; putting a fork in her back; placing an iron on her body; strangling; throwing her from the staircase; breaking some vertebrae; keeping her awake day and night by threatening her with a knife.

Many women told us that they had tried many times to escape, but failed for lack of a safe place to go. They usually fled to families or friends, but then their husbands knew immediately where they could go to find them. The official welfare and service institutions don't take their problems seriously, and try to get them back where they think they belong—at "home."

Police refuse to note down women's complaints about battering. "This is a marital fight, ma'm. We can't do anything for you. You'd better go home."

Doctors give some first aid, but they often refuse to give a certificate which a woman can use at the police station. They want to stay "clear" from providing any evidence whatsoever.

Lawyers also keep women at home by telling them that they lose their right to the house when they leave "voluntarily." This is totally untrue. A lot of women have claimed their houses and gotten them back. Lawyers also advise women sometimes not to get a divorce because "you mightn't get out alive." Moreover they don't offer help in finding a safe refuge. They hold the opinion that "a blow happens in any good marriage."

Social work and therapeutic institutions assume that a non-existent equality exists between the partners. Both partners have to tell their own stories, listening to the other partner. The therapist listens to both of them and stays "neutral." He or she supports *de facto* the right of the strongest one, which is the man. What usually happens is that they come home and the man makes his wife feel that he didn't like what she just told the therapist. Next time the woman won't tell anything.

Family and neighbors usually don't know anything about the problems of the woman. Women don't like talking about the battering out of fear or shame. Some of them start disbelieving the repeated story about "having bumped into a door," and sometimes they offer help, for instance, room in their own home. But this often causes many problems: the husband might start threatening the family and/or neighbors as well, and he can find his wife easily. And sometimes they start helping the woman, but can't continue due to the lack of space in their own home. Also some try to persuade the woman to go back home to "save the marriage."

When a woman has been battered a long time, one year after the other, she gets other problems as well: she loses weight, or, on the contrary, crams herself continually with food, gets skin rashes, becomes irritated, also with her children. She might become "crazy," walking in the streets shouting and crying, or "seeing things." Then she'll be threatened with being committed to a psychiatric hospital. Men are aware of this: "I'll pester you until you get admitted to an asylum," said one husband. Women in this situation find themselves in a vicious circle: when they are battered and stay home, they'll be labelled as masochistic, neurotic, or hysterical, but when they leave home they find themselves labelled as irresponsible and not able to care for themselves and their children.

Since we started, the problem of battering has been recognized more than before. Although a lot of people still start laughing and ignore the problem, this reaction has diminished. Women must realize that they *can* leave home if they want to. But there should be more houses for battered women. Some women, we presume, don't come to the refuge because they consider Amsterdam too "far out" for them. There should be more houses in other regions of Holland.

Another problem is getting permanent housing facilities for battered women. It turns out that a lot of women have to stay in the refuge for a long period of time because they can't find suitable and safe accommodation for themselves and their children.

The starting point is still that women have to speak up about this specific crime against them. Only then can they find and create solutions, and in the long term, press other people to set up the facilities they need and have right to.

♀ ♀ ♀ ♀ ♀

What is astounding about the testimony on woman battering is that the police and most social agencies accept even the most extreme forms of violence occuring in the home. Modern societies are supposed to take murder seriously, but women can be all but murdered by their husbands without receiving any protection or even human compassion from those paid by the state to help and protect its citizens.

FORCED INCARCERATION IN MENTAL HOSPITALS AND MARRIAGE

The situation of battered wives is aggravated greatly when divorce is not permissible in a society. Forcing women to remain married when they are subject to cruelty is an example of how barbaric patriarchal laws sometimes are. Testimony from Ireland follows.

Witness : Ireland

My name is Josephine McCormack. I am 51 years old. I have been married for 24 years and I have 9 children, ranging in age from 8 years up to 23 years. My husband is a railway porter and a signalman. Almost from the beginning, my marriage was a failure. My husband was an oppressive man who dictated what life should be for me. He believed I was his to do with what he pleased. If I disagreed with him, or displeased him, or even if he was in a bad mood, he beat me. Our home was in a small rural community in the west of Ireland. My life consisted of my home and my children. I lost contact with other people down the years since my friends were not allowed to visit me in my husband's house.

My marriage deteriorated to the extent that my husband and I no longer spoke to each other. He conveyed messages about domestic issues to me through one of our children. This total lack of communication existed during the last 6 years of our life together, though we lived in the same house. During that time there was no one I could turn to for help. There is no divorce in Ireland. I could not afford the legal expenses of a High Court separation. When my marriage failed, I had two choices: either leave the family to make a new life on my own, or stay with my husband and children. The house belonged to my husband. I had no money, no job, and no legal right to my children. But I loved my children and could not leave them.

In August 1974 the strain of my life became intolerable, and in desperation, I planned to leave and take my 5 youngest children with me. I hoped to travel to England, find a job and work to establish a new home there. I did not inform my husband of my decision.

My home was in Galway, and the journey from there to Dublin is approximately 150 miles. We boarded the afternoon train on the day of August 9, 1974. When we stopped at the first station on route to Dublin, two plainclothes policemen came aboard. They established my identity and interrogated me. When they asked me to get off the train with them I refused, and they agreed that I had committed no crime to justify their action. They admitted they were acting on instructions to intercept me and the children and detain us. At the next station, two uniformed policemen confronted us. They also said I should leave the train and accompany them. Again I refused, and they would not tell me on what authority they were doing this. I also refused to tell them where I was going. First they cautioned me, told me they had the power to restrain me, and then they bodily lifted me and my children out of the train and into a police car. I was frightened and distressed, and my children were hysterical.

At the police station we were detained in a room, and given no information whatsoever. At midnight, one policeman suggested I was sick and should go to the hospital, and should accompany him quietly. I refused to leave, said I did not need hospitalization, and asked to see a solicitor or doctor. My request was refused. My children were separated from me and sent back to their father. I was caught roughly by the arms and legs and carried once more to a waiting police car. I arrived at the hospital with my arms pinioned behind my back, having been kept in a kneeling position in the back of the police car. But the more I resisted my detention, the more brutal the treatment got.

Next day I found myself in a high security ward, allowed no outside contact and no information. Going to Mass escorted by a nurse was the only concession to free movement. After three weeks, during which time my requests for information were either ignored or refused by the doctors, I went on a hunger strike. I informed a doctor of my decision, explaining that it was to protest my illegal detention. I was penalized forthwith by having my cigarettes confiscated, given an injection, and put to bed. But I persisted with my hunger strike, and resisted attempts to force feed me. For five days I lived on liquids, and was then informed that my case was being considered and I would be transferred to another hospital for "discharge purposes." By that time I had been detained for one month, and had written a letter of complaint to the Minister of Health.

I was transferred under guard to another hospital, but was not, as promised, released. Instead, constant pressure was put on me to agree to shock treatment, which I refused. I suspected my case might be under investigation by the Department of Health, since I had written to them, and a course of treatment would have regularized the hospital's situation in the matter and might appear to justify my detention.

As my husband had signed me into the hospital, I needed his signature to release me. He adamantly refused to give it, and told one doctor he "never wanted to see me again." My 21-year-old daughter Margaret, who is estranged from her father and does not live at home, visited me often. She became worried about my situation, and consulted a solicitor about the legality of my detention. She learned that she could sign for my release, if she accepted full responsibility for me. When she informed the hospital of this, they insisted that first my husband should be consulted and informed of this decision. But it was a formality, and 3 weeks after my daughter signed the form of responsibility, I was released. On November 7th, 3 months after my removal from the train, I was a free woman again.

I could not go home, so I was unable to see my children. They had no one to care for them and were neglected and unhappy. For some weeks I worked as a cleaner in a hotel, until I collected a little money and was sufficiently recovered in health. Then with the assistance of my daughter Margaret, I kidnapped my children from home, once more got on a train for Dublin, and this time succeeded in escaping to a new life. For more than one year my younger children and myself have had a very happy life in Dublin.

Since then, I have tried unsuccessfully to get an explanation of the crime against myself and my children. But in cases like this, both the legal profession and the medical profession close ranks, and I have found it impossible to penetrate the barriers of secrecy and so-called ethics. Some things I have learned however. My husband's accomplice in having me incarcerated was our local priest. He was a friend of my husband, who knew of the conditions in our home, had seen me after my husband's beatings, but he never saw fit to help me or the children. This priest used his influence, and the fact that in 1971 I had been a voluntary patient in a hospital for treatment of anxiety and depression, to have us removed from the train. He gave instructions to the police by telephone.

It was not my choice to live in such a marriage, but I was trapped because I loved my 9 children. Ireland does not allow divorce. Our country has no provision for women who find themselves in my position.

♀ ♀ ♀ ♀ ♀

The violent behavior of this woman's husband is not as shocking as the fact that the laws so clearly protect his whims, that they fail so completely to protect the interests of women, and that the priest, the police, and the doctors in the mental hospital, all actively cooperated or supported the violent and criminal behavior of this man. Complicity of this sort among men is surely one reason why there are many more women in mental hospitals than men.

ASSAULT

With awareness about rape and woman battering spreading fast, the problem of non-sexual assault on women outside of marriage is sometimes forgotten. Men's greater physical strength and generally greater readiness to use violence affects all relationships between women and men, even if we are not aware of it, or have never been the victim of violence in our own lives. I doubt that there is a woman alive in the world today who has never feared male violence, and fear, of course, affects behavior. The following testimony is about a German woman who was assaulted by a man during the days of the Tribunal.

Witness: Belgium

There is a group of about fifty women staying in a youth hostel in Brussels, and we have been subjected to a lot of verbal humiliation and violence from the owner ever since we first got there. We haven't taken any action until now, probably because as women we are used to this kind of stuff. But today, one of the women staying in the hostel, a German woman, went to the bathroom after breakfast and couldn't get the door unlocked to get out again. So she yelled for assistance. The owner had to open the door with a pair of pliers. Once he got the door open, he was so enraged that she had gotten herself locked in, that he hit her on the back with the pliers. We were getting dressed up in our room—it was right before the Tribunal—when she came upstairs really hysterical. Immediately after her came the owner, yelling at her, telling her to pack her bags and get out of there, that she was no longer welcome in the hostel. Well, naturally she refused, and we all stood by her. Like the rest of us, she had already paid for all 5 nights. The man left, and since she was surrounded by a group of friends, about nine women, the rest of us thought that the matter was over, but that we would bring it up at the Tribunal this morning.

Soon afterward, we left, and the assaulted woman and her friends prepared to leave. However, when they went downstairs the owner put himself in front of the door and would not let them go out. He said that he had called the police, and that they were to wait. The police finally arrived, demanded the women's passports, addresses and so forth, but the women refused, asked them why they were being detained, and what they had done wrong. Because they refused, the police threatened to take them to jail, and ordered a police wagon. Another police car arrived with sirens sounding, and lights flashing, designed to intimidate the women. Still the women refused to cooperate and the head of police was finally called. He demanded their passports and took their addresses down. When the police found out that these women were from the Tribunal, their faces suddenly dropped, and they all retired to a little room, leaving the women to wait outside. They talked among themselves for half an hour, then came back out, and the head of police told the women that if they would promise to remain calm, and be good, that they would be allowed to stay one more night. Remember, we had all paid for five nights, but we were to be *allowed* to stay!

Meanwhile the owner of the hostel is calling the women of the Tribunal lunatics and idiots. So what we want to do is warn the women who are staying in the International Hotel des Jeunes, to please meet behind the assembly hall here so that we can decide what to do. We also want to put the following resolution to you: "We, the women of the International Tribunal on Crimes against Women, demand an immediate investigation of the owner of the International Hotel des Jeunes, Rue du Congrès, Brussels, with the purpose of revocation of his license. This man has committed crimes against women." (Resolution passed by acclamation). Finally, please try to put pressure on the local community to do something about this man. We think he is dangerous.

FEMICIDE

We must realize that a lot of homicide is in fact femicide. We must recognize the sexual politics of murder. From the burning of witches in the past, to the more recent widespread custom of female infanticide in many societies, to the killing of women for "honor," we realize that femicide has been going on a long time. But since it involves mere females, there was no name for it until Carol Orlock invented the word "femicide." Testimony from the U.S.A. and Lebanon follows.

Witness 1: U.S.A.

Some wifebeating escalates into wife killing. One study found that in 85% of domestic homicide cases, the police had been called for help at least once, and in 50% of such cases, the police had been called 5 or more times prior to the murder. The inadequate handling of violent husbands results in immeasurable pain and suffering for many women, and contributes to this form of femicide.

One out of every 10 female murder victims in the U.S. is killed during rape or other sexual offenses. Brownmiller in her recent book *Against Our Will*, estimates that in the U.S., four hundred rape-murders are committed by men every year. Fear of death in the hands of rapists is much greater than this figure might indicate. We do not know how many of the 55,210 women who reported being raped in the U.S. in 1974, or how many of the larger number who never reported their experience, submitted because of their fear of being killed. But we *are* sure that they are *many*. This form of femicide—rape-murder—has consequences far beyond the estimated 400 victims. It terrorizes many of us whether we become rape victims or not.

The following cases of femicide were gathered from the pages of San Francisco newspapers by Louise Merrill.

Janet Ann Taylor (age 21): Strangled and dumped by the side of the road in San Mateo County.

Mariko Sato (age 25): Stabbed, hacked and shot. Her body was stripped from the waist down, wrapped in a blanket and stuffed in a trunk in a San Francisco apartment.

Darlene Maxwell (age 28): Tied at the neck, wrists, and ankles with a rope. Gagged with her own underwear, strangled and left in an industrial area of San Francisco. Her body was not identified for 2 days after being found.

Betty Jean Keith (age 25–30): Stabbed in the throat and left in the water off Richmond sometime between midnight and five A.M. Her body was found the same day, but not identified for three days.

Mary E. Robinson (age 23): Stabbed eighteen times by her boyfriend. "She called me a coward," he said. "She said I was afraid to fight for my rights." San Francisco.

Lucy Ann Gilbride (age 52): Slashed and clubbed to death in her home in San Rafael.

Cassie Riley (age 13): Beaten, stripped, raped, drowned. Union City.

Sonya Johnson (age 4): Raped and clubbed, possibly strangled. She was missing eleven days before her body was found and identified. San Jose.

Diane David (age 36): Beaten, tied, gagged, and stabbed, and left in her apartment in San Francisco.

Arlis Perry (age 19): Stabbed, strangled. Raped with altar candles in a church on the Stanford campus. She had been stripped from the waist down.

Linda Faye Barber (age 24): Beaten to death and left naked near the golf course of the Castlewood Country Club.

Maude Burgess (age 83): Left naked and spread-eagled on her bed, her arms and legs tied with sheets. It was two days before her body was found. A pillow slip had been pulled over her head. San Francisco.

Josephine de Caso (age 27): Stabbed and beaten and left in a deserted stable. Milpitas.

Darlene Davenport (age 16): Stripped and hacked to death. Left in a parking lot in Oakland.

Susan Murphy (age 19): Beaten to death in her living room in Oakland.

Debra Pera (age 19): Lived three days after having been whipped and beaten by her boyfriend. San Francisco.

Rosie Lee Norris (age 32): Stabbed to death in her apartment in San Francisco. Her body was discovered, with her robe and night gown down around her waist, on December 24. The public was spared news of the killing until after Christmas.

Men tell us not to take a morbid interest in these atrocities. The epitome of triviality is alleged to be a curiosity about "the latest rape and the latest murder." The murder and mutilation of a woman is not considered a political event. Men tell us that they cannot be blamed for what a few maniacs do. Yet the very process of denying the political content of the terror helps to perpetuate it, keeps us weak, vulnerable, and fearful. These are 20th century witchburnings. The "maniacs" who commit these atrocities are acting out the logical conclusion of the woman-hatred which pervades the entire culture. Recently, this has resulted in several pornographic movies whose climax is said to be the actual killing and dismembering of a woman. These so-called "snuff" movies are now being imitated. For example, a movie shown in the U.S. is advertising that it is impossible for the audience to tell whether the killing of the woman is real or not.

The women slaughtered in these movies have no names. The names of those I have read out to you today will soon be obliterated. No demonstrations have accompanied them to the grave, no protests rocked the city, no leaflets were passed out, no committees were formed. But today we have remembered them. And tomorrow we must act to *stop femicide!*

♀ ♀ ♀ ♀ ♀

Witness 2: U.S.A.

This testimony was presented in the form of an unpublished poem. Pat Parker wrote *Womanslaughter** about the murder of her sister by her sister's husband, and read it at the Tribunal. Since it is a very long poem, we reluctantly include exerpts only.

WOMANSLAUGHTER
(Excerpts from a poem by Pat Parker.)

Hello, Hello Death
There was a quiet man
He married a quiet wife
Together, they lived
a quiet life.

Not so, not so
her sisters said,
the truth comes out
as she lies dead.
He beat her.
He accused her
of awful things
and he beat her.
One day she left.

She went to her sister's house
She, too, was a woman alone.
The quiet man came and beat her.
Both women were afraid.

"Hello, Hello Police
I am a woman
and I am afraid.
My husband means to kill me."

"Lady, there's nothing we can do
until he tries to hurt you.
Go to the judge and he will decree
that your husband leaves you be!
She found an apartment
with a friend.
She would begin
a new life again.
Interlocutory Divorce Decreeing
the end of the quiet man.

*Copyright: Pat Parker, 1974.

He came to her home
and he beat her.
Both women were afraid.

"Hello, Hello Police
I am a woman alone
and I am afraid.
My ex-husband means to kill me."

"Fear not, Lady
He will be sought."
It was too *late,*
when he was caught.
One day a quiet man
shot his quiet wife
three times in the back.
He shot her friend as well.
His wife died.

What shall be done with this man?
Is it a murder of first degree?
No, said the men
It is a crime of passion.
He was angry.

Is it a murder of second degree?
Yes, said the men,
but we will not call it that.
We must think of his record.
We will call it manslaughter.
The sentence is the same.
What will we do with this man?
His boss, a white man came.
This is a quiet Black man, he said
He works well for me
The men sent the quiet
Black man to jail.
He went to work in the day.
He went to jail and slept at night.
In one year, he went home.

Sister, I do not understand,
I rage and do not understand.
In Texas, he would be freed.
One Black kills another
One less Black for Texas.

But this is not Texas.
This is California.
The city of angels.
Was his crime so slight?
George Jackson served
years for robbery.
Eldridge Cleaver served
years for rape.
I know of a man in Texas
who is serving 40 years
for possession of marijuana.
Was his crime so slight?
What was his crime?
He only killed his wife.
But a divorce I say.
Not final; they say;
Her things were his
including her life.
Men cannot rape their wives!
Men cannot kill their wives.
They passion them to death.

The three sisters
of Shirley Jones
came and cremated her.
And they were not strong.
Hear me now–
It is almost three years
and I am again strong.
I have gained many sisters.
And if one is beaten,
or raped, or killed,
I will not come in mourning black.
I will not pick the right flowers
I will not celebrate her death
and it will matter not
if she's Black or white–
if she loves women or men.
I will come with my many sisters
and decorate the streets
with the innards of those
brothers-in-womenslaughter.
No more, can I dull my rage
in alcohol and deference

to men's *courts.*
I will come to my sisters,
not dutiful,
I will come strong.

Witness 3: Lebanon*

I want to relate to you two extreme examples of deprivation of freedom for women in Lebanon. Last year a brother cut the head off his sister because she married the man she loved. Another brother killed his sister whom he believed to have been unfaithful to the very rich man her family obliged her to marry. Autopsy proved that the girl was still a virgin and that her husband must have been impotent.

THE CASTRATION OF FEMALES: CLITORIDECTOMY, EXCISION, AND INFIBULATION

The word *castration* almost always refers to men; but anxious as men appear to be about it, females are much more widely subject to castration. We use the word to refer to clitoridectomy (the removal of the entire clitoris), excision (the removal of the clitoris and the adjacent parts of the *labia minora* or all the exterior genitalia except the *labia majora*), and infibulation (excision followed by the sewing of the genitals to obliterate the entrance to the vagina except for a tiny opening). In the testimony on medical crimes, the German women referred to the removal of a woman's uterus and ovaries as castration; but we feel it preferable to use the word for the destruction of our sexuality.

The following testimony from Guinea was not given personally, but was brought by a group of French women who have been researching this topic for some time.

Witness 1: Guinea

There was a wall around the place where we lived, from which you could see the big baths where women and men came to wash. It was there that one day I saw myself the savage mutilation called excision that is inflicted on the women of my country between the ages of 10 and 12, that is, a year before their puberty. *F.*

*This information was contained in a letter to the Tribunal.

was stretched out on the pebbles on the ground. There were six women surrounding her; the eldest, the woman who was to do the excision (the exciseuse), was of her own family. *F.* was being firmly held down by the women, who held her legs apart and made every effort to keep her still despite the desperate convulsions of her body.

The operation was done without any anesthetic, with no regard for hygiene or precautions of any sort. With the broken neck of a bottle, the old woman banged hard down, cutting into the upper part of my friend's genitals so as to make as wide a cut as possible, since "an incomplete excision does not constitute a sufficient guarantee against profligacy in girls."

The blunt glass of the bottle did not cut deeply enough into my friends genitals and the exciseuse had to do it several more times. The blood gushed, my friend cried out, and the prayers being intoned could not drown her screams. When the clitoris had been ripped out, the women howled with joy, and forced my friend to get up despite a streaming hemorrhage, to parade her through the town. Dressed in a white loin-cloth, her breasts bare, although prior to excision women never appear naked in public, she walked with difficulty.

Behind her a dozen or so women, young and no so young, were singing to the accompaniment of an instrument made of rings of gourd. They were informing the village that my friend was ready for marriage. In Guinea, in fact, no man marries a woman who has not been excised and who is not a virgin, with rare exceptions.

The wound takes 2 to 3 weeks to heal, and is horribly painful. My friend screamed every time she urinated. To alleviate the pain she carried a little jug of water with her, which she poured on herself as she urinated. She was lucky enough not to suffer complications; infection and painful side-effects due to the cutting of the urinary tract or the perineum frequently occur.

Among some of my friends a "nevrome" formed at the point where the nerve had been cut. This sets off flashing pains similar to those felt with amputated limbs.

In my country, Guinea, 85% of the women are *today* excised, and my country is said to be progressive.

Clitoridectomy is practised in the Yemen, Saudi Arabia, Ethiopia, Sudan, Egypt, Iraq, Jordan, Syria, the Ivory Coast, among the Dogons of the Niger, the Mendingo's of Mali, the Toucouleu in the North of Senegal, and the Peuls, and among many other African tribes.

I would like to add that in some other countries this savage mutilation is not enough; it is also necessary to sew the woman up in order to really dispossess her of her body. After having cut, without the benefit of anesthetic, part of the large lips, they are brought together by piercing them with pins. This way they grow together, except for a space for the passage of blood and urine.

The young wife must, before her wedding night, have it reopened with a razor. Her husband can, moreover, always insist on having his wife sewn up again if he is thinking of leaving her for some time.

I appeal to the solidarity of women to make their dignity as human beings recognized, dignity which is denied by the dispossessing of their bodies and souls.

I appeal to the solidarity of women to end patriarchal oppression and violence founded on the fear and hatred of our bodies.

I appeal to the solidarity of women to end these barbarous mutilations.

In countries, such as the U.S. and Britain, where the physical castration of females is no longer practiced, psychological means often achieve a similar effect—totally cutting women off from their own sexuality.

VIOLENT REPRESSION OF NON-CONFORMING GIRLS

While there is only one testimony from France about this crime, it is of course not unique to this country. If girls reject the role they are supposed to play, society tries to force or manipulate them into changing their minds. And a double standard invariably operates, particularly where sexual behavior is concerned. A sexually active young woman can be institutionalized for behavior that would be bragged about by a boy.

Witness 1: France

I would like to speak about female delinquency, the type of rebellion specific to women. It's very difficult. They are even called "difficult women." Most of these women are 12 to 13 years old. Women running away from home, stealing, and committing acts of violence, are on the increase everywhere. These are children who speak, who act, who present real opposition to the system. Those concerned in the struggle must absolutely not remain unaware of this. We must no longer ignore the fact that children are a section of society, and that the struggle of these women is genuine.

I presume that among you here there are some women who are teachers and who have jobs in which you are in contact with children. And I hope you will take note of what I say. Because I want to speak about how children are repressed, and to say that we should now be able to let these children speak. These young women have rebelled in exactly the same way as the guys, but they are tried in five minutes and the sentences can be up to four years imprisonment. They are often violated while they are running away by men who offer them a place to stay, or by truck-drivers when they try to travel. They are also often raped by the cops. And at the police station they are made to go through vaginal examinations, blood tests and repeated psychological tests.

I would also like to point out that the only attitude of the children's courts towards these women is that of repression. Repression no longer means shutting people up within walls. Walls have been replaced by structures, by a logical system, scientific, subtle and phallocratic. Repression can be exercised by severe or mild methods. The children's courts do not accept rape as a cause for revolt among women; they do not consider these women's backgrounds. They do not listen to the questions of these women, nor do they really look into the cause of the revolt. Repression is now called therapy. It poses as redemption, re-education. They take away your right to speak, they deny you, they sterilize you, they call you a problem-child, they put you into categories, they make you undergo humiliations at the police station.

The apparently open-minded system, of course, has but one goal—social rehabilitation, work at any price, marriage and motherhood. At St. Omer, for example, there is a special service set up for difficult women. This consists of therapy. In my opinion, this therapy is one that instills the greatest feeling of guilt. You get every comfort—you have the right to knit, you have the right to thread beads. What does this amount to? You are put into a position where you can only receive. These forms of therapy firmly instill only feelings of culpability, and misery! It is applied like a cane to instill obedience. All the protection they appear to be offering, makes you sweat blood. The repression is being completely concealed. All the security is only a phantom through which can be seen slavery and its rotten implications.

TORTURE OF WOMEN FOR POLITICAL ENDS

Elsewhere we have suggested that violence against women in general serves a political function in maintaining sexism. In the following testimony from Korea, however, rape and torture are used for more organized political ends. Of course men are tortured for the same ends; nevertheless an additional oppressive factor is introduced by the fact that these women are tortured by men, and are helpless prey of their captors' sexist sadism.

Witness 1: Korea

I am a 2nd-generation South Korean woman, born in Japan, where I also live. My name is Kwon Mal-Ja. I am 26 years old and a second-year student at Seoul University, South Korea. Last summer while I was studying in Korea, I was taken to a KCIA (the Korean secret police) office and sexually assaulted. This unbearable experience completely shattered my hopes for the future.

I had decided to go to Korea to study, because I did not know the language of my homeland nor the facts about my home country. I wanted to live as a Korean woman, proud of the heritage of the Korean people. One day in March 1974, I travelled to South Korea. University life was quite enjoyable. I made deliberate efforts to learn Korean customs by making friends with as many Korean students and visiting as many Korean homes as possible.

One day, a KCIA agent came and took me to his office. It was so unexpected. I clearly remember the day. It was August 5, 1975, around 11:30 in the morning. I was alone in my room, reading a book. My roommate had gone to school, when a man quite unexpectedly came into my room and asked me to go with him, showing his KCIA ID card. He was the kind of person who could easily send a shudder through your frame when you looked at him. A car was parked outside and another tough-looking man was standing by the car. I was driven to a certain two story house near the KCIA headquarters in Namsang. The house looked like any other ordinary residence. I was nervous and anxiously wondering what would happen.

After lunch, several men began to interrogate me in frightening voices. The first question they asked me was, "You know why you were brought here, don't you?" I said, "No." He insisted that I knew, saying, "I bet you know. Just ask yourself!" I again had to say, "No!" For a few moments, exchanges of the same question and the same answer ensued. The interrogators threatened, "You know what this place is. It is entirely up to us whether we kill you or leave you alive, so you'd better tell us the truth." They demanded that I give them names of Korean friends from Japan. I gave them a few names. Then they asked me to write a statement to the effect that I was engaged in political activities with these friends. Since I was not engaging in any such activities, I didn't have anything to write. So I wrote about my relations with them, as they were. Upon the completion of my statement, they said, "You are not sincere, nor cooperative," and suddenly hit me on the cheek. They threatened, "If you don't tell us, they are ways to make you speak. We can also go to another room to continue our interrogation. There are torture specialists in the basement, who can do anything they want. You may not get out of this place alive." Then they began to read testimonies of the victims of torture which were reported in the newspapers, and compared me to them.

I was completely out of my mind with fear. I cannot even remember—except fragmentarily—what I said during the interrogation, which lasted for ten days. They asked about every detail of the trips I made in Japan and in Korea, of my extra curricular activities at the university, of the purpose of my study in Korea, of my work as a teacher at the Tokyo Korean School, of the people I got acquainted with in Japan and in Korea, and they made me rewrite the statement many times. They sometimes continued their interrogation throughout the night and gave me little sleep, if they allowed me to sleep at all.

One day when I was half dazed, I overheard conversations among the men. "We will just make use of her as much as possible. If she is not cooperative, we will wipe her out," they said. I was so frightened thinking that I could never get out of this place alive, I burst into tears. Faces of my parents, brothers and sisters and friends passed through my mind one after another. After that, I confirmed whatever they wanted me to, whether it was true or not. They did not hesitate to use obscenities in front of me and to offer me drinks. One such night, I felt a man's hand pawing my body. I was startled and got up. The man went out quietly. I think it was August 14, the day before I was released, that a man came into my room and tried to assault me sexually. I resisted him to the utmost of my ability. The man finally gave up and reluctantly went out of my room.

On the day that I was released, a KCIA man came to my apartment and threatened me, saying, "Unless you allow yourself to sleep with me, I will again take you to the KCIA, and will not give your passport back." Then he jumped on me like a beast and assaulted me sexually. My virginity was taken away by force and I suffered from unbearable shame. The man went out of my room and I was left there almost unconscious, thinking vaguely of my parents and brothers and sisters and my future.

Before I was released on August 15, I was forced to sign a statement which roughly said, "I will not tell anybody whatsoever about the investigation I went through at the KCIA office. If I do, I shall have to be taken to the KCIA again and punished." I was asked to write a statement of repentance to the effect that I would actively participate in the activities of the Student's Defense Corps and work for the Yushin Regime.

After I was released, I was asked to go to the Prince Hotel on the 21st, and again was sexually assaulted by KCIA beasts. They also checked the date of my departure for Japan. I received a phone call from someone, probably in a higher echelon of the KCIA. He had the nerve to say to me, "Please, come to see us again when you come back to Seoul. We will take care of everything, your registration at the university, living, job-finding, and everything else."

I went back to Japan with a deeply wounded heart—quite unlike the time I was leaving for Korea. Though I felt relieved at home, I could not get over my bitter feelings about the merciless acts performed on me in Seoul. Of course, I could not talk about them with my parents. As days passed, I became even more embittered against the Park regime and those hateful KCIA beasts.

Towards the end of September, I received a letter from a man in the KCIA. He said in the letter that I should return to Korea as soon as possible, and that he could help me through some agents in Japan. My bitter feeling against them was renewed, though at the same time, I felt very worried because of the KCIA agents in Japan. Who can tell what they are going to do to me here? I decided not to go back to Seoul which meant that I had to give up my hope of becoming a teacher. I also realized I could not get married, being a deflowered woman. A close friend whom I told about my asault encouraged me not to give up my desire to live.

On November 22, the KCIA made an announcement about an alleged "spy plot of Korean students from Japan." To my great surprise, I found, on the list of those arrested, the names of my friends whom I had mentioned during the course of my investigation at the KCIA office. I felt ashamed and had to blame myself for the fact that they were arrested for framed-up crimes, simply because I had mentioned their names. I realized for the first time that I had been used for the purpose of implicating many Korean students from Japan. My understanding of this is what prompted me to talk about it.

I can say unequivocally that the spy plot by the Korean students from Japan was a complete frame-up. The Park regime and the KCIA not only destroyed my life as a woman, but also used my forced confession to fake an entirely groundless spy plot. I had heard many stories of tortures and sexual assaults which Korean women students suffered, and after my own experience I know that these must be true.

I decided to make this story public in the hope that democracy will be realized in Korea sooner. I sincerely hope that the days of the Park regime are numbered. I could have kept my shameful experience to myself. I have to carry the burden of it being known publicly that I am a "marred woman." I was fully aware that the act of making the story public would have other negative effects on me. The astonishment of my parents when they were finally told about my experience was indescribable. Who knows whether the KCIA will not take my life away? Nevertheless, I decided to publicize what happened to me so that more young people like myself may not suffer from the same shame, and so that the unification of my home country may be realized sooner.

BRUTAL TREATMENT OF WOMEN IN PRISON

While men are also treated brutally in prison, sexism adds another dimension to the experience of women in prison. The testimony of Lidia Falcon from Spain is particularly eloquent in explaining this.

An Indian woman living in England who chaired the panel on this topic also gave the following introduction to it. Testimony follows that from Iran, Chile, India, Spain, Greece, the Soviet Union, Northern Ireland, Switzerland and West Germany.

The workshop on women in prison yesterday expressed the feeling that women, because of their position in society and their relationship to the reproductive process, are oppressed in every kind of way. Therefore, if they end up in prison, they cannot really be seen as divorced from this system which sends them to prison, and therefore all women are political prisoners in a very broad sense. However, it was also felt that there are women who have organized with males working for similar causes. These women, being in a much more exposed situation, tend to be more viciously and more brutally treated when they are arrested, when they are interrogated, when they are put into prison. So, women as political prisoners in this sense, are in a much more difficult situation, face a much harsher reality, and therefore we have to deal with the problem in a slightly different way.

We felt that though women in this conference are generally from Western Europe, and generally from the non-communist world, we would like to point out that political prisoners exist everywhere. In the Third World, especially where poverty and the lack of development of the economic system makes it so difficult for the ruling class to deliver the goods to its people, women at even the lowest levels increasingly come into conflict with the State. In India, for example, if you just go out on a demonstration protesting high prices, if you just walk down the street with your pots and pans, you might end up in prison and be treated as a political prisoner. You might object to the way in which children are deprived of textbooks and education in school, and you might end up being a political prisoner.

Therefore, depending on the level of development of different countries, women who seem to be struggling on a non-political level, end up in a very political and difficult situation. This is the background for the reports that you now will hear.

Witness 1: Iran

The fascist regime of Iran, which the U.N. Human Rights Commission has declared as the second worst offender after Brazil in the use of torture on political dissidents, has once again on the occasion of International Women's Year, embarked upon another large-scale public relations ruse, at great cost, in order to hide its ugly face behind a torrent of boastful propaganda.

Princess Ashraf, the Shah's sister, was the spokeswoman of the regime at the U.N. International Women's Conference in Mexico City, masquerading as the representative of Iranian women, who have, according to her, achieved their rightful freedom and liberty and are actively participating in the political and social affairs of their country. Princess Ashraf, as usual, laced her misrepresentation with a $2 million donation to the research program endorsed by the Conference.

The Shah himself claims that since the launching of his so-called "White Revolution," ultimate liberty has been granted to the women of Iran by their right to vote. The Shah has ordered that Iranian women must celebrate International Women's Day not on March 8, as elsewhere in the world, but on February 27, marking the date on which women's enfranchisement was decreed by his Gracious Majesty!

In this farcical system, Iranian women are represented by the Organization of Iranian Women, once again presided over by Princess Ashraf, in which a medley of upper class dilettante women join in a chorus of praise for His Majesty. In this carnival the laboring millions of Iranian women have no properly elected delegates.

The truth is that under the existing dictatorship in Iran, the vast majority of citizens are utterly deprived of the most elementary forms of political expression, let alone the women of the countryside who are among the most deprived anywhere, despite the enormous oil revenues, and the regime's boastful schemes to abolish illiteracy. According to the government's own statistics, some 80% of Iranian women are illiterate. This percentage is even higher—up to 96%—at the rural and village level.

These statistics, reflecting the pathetic state of women in Iran, give the lie to the statutes purporting to protect women and their families. Ignorance arising from sheer illiteracy would preclude effective use of the law by these women, assuming that the law were on their side, which it is not. In reality, and despite grandiose schemes and declarations by the regime, there are fundamental inequalities existing between men and women in the law which have not been remedied. The man is considered the head of the family, can marry more than one wife, and his testimony in any dispute counts as twice as effective as that of a woman. The woman is subordinate and cannot travel without her husband's permission.

Many Iranians, having recognized the anti-popular nature of this CIA-backed regime, have struggled against it. In recent years the extent and momentum of this struggle has enlarged in proportion to the brutality and repression of the regime. Amnesty International in its latest annual report estimates from 25,000 to 100,000 political prisoners in Iran, among whom there are 4,000 women. Most of them are, or have been, subjected to maltreatment or barbaric tortures such as beatings, whippings, the application of cigarette burns, slow roasting on electric grills, shock treatment to genitalia, avulsion of nails, rape, and maltreatment of children in front of captive mothers. And, usually, when they capture a man, they rape his wife in front of him, to psychologically weaken him. A woman political prisoner who managed to escape from prison, has written about her torture. In it she tells how they spoonfed her with urine and excrement. Many of these militant women political prisoners, if they have survived their torture, have become paralyzed, blind, or have lost their arms or legs.

Witness 2: Iran

I am one of the delegates from the Confederation of Iranian Students. I am going to tell you about the torture in the prisons of the Shah—the torture of children and the relatives of women prisoners in front of them to make them confess, the taking of hostages from members of their families, repeated rape, hot tables, whips etc. This torture has created an unbearably terrifying situation for an entire people. And I will quote a few extracts from the *Epic of Resistance* by Achraf Tehrani, written after her escape from prison.

Achraf Tehrani is a member of the People's Feddayin Guerrilla Organization. She was arrested on March 19, 1971, at the age of 21 years. Her case was heard in secret and she was sentenced to 10 years imprisonment. She managed to escape on March 25th, 1973. This is how she described some of what happened to her.

> He suddenly got angry, . . . and he said to the others, 'Beat this whore up.' He tied me onto a bed while he was insulting me. The room was full of cops, some of them had come to watch. But of course, if need be, they would help the torturers. They were there, above all, to watch a revolutionary woman being tortured. They found the show very amusing. Some of them even seemed calm and looked as if nothing abnormal was happening, which surprised me because I could never have imagined that a torturer could be that way. Captain Niktab was the main one, the others helped him. The whip was passed from one pair of hands to another. One by one they struck the soles of my feet. The pain was intense but I recited poems and shouted slogans which gave me more strength. This infuriated them. And the blows from the whip got more and more severe. Nothing incensed them more than my insults against the Shah. I had given them an opportunity to show their enthusiasm for him. The whip lasted a long time. A bit later on, they got an electric bludgeon to torture me. At first they used this thing to break my morale as much as to make me suffer physically. They undressed me, shouting the most vulgar insults at me. They put this bludgeon onto the most sensitive parts of my body. Niktab, the swine, was not there yet. But later he came into the torture chamber. He had such a repulsive face that I wondered how he could have sunk into such a state of degradation and vileness. . . .
>
> They put me flat on my stomach on the bench. He took down his trousers, sordidly, in front of his colleagues, and lay down on me. He raped me to humiliate me and break my morale. I was mad with rage but tried to look calm and indifferent so that it would be them, and not

me, who would feel humiliated and degraded. In this way, I made them aware that their low behavior had not affected me. And really, what importance did it have, what difference was there between that and the whip? They were both means of torture. And both had the same sordid aim—to drag secrets from me.

They tied me to the bed again and started to whip me. This time, the pain on the soles of my feet was more acute. I could stand it by my own strength of will and the powers of suggestion, in which I have great faith. Thus I gained a kind of moral strength which gave me the impression that I was no longer being tortured but was merely observing the torture of someone else. However, the whip was concrete reality and the idea was not enough to get me through it. To be able to fix my thoughts I needed an objective reality. The pain of the whip got worse and worse. I called out Ipak, Kayhan, Rohab, Ghassem and the others. These were oppressed, hard working men and women from the village where I used to teach. I could feel their eyes fixed on me. I could feel physically that they really wanted to believe in my loyalty and affection for them. I could see in their eyes their totally justified expectations of me. I do not know how long I lay there, tied to the bench. Perhaps I lost consciousness or fell asleep. When I regained consciousness they started threatening me. 'You haven't seen anything yet. We aren't agents of the Savagh. When you get to them, at Evine, they'll force you to speak. They are terrible. You'll see. We're going to take you over there tonight.' "

I would like to present a resolution against these barbaric tortures. (See section on resolutions—Ed.)

Witness 3: Chile

In September 1973, a military coup supported by the national bourgeoisie, assisted and financed by the CIA and multinational companies, took power in Chile. I was among those imprisoned from the start of the dictatorship until June 1975. Political consciousness in Chile is repressed by prisons, tortures, and threats of death. Right from the beginning of the dictatorship, women and men were arrested, thrown in makeshift detention centers and subjected to the same treatment, the only differences being in the way sexism is used.

In the last two and one-half years, the junta has refined its system of torture, imprisonment, and assassination. A secret police has been created, the DINA, with unlimited powers. At their disposal is a network of secret prisons and concentration camps throughout the country. Political repression in Chile always has two stages for its victims. The first is the secret prison, where the prisoners are massed together and subjected to interrogation and torture. They are kept there for days or months, and there are many who never leave. The time spent in the secret prison is the most degrading and brutal period of physical and mental torture. Threats against children are made to put pressure on the prisoners, a method that is used in the extreme against women. Women prisoners are always naked when interrogated, their defenseless bodies being easy targets for blows and sexual aggressions. Sexual aggression is a frequently used weapon against the women, and rape is only one of the manifestations. In Villa Grimaldy, they keep a dog specifically trained for this type of violence against women.

There is no rest; night and day the guards and torturers take turns working on the prisoners. There is no escape from this treatment for women who are pregnant. Solitary confinement, beatings, electric shocks are all used. Mind-transforming drugs are also used during interrogations so as to undermine the will of the prisoner and put her at the mercy of the torturers. Many of the pregnant women lose their children; the stronger have their children and keep them in the prisons. They have to suffer the anguish of the uncertainty of their children's fate inside or outside of prison.

In the second stage, they are transferred to the concentration camps or to the ordinary prisons. The only concentration camp where women are allowed is Tres Alamos in Santiago. Since December 1974, they had never been less than 100 living there.

The fate of those women held in normal prisons is practically the same. The guards try to turn the ordinary prisoners against the political prisoners through lies and deceit. The political prisoners eventually undergo a farcical trial and afterwards must live condemned by this "justice."

Women have been detained as hostages for their husbands, sons, and daughters, or the authorities detain or threaten to detain their children as hostages. The torture suffered by thousands of people is multiplied many times because behind each prisoner we find their family, friends, work mates, and sometimes their political colleagues.

Women who take on the task of assisting those in prison, are given a very hard time, with endless hours in waiting rooms and exposure to much verbal abuse. It is often the women outside of prison who keep the prisoners in contact with the outside world and sustain them materially during their time in prison. The women related to political prisoners have organized themselves so as to better help those in prison. Women who perform these tasks also suffer repression, and in many cases, they themselves end up in jail as political prisoners. The wives of political prisoners frequently lose their jobs and consequently suffer great economic hardships. In the minds of employers in Chile, it is a stigma to be the wife of a political prisoner. This stigma also affects those who do not work.

The ex-political prisoners, those still in prison, and the Chilean resistance movement, are grateful for the solidarity we have received from some of the European women's movements. We want this solidarity to be extended to our sisters imprisoned in Bolivia, Argentina, and Paraguay, who are suffering similar tortures and assassinations by the police in their countries. We ask women to promote campaigns in their countries to denounce these crimes against women and their loved ones.

Witness 4: India

I have come a very long way to speak to you, and I have waited for this opportunity for a very long time. I have come here to speak about the oppression of women in my country, and in particular those women who have been put behind bars. Women from my country suffer from a triple sexual exploitation. They are exploited by the men in their families, they are discriminated against by the State, and they are sexually victimized by an international system of male complicity. I think that it is very important for sisters here from Europe and America to realize that a lot of the exploitation which happens to women in our country is directly organized and institutionalized by a system of male domination.

Another woman and I got involved in politics about five years ago. We were very upset about the condition of our country, about the poverty, about the oppression, and we wanted to do something about that. We got involved in a left movement—the Naxalites—and we tried to organize women into groups. But it was very difficult to bring to them ideas of independence because they had come from such traditional structures. On the other hand, it was very easy for them to relate to a left movement because they were seeing the police brutalizing them continuously, and they came forward very quickly in support of the movement.

As a result of our activities, we were arrested. In prison we tried to organize solidarity with the other women prisoners, because we felt that the women prisoners who were there, were also there for political reasons. Although we were consciously political, they were not arrested for any consciously political action, yet it was the system in which all of us were trapped which had landed us all in prison. We organized the resistance, and we found ourselves in direct physical confrontation with the jail authorities who were continuously trying to torture us, and continuously trying to prevent us from knowing what was going on within the jails.

The political prisoners are the victims of the most vicious tortures, and if they are killed no one will know about it. For example, when a friend of mine was arrested, she was bayonetted, and brutally tortured. She was hanged upside down, hot irons put into her rectum. She was raped. She was placed in solitary confinement, and guarded by two warders. She is still in prison.

I want to ask for your solidarity with the movement of women in India, so that the feminist movement proves itself an international force and intervenes in opposition to the exploitation of women.

Witness 5: India

Indira Ghandi has done much to enhance India's image—an image carefully preserved until the emergency of June 26, 1975. Seeing a woman as a figurehead of the second most populous nation in the world, many people assumed that Indian women are emancipated in relation to their sisters in other Third World countries. Unfortunately, Indira Ghandi has never been representative of more than a tiny elite among Indian women. She and a few other women in prominent positions are far removed from the peasant and working class women who form the bulk of the population.

There is also another, more typical, face of Indian womanhood. Eighty percent of Indian women are poor peasants who are the victims of an oppressive, unenlightened, corrupt society; women who are victims of rape, forced into prostitution, driven to dangerous abortions; women who, because of acute poverty, are sold into slavery, women persecuted for marrying outside their caste; and the daily oppressive life of the *Harijan* (untouchable) women and of minority groups and lower castes. The relationship of the *Brahmin* (highest caste) to the *Harijan* is clearly illustrated by the following incident. In a rural area of East Tanjore in 1972 untouchable women could not walk on the same road at the same time as the Brahmin. Through the organization of a women's movement, untouchable women gained confidence to do this. The landlords and the Brahmins of the community were enraged by this blatant revolt against all caste rules. As a token of "revenge," to set an example, and to maintain their class position, 44 women and children were put in one hut and burned alive (Minority Rights Report). In such oppressive and tragic circumstances, it is not surprising that Harijan women are extremely militant when aroused.

A campaign for the release of Indian Political Prisoners (CRIPP), which is sponsored by the Bertrand Russell Peace Foundation, has recently produced a 50-page brochure documenting the conditions and treatment of political detainees.

Torture is actually commonplace, and varies from cigarette burns on the body to electrical shock treatment on the genitals. The All Bengal Women's Association reported on the forms of torture and sexual abuses of women prisoners. After arrest and the usual form of police interrogation, often including beatings with hands and rifle butts, suspects are detained in jail. After one month in prison, girls undergo further interrogation. They are stripped naked and made to lie on a table where they are burned with cigarettes on all soft parts of the body, accompanied by all unimaginable humiliations. If they fail to answer questions satisfactorily, an iron ruler is inserted into the rectum. As a result of repeated torture, the rectum and the vagina become one. Twenty days later the same treatment is repeated.

Amnesty International has documented 88 cases of prison deaths, which is, no doubt, a gross underestimate. It is known that among the dead are many women, although figures, of course, are impossible to obtain. It is clear that only the strongest pressure brought to bear on the Indian Government will have an effect. Let our sisters in India know that we here are with them mentally, if not physically, and that we will not forget them.

Witness 6: Spain

My name is Lidia Falcon and I was imprisoned in Spain by the Franco regime. In the first place I'd like to announce that I don't make any distinction between the conditions in the Spanish prisons for those arrested for political activities, and those arrested for common crimes, for 2 reasons—in the first place, because it is understood that all imprisoned women suffer from sexist repression, and in the second place, because the conditions in which this repression occurs, is much the same for both.

In Spain, more than 100 women are imprisoned for political reasons. Some of them exclusively for the offence of assembling for a public demonstration or for organizing. In the last 100 years, during which the Spanish women have suffered the multiple aggressions of which they have always been victims, no other epoch has been so continuously sinister and ferocious as the one we have lived through in these last 37 years. The suppression and exploitation of women has been intensified on all levels. We have been humiliated as human beings, as sexual persons, and as laborers. We have been used as brood mares and we have been manipulated as economic tools of the family unit, which is the social base of the new state.

The deeply internalized mystification about the physical and psychological inferiority of the female sex, and the irreplacable role of the girl, wife, or mother, has not prevented the exploitation of cruel police and prison repression of women in our country at the first sign of individual or collective rebellion. The crimes committed against women in the police stations and Spanish prisons can be classified in two main groups: according to the crime committed, and according to the special situations of women prior to detention in prison. As far as the offense is concerned, Spanish legislation is very sexist. For instance, a woman who has intercourse even once with a man other than her husband is considered adulterous, while for the man to be found guilty of the same offense, it must be clear that he keeps a concubine at his home or elsewhere. Therefore we find ten times as many women imprisoned for the offense of adultery than men, with sentences of up to 6 years.

The illegality of contraception turns approximately 800,000 Spanish women into criminals. According to the official statistics, this number of Spanish women use ovulation-interrupters, without counting the other methods of birth-control which are regarded as unnatural by the Catholic Church, as, for example, coitus interruptus. The illegality of abortion has increased the female population in Spanish prisons by 30%. These women are double victims. First, because of the physical suffering involved in an abortion, and second, because of the punitive law regarding abortion.

In the case of other offenses such as abandoning one's family and children, where the offender may be a man or a woman, it is the woman who gets the more severe sentence, even though this is not written in the law.

Nobody knows where the women's prisons are even situated in Spain. Nobody remembers that in them accumulate the miseries and pains of hundreds of women who suffer confinement without any economic or moral support, and who are maltreated without any sexist indulgence. Women who enter prison pregnant are obliged to have the child, not being permitted an abortion, whatever their physical or psychological needs. They have to give birth in the most precarious sanitary conditions in the country, and then return to their cell with a newborn baby of whom they are supposed to take the utmost care.

It is generally believed that being confined in prison is the same for men and women. This is absurd. In a masculine world, all the agents of repression are men. Equality has never existed in a male world. Throughout her detention a woman has a man watching her, a man who takes a special interest in her physical needs. In the cells of police stations the toilets consist of a hole in the floor, and the policeman who has a woman in custody will stand near the cubical to look under the door. This woman cannot wash or even use the cold water without a policeman watching her. And torture is performed as systematically in Spain as in the other countries of which my comrades have spoken. In the same way the beatings, rape, and other sexual abuses are repeated in all prisons and police stations.

The fight will be long and violent. Until we succeed in taking over the power, men will always suppress and exploit us. Every form of reformism is outmoded. The hour of the suffragettes has gone. It should be clear that this structure, dominated by male power, will not be changed by reformed legislation on abortion, on divorce, on homosexuality, nor by denouncing it. Only the triumph of the feminist revolution will modify the relations between men and women, and build from here on, the new world we all desire.

Witness 7: Greece

My experience, together with that of so many others, began on the first day of the military coup on the 21st of April, 1967, when they knocked on the door of my house for the first time. Fortunately, because a friend had warned me, I had the opportunity to escape. After that I lived underground.

The first month after the coup, we began to form an organization with the name E.K.D.A. Unfortunately after the first pamphlets we distributed, they arrested us. I was arrested by the police in August 1967. They took my books, personal things and anything else that they wanted. For the next one and half months I was in complete isolation from other prisoners. Every day for one month I was interrogated day and night. When they did not interrogate me they would put me in the dirtiest and darkest cell, full of dirty water and mice. I will never forget how I was constantly standing up, being afraid to touch anything because the cell was so full of mice.

They also involved my mother in this. During the last days of isolation when the interrogations were over, they tantalized me by letting me see my mother for a few minutes. They wanted me to sign a statement and they tried to break my morale to get me to do so. They put me in a cell with 20 other women who had had about the same experiences as I had. Eleni Boulgari, Ermans Nahuikian, Evtyhia Manteou, Niki Fountourathaki and Kakia Ioannidou were among them. They were blackmailing us and telling us that we were not political prisoners, but criminal prisoners. A few months later I was tried in a martial court.

When I was finally freed I left for Paris. In 1969 I decided to go back to Greece, where I was arrested again and interrogated about the organizations abroad and my participation in them. They let me go, but in August 1971 the military police (E.S.A.) arrested me yet again. I was told that if I would not speak, I would not leave the E.S.A. alive. They played a tape on which it was said again and again, "Moraitou is crazy," "Moraitou is crazy." They would talk outside my cell, saying that my mother was dead, and they threatened my mother that if I did not speak, she would find me dead. One month later they let me go. By then I suffered amnesia and my left side was paralyzed.

Witness 8: Soviet Union

I am from the U.S., and I would like to speak to you about our sisters who are in prisons in the USSR. I will quote what Rose Styron of Amnesty International has to say about them.

"Women in the Soviet Union have been condemned to jails and camps and psychiatric hospitals for their ideas, their religion, the books they read, or for petitioning for national rights and the preservation of a national heritage, for advocating legal reforms, for defending their friends and colleagues, for refusing to denounce their kin."

In prison these women are punished by solitary confinement, reduced rations, and denial of their children's once-a-year visiting privileges. They suffer from maladies like breast cancer, tuberculosis, paralysis, but do not receive medical treatment.

I will now give you a short testimony from Ukranian sisters. She is one of many who appealed to the government of the USSR to allow them to emigrate. Permission was denied.

"We send you this appeal" they have written, "like a note in a bottle, cast out to sea, not knowing who it will reach." Then one of them wrote, "They came to my home. 'We have come to search you under Code 62,' they said. 'What is code 62?' I asked. No answer. Five of them took me into the bathroom. They took off my clothes. They put their hands into my hair, my ears, my mouth.

They put them into my vagina, me rectum. 'What is it you seek?' I asked. 'A manuscript,' they replied."

Others wrote of similar experiences.

Witness 9: Northern Ireland

Two weeks ago a young housewife went into the center of Belfast to pay her rate bill. As she was walking along Royal Avenue an armored car pulled up beside her. Two policemen and four soldiers jumped out and arrested her in the name of Her Majesty the Queen. She was suspected of being attached to the I.R.A. In reality she has never at any time been involved with this organization, but her husband had been interned for two years. She has had to look after her three small children, who are all under the age of 8, by herself. This responsibility, in conjunction with the continual army harassment, has completely wrecked her nerves.

She was arrested at 12:45 P.M., and for the next 54 hours she saw no one other than the Special Branch Police. The Special Branch questioned her for hours on end. Then she was put in an underground cell and locked up. She did not know when it was night or day. They took her watch, shoes, chain and cross. Their excuse was that it was for her own safety. The policewoman deliberately dropped the woman's glasses when she was handing them back to her because she had complained that she could not see without them. She was hardly able to sleep in the cell since they continually woke her up for more questioning. The Special Branch did not inform her husband that she had been arrested until 6 hours after her arrest. But for the fact that a neighbor took her three children into her home, the children would have been left out in the street.

The woman's state of mind on release was terrible to see. She was in a complete stupor for three days. When someone asked her a question you could see it had not registered in her head. This woman is now afraid to go out of her home in case she is again arrested for nothing.

Witness 10: Switzerland

Up to now, we have been talking about repression in prisons in fascist countries, or countries which are repressive. I want to testify about repression in a so-called democratic country, Switzerland. A trial will take place on March 9 in a small Swiss town—a trial brought against the Women's Liberation Movement. On March 8, 1975, we put up a stall and exhibition in the town. The police tried to stop us. The first thing they did was to try to stop us putting up an exhibition on crèches. We condemned the total lack of crèches in the town; the town is completely working class; many immigrant women work there, and there are no provisions for their children. The police succeeded in taxing our advertisements and our leaflets. Next they tried to stop us exhibiting and selling other books, which they claimed to be subversive and pornographic. These were books on contraception and abortion, and the struggles of our Vietnamese and Chilean comrades. They withdrew this charge when they saw the extent of the campaign of solidarity and denunciation which we had led in the town. Finally, their latest charge, to which we have to reply on Tuesday, March 9, concerns our papers which they are questioning.

We want to publicize as widely as possible the obstacles which are put in the way of women's freedom of expression in Switzerland. Every other political group in the town has the right to express itself without any problems. I am involved in other political groups working in Spain and Chile, and as a political militant, I have no problems. As a feminist, I bring in books on Chile, Spain or Portugal, or on abortion, and my comrades and I are stopped.

Witness 11: Argentina and Spain

We are a group of women of different nationalities living in Munich and working against the torture and suffering of our sisters in patriarchal societies, including our sisters imprisoned in Spain, Chile, Uruguay, and other parts of the world. All the existing organizations are neglecting the particular problems of women, who suffer double injustice and discrimination in prison. Women do not have the rights that men enjoy in Spain and Argentina. In contrast to the men, women cannot have access to newspapers, canteens, and bookshops. In addition to the torture to which men are subjected, women prisoners have to put up with rape and sexual torture. We want to free these women from their isolation and give them a feeling of solidarity so that they can find strength to continue their fight. We have received letters saying that women prisoners have not got the same rights and privileges as male prisoners because of women's lack of solidarity.

Our group raises money and sends parcels to these women. With the help of Amnesty International and other organizations, we are supporting them in their struggle by trying to pay lawyers for them during their trials, and in other ways. We are looking for other groups like ours in order to co-ordinate our efforts in the most efficient manner possible.

Violence Against Women in General

While many examples of violence against women have been testified about, there are still gaps. Particularly striking is the lack of a single testimony on child molestation and incest, most of which (need it be said?) involve females as victims and males as aggressors. They remain extremely widespread and neglected crimes.

The very last testimony in this section focuses on the tremendously important problem of nuclear waste poisons, and especially their effects on women and children. The dangers of contamination have increasingly been thrust on an uninformed public by a male brotherhood—regardless of the terrible threat to human lives.

The following testimonies are about crimes of violence in Ausralia, Italy, and the U.S.A.

Witness 1: Australia

Australian culture is based on the myth of "mateship." Mateship is the word used to describe the bonding between men: that deep spiritual relationship that allows them to exclude women as trivial, as objects of disdain, in the light of the real achievements of men, particularly in the early days when they explored and looted the bush and the great outback, in the two world wars, and in sport.

Mateship is the most celebrated national quality, taught and glorified in schools and exported in films. The violence inherent in the mateship ethic has never been hidden. The bushrangers, the soldiers, the footballers, all use violence to put down the other side. Violence performed by groups of men, or at least sanctioned by the group, is the historical heritage that provides Australian men with their mystical feelings about each other and their feeling of real power. Violence towards women is the means by which they impress upon women the fact that they are forever powerless.

Homosexuality is the most despised sexual activity of a man, and homosexuals are bashed and murdered by groups of men. As heterosexuality is mandatory, but women are hated, heterosexual intercourse is called "having a naughty," implying that to have sex with a woman is to stray from the man's role. A more recent term is "to have a nasty," which relates more strongly the unpleasant feeling about this act, and the wickedness and uncleanness of women. There is no erotic culture in Australia. There has never been any attempt to beautify sexual intercourse. There is only skin-flick pornography which concentrates on women as passive and ugly receptacles for men's sperm.

Women are, of course, necessary to free men for their group pursuits and fantasies, to mind the children during their long absences from home, to make excuses to the boss when a hangover precludes work, and to prepare the evening meal in perfect timing for the daily return of the man. An Australian man can manage to control his hatred of women in his marriage in most cases, as long as there is no possibility of her usurping his role. On the other hand, many women are bashed by their husbands for imaginary acts of revolt. I have talked to hundreds of women who have been repeatedly assaulted by their husbands. The most common prelude to an act of violence by a husband is that the wife has failed to serve the dinner in the required manner. Along with this goes the accusation of infidelity, so that you often hear women say, "I had to walk along the street with my eyes glued to the ground."

In Australia, rape is a crime against women that puts them "in their place." Rape constantly reminds a woman that she is the servicer of men. It divides women by the stigma that they bear for having been raped. "Pack" rape in Australia is devised by a group of men as an event that they share in common as a celebration of their group identity and power. Pack rape is seen as an honest embodiment of Australian mateship. It is not related to class, as mateship itself cuts across class barriers. Mateship has done much to give Australia the appearance of a classless society. While the sons of wealthy parents, educated at church schools, fantasize together, and then go out and "bring down" a girl they consider to be above herself, the sons of laborers and factory workers comb the streets for girls they term "cases," girls and women they feel need, or want, to be raped by them.

Men who pack rape don't necessarily belong to the same age group. An older man may rape with a group of younger men to prove to the other men that he is still virile. A husband may arrange for his mates to rape his wife or he may condone it. There seems to be increasing evidence that this practice is almost like a betrothal custom. A woman will conceal rape where possible, especially from her husband, for whom she feels she must remain untainted, or he may be provided with the satisfaction of knowing his wife is not pure, and indeed a "nasty"—that is what he wants.

Australian women, whether they work or stay at home, are

isolated from one another. The mateship ethic, which denies them any role of achievement, relegates them to the position of "having no soul." They must vie among each other for acceptance by men. Australia has an incredibly high rate of fatal kidney diseases in women, due to the abuse of headache powders, self-prescribed, to ease the pain of their lives.

Witness 2: Italy

I belong to a group in Naples called "Le Nemesiache" (the Furies). We have prepared a paper denouncing violence. We include the subtle violence which our Le Nemesiache fights against; the violence which is used against beauty, tenderness, against the nuances of colors and sounds, against the internal rhythms of our lives. Our creativity has been confined, exiled, violated, thrown to one side by abstract rationalizing, by legal organizations, by being beaten down, and by the practice of ridiculing and despising all dimensions which are not considered to be efficient or productive. This is the kind of violence which leads to the taming of, and shame for, one's own sensitivity and intuition. This is the kind of brutality which right from the cradle forces the female to imitate the male. This is the kind of violence which undermines us, making us insecure and forcing us to imitate men instead of realizing who we are.

We don't believe in legal machinery, because violence from men is not any the less real for being backed up by an organization. There is no way in which any law can restore life or prevent the violence which has already taken place. We denounce the kind of violence which penetrates and shatters our autonomy. We must not forget that men's violence is supported by the social, legal, economic, historic, scientific, bureaucratic and professional organizations.

We give testimony of the specific kind of violence we have discovered through self-awareness: the inability to speak out, paralysis of our bodies, the feelings of insecurity which move us to support fights which are not ours. The crime of being seen merely as a sex object, of always seeing oneself reduced and confined to sex, the violence of seeing ourselves reduced to morons who have no problems because we have used up all our energy and strength for the benefit of others—there lies victimization and desperation.

There is also the terrible violence which the whole male cultural organization has used against beauty and which has been adopted by many women too. Beautiful women are associated with stupidity and the superfluous. The idea that there is only one right and valid way of examining problems—this kind of violence prevents us from communicating, colors our way of looking at ourselves and others, causing us to undervalue the richest parts of our history and our struggles. Our struggle lies in trying to reduce violence in ourselves, not to let it infiltrate us, or set up barriers within our thoughts, our intuitions. Let's not set up legal machinery ourselves. Let's not elevate professionalism to the level of a myth. Let's not support power or insensitivity.

Witness 3: U.S.A.*

I would like to talk here about the power which comes from atomic energy, and which will affect us all in one form or another as soon as the ambitious plans of operators and politicians will be realized. This technology, developed, planned, approved, built and operated by men, can destroy all of us and our living space. However, those who will have to bear the greatest burden are women who are hit during pregnancy by radioactive substances and give birth to deformed, weak-minded, crippled or mentally backward children for whom they cannot expect any help. Statistics from areas influenced by atomic plants in the U.S.A. show that there are hundreds of miscarriages, deformed babies and deaths, as well as leukemia and all other types of cancer in these areas. The men who want to build the atomic reactors and plants at any price, say that atomic energy is not harmful. They say this because those substances which are distributed from the chimneys of reactors into the environment, and from cooling waters into the rivers, cannot be seen, smelled, tasted or touched.

Atomic reactors are being built in almost all countries all over the world. Whoever possesses atomic reactors is also able to build an atom bomb. It is not us women's fault that the world has become what it is today: boundless wealth and power for some, barbaric poverty conditions for others. Contamination, damage, destruction, and annihilation of our environment increases rapidly. But women do not want to take risks to us and our children out of all proportion to what can be gained.

Women! Start action groups against the dangers of atomic energy, or join existing groups and enrich those with your imagination and creative initiative.

*This testimony was presented by a German woman.

CHAPTER 13

Sexual Objectification of Women

If men were not encouraged by their socialization (we optimistically assume socialization is responsible!) to divorce their sexual response from their feelings of liking, respect and love, that is, if their sexuality were better integrated with their positive feelings, they would be as uninterested as most women are in buying sex from unknown persons. Men also would not be interested in what has come to be known as pornography because it turns men on. Further they would be less interested in rape.

PROSTITUTION

No one at the Tribunal offered testimony about young girls and women sold into prostitution by their families or slave traders, though this is still happening in many parts of the world today. The testimony from Japan and Korea indicates that women are forced into prostitution because of the lack of alternative jobs. This horrendous situation is nevertheless a little better than the literal enslavement of women for sex that still flourishes undercover in many places.

Of course, the deliberate choice to become a prostitute is an entirely different situation. But the conscious choice to become a prostitute often turns out to be based on a lack of alternative job opportunities or extremely poorly paid ones. In these cases, whether or not prostitution is a genuine choice, is rather questionable.

Testimony on prostitution follows from Japan, Korea and the U.S.A.

Witness 1: Japan

Abolition of state-regulated prostitution and the coming into effect of the Anti-Prostitution Act of 1958 liberated many prostitutes who had been the victims of a centuries-old flesh traffic. Nevertheless, the continued demand of men for slave-like sexual service, combined with the oppressed status of women, allowed an underground prostitution market to survive, and today in Japan, the turkish baths are among the most common places where "controlled prostitution" is performed under the guise of the public baths business.

I would like to denounce this exploitative system which has survived in spite of our repeated protests.

Turkish bath houses usually charge customers between 2,000 and 5,000 Yen ($7–$17) depending on the class of the house. This is only the amount for taking a bath and having your body washed and massaged by a masseuse called "Miss Turkey." Of course they are Japanese, not Turkish. These women are not licensed masseuses, but no one cares because the customer's purpose in going to a Turkish bath is not just to take a bath and be massaged.

According to one of the Miss Turkeys with whom I talked, her bath house charged 2500 Yen ($8) per customer, and out of this 2500 Yen, her share is supposed to be one-third—800 Yen ($2.70). But of her 800 Yen she has to pay herself for the soap, towels, and all other utensils she uses for her work. Some refreshment such as cola is served to each customer, often at the expense of the women, depending on the system of the house.

I learned that a certain house charged the Miss Turkeys 60 Yen for one bottle of cola when its original price was 30 Yen. They also charged 60 Yen for a rented towel, when the laundry charges only 10 Yen for its rental. Five towels are used for one customer. Not only are these costs laid on the women but the houses also rake off additional profits on other indispensible expenses. One set of gowns and uniforms has to be covered by the Miss Turkey herself. Another payment she has to make every day is 500 Yen ($1.70) to the manager who allots customers. If she doesn't give this money to the manager, the manager might give her regular customers to her colleagues.

After everything, because of these expenditures, not more than 500 Yen ($1.70) is left as pay for their 50 minutes of physical labor. What do you think you can buy with 500 Yen in Japan? A cup of coffee in a typical coffee shop in Tokyo costs 250 or 300 Yen. How can you make your living with this? This is how the masseuses are forced to make money by extra work, that is, prostitution.

A compartment with a closing door is provided for each Miss Turkey, where she can fulfill the requests of her customers. Again Miss Turkey has to pay—4,000 Yen ($13) for the compartment, which amounts to more than her regular income. Then the employers order the women to keep the charges for the prostitution as low as possible so that customers will not move away to rival houses. So, the Miss Turkeys have to take as many customers a night as possible to keep up with the excessive payments to the house they belong to.

Another means of exploiting the Miss Turkeys is the strict time charge. Even for 5 minutes overtime, the Miss Turkeys themselves have to pay the charge to the bathhouse. I know of a case where the over-time charge snowballed day by day, and in order to wipe out the debt, the woman came to depend on a drug to keep her awake until she totally broke down after a few months.

So, Turkish baths in Japan, actually prostitution houses, profit off the sacrifice of women's slave-like labor. Some of you might wonder why these women do not quit such a hard and unfair job. Nobody, including the Miss Turkeys, wants to do unprofitable work *if* there are other possiblities. But in Japan, big enterprises use every possible means to discourage women from continuing to work. They try never to employ women over 30, or even in their 20's. Being forced to quit their jobs at an early age, women in general try to get the position of "wife" which is regarded as the most respectable position for a woman. Thus, economically dependent women are mass-produced by a system of "retirement at marriage," and without the total breakdown of this system, we cannot get rid of forced prostitution and exploitation in any profession.

Witness 2: Korea

I am reading a testimony which was actually written by my colleague, a Japanese journalist named Matsui Yayori, about the way Japanese men sexually exploit Korean women. She writes:

> Everyday hundreds and thousands of Japanese men travel to Korea with large wads of money which they use to violate women in our neighboring country. The number of Japanese tourists going to South Korea has doubled yearly since 1965. By 1973 over 80% of the 500,000 foreign tourists to Korea were Japanese. Since the great majority of them were and continue to be men, it is like a giant parade of lechers. At Seoul's Kimpo Airport, jumbo jets completely filled with Japanese men land in a steady stream. In this way, upwards of two thousand Japanese men a day enter the country. These men have been lured by prestigious Japanese travel agencies who advertise, for example, "Complete *Kisaeng* service; a man's paradise." (Korean prostitutes are referred to as *kisaeng*.) As a "morale booster," Japanese companies reward their outstanding branch office managers and salesmen with all-expenses-paid tours of South Korea's brothels. One or two nights of *kisaeng* parties are invariably included

in the schedule, but recently, as a matter of courtesy, an "optional feature" has been actually written into the tour brochures. Chartered tours of two nights and three days cost no more than $200—including the price of sex.

"I go to Korea two or three times a year with my co-workers, telling my wife that I'm going to visit Kyushu," says a taxi driver. "You can't find a decent geisha in Japan, even at a hot springs resort. South Korea's much better," claims the owner of a small factory. "In South Korea the spirit of rendering oneself completely to a man still exists among the women, and their exhaustive service is irresistible," claims a white-collar worker, his eyes glistening.

Many Japanese men fall for stories of *kisaeng* girls in their colorful native dress waiting on men at parties and even putting food into the customer's mouth for him. It is advertised that the *kisaeng* spirit is so self-sacrificing and dedicated that when a man brings a *kisaeng* girl back to his hotel, she will even do his laundry if he will leave her a big tip. Tales abound of Japanese tourists sallying forth to a *kisaeng* party in one bus and then returning to their hotel in two buses, each man accompanied by a young woman who has changed into her street clothes. They are truly sex-hungry males, swaggering about without any concern for where they are.

There are said to be more than 8,000 of these *kisaeng* who act as "receptacles for Japanese men's psychological discharges." Approximately 2,000 of them are reported to be authorized prostitutes who hold official registration certificates and undergo tests about twice a month to check for venereal disease. The South Korean Minister of Education has decreed that "the sincerity of girls who have contributed with their cunts to their fatherland's economic development is indeed praiseworthy." This statement about national pimping has become notorious in the Korean community in Japan. It is even reported that prospective *kisaeng* must endure lectures by male university professors on the crucial role of tourism in the South Korean economy before they can get their prostitution licenses.

If the women who become *kisaeng* were to work in a factory, their salary might not even reach thirty dollars a month. But as *kisaeng* they receive a larger income for the labor of spending a night in a luxury hotel. South Korea has no social security or public health insurance, so when a working person loses his or her job or becomes ill, the whole family faces the specter of literal starvation. Under these circumstances some women are forced to sell their bodies just to stay alive.

An angry reaction against Japanese *kisaeng* tours has been spreading quietly but steadily inside South Korea. In December 1973, students from Ehwa Women's University demonstrated against Japanese men arriving on *kisaeng* tours at Seoul's Kimpo Airport. They demanded, "Behind the facade of promoting tourism in our country our fellow women are being made into commodities and their precious human rights are being ignored. We can no longer permit

> our sisters' bodies to be sold to bring in foreign capital. What good will come of corrupting the spirit in order to earn dollars? Many years have passed since our country was liberated from Japanese colonial rule. Why must our women still act as commodities to be sold for filthy Japanese money? We demand an immediate end to brothel tourism which is making our country into a sexual playground for Japanese men.

For a while the Japanese women who opposed *kisaeng* tours were unsure about what action to take, but the powerful appeals made by Korean women had a galvanizing effect. In December 1973, the "Women's Group Opposing *Kisaeng* Tourism" was established in Tokyo. Two days after the demonstration held by the students at Ehwa Women's University, Japanese women demonstrated at Tokyo's Haneda Airport on Christmas Day. About 50 women—students, housewives, and workers of all ages—confronted the Japanese male tourists leaving on *kisaeng* tours with leaflets and with slogans painted on their vests, including: "Aren't you ashamed to go on group brothel tours?" and "Go to hell, sex animals!" Indignantly they also stated: "Previously, Japan colonized and pillaged Korea, raping many of her daughters as army prostitutes. Now they go back to the same land and disgrace her women again, this time with money. The Japanese government, under the name of economic assistance, is actively cooperating with the institution of brothel tours. We must not permit our husbands, lovers, brothers, and associates to go to South Korea to buy women." Even this small demonstration was suppressed by the Japanese police; but their power could not crush the budding solidarity between women of both countries.

The distorted and numb sensitivities of Japanese men can be seen in their relationships with women in general. For most of them the word "women" means only domestic servants who, under the label of wife, are driven relentlessly with housework; or it means prostitutes who, labelled "bar girls" or "massage parlor girls," act as instruments to drain off the fluids of the lower male body. Because Japanese men debase their own women as house slaves or prostitutes, Japanese men feel no compunction about raping foreign women with their money.

Witness 3: U.S.A.

I am Margot St. James from the United States. I am a whore. I was labelled a whore in 1962 when I was forcibly arrested. I am obliged to remain a whore for the rest of my life. I have never been able to get a job since I was so labelled, even though a higher court found me innocent two years later.

Streetwalkers in America are the most oppressed women, the most oppressed workers in the country. They are mostly minority women, and they are discriminated against by the hotels and the parlor owners, who I call legalized pimps. The parlor owners take at least 60 to 75% of the money, and give the women no benefits and no job security.

Forty-eight thousand women in the United States are arrested every year for prostitution. They are so labelled by the police, by the courts, by the traditional sexist legal system, for providing sex for establishment men. Seventy percent of the women in prison in the United States today were first arrested for prostitution. They learn other ways of earning money faster once they go to jail. They learn how to steal and sometimes they go into drugs. Eighty percent of juveniles—girls under 18 years—who become prostitutes, were first incest victims in their own families. This is something that is never talked about.

If we are to do something about the juveniles in prostitution, we must go after the men who buy those girls. In the U.S.A, only the women are arrested. In France, only the women are arrested. Everywhere it is the same. Only the women are put in jail or arrested for prostitution. The enforcement of prostitution laws against women makes the prostitute an object lesson to all women that they had better stay home and they had better live within the roles defined by men.

The illegality of prostitution, the laws which are enforced against the women, make the women easy victims for any sadistic man who wants to go and rip her off and brutalize her, or even murder her. Twelve prostitutes were murdered in San Francisco in 1974. That is one a month, but not *one* of them got a story in the paper. Yet, when one policeman gets shot it is a headline for three days!

On Mother's Day in 1973, I started an organization to combat this blacklabelling process, to combat the divide-and-conquer technique used by men. I called it COYOTE: Call Off Your Old Tired Ethics. Men call prostitution the oldest profession. I call it the oldest injustice. The enforcement against women only promotes the rape ideology. As the woman from Japan pointed out, the women themselves get hardly any of the money. Ninety percent of their income is taxed away informally by anyone who is in a position to know what they do, and that what they do is illegal: the landlord, the hotel manager, the policeman.

The problems are the same in whatever country I have been

to. They charge you for soliciting even when being a prostitute is not against the law. They arrest your boyfriend or your husband and say he is living on your earnings, which is immoral. Yet many countries, like Germany, want to have government-run houses. But the government is the worst pimp of all!

PORNOGRAPHY

The testimony on pornography from Denmark included a short movie distributed in Denmark showing three men raping a woman. It was so horrifyingly realistic that some women viewers insisted it be stopped after two or three minutes; but even this brief viewing made the point. Pornography has been an issue too long neglected by feminists, many of whom are still swayed by notions of liberal tolerance. Of course, liberals wouldn't tolerate movies of whites beating Blacks, or Christians beating Jews, but if it is called pornography and women are the victims, then you are a prude to object.

Witness 1: Denmark

On July 1, 1969, pictorial pornography was legalized in Denmark. Prior to this there was a big debate about whether or not to legalize it. One of the strongest arguments for changing the law was that women would not be raped as much as they had been before. So we should be happy, because men who would like to rape us will go out and buy a porno magazine instead. But it is a big fat lie. With the legalizing of pornography it is also legal to regard women as sex objects, to rape and accost according to need, because pornography ideologically establishes that women's innermost wish is to subject herself to men.

It is a crime against women that some make a profit out of such an ideology. It is violence against women to be exhibited as sex objects and nothing else. So why did our government agree to legalize pornography? Who does it serve other than capitalists? Even before the change in the law they made money by sending magazines and films abroad. Uncensored pornography means even more profit.

Who are the women who agree to be photographed for pornography? They are housewives, young women who can't earn enough money, women students who haven't enough understanding of what it is to be a real woman, women who do not have the possibility of becoming economically independent of men. Should we blame these women who have been told their whole lives that they are sex objects, and that this is their most important role in life?

This society is organized according to the needs of capitalism and men, and it is a threat to capitalism and male structures if women start to believe in themselves, because then they will start to struggle against every form of economic and ideological oppression. It is quite clear that it is in society's interest to legalize pornography because pornography helps to deepen woman's alienation from herself. It alienates her from her own body and her own sexuality. It is a way to strengthen and justify the male ethic that men can direct their potency and aggression towards women, and that women shall passively submit to them. But here in Denmark we are so sexually liberated, or so it is said, that it is considered to be in women's interests that everything is allowed, pornography too.

Let us go back to those who let themselves be photographed. Yes, I am one of them. I believed that I was so liberated that nothing could touch me. Nobody could exploit me. Why did I do it? I had to get a lot of money fast and that was the easiest way. It paid well. But how I felt doing it was something else! I felt it as a violence against my body to be exhibited like a piece of meat, and as a violence against all women. All women suffered because I supported the porno industry.

The many women I talked to during my three months as a porno model often hated themselves. But it was very often of bitter necessity that they did it. They had to. Their husbands drank, or they were single mothers. Others felt they had to compete by wearing smarter clothes. For some it was just to be the one time, because they wanted to buy this or that. But for me it was many times. For me too it was almost impossible to get out again. The money is good and for many women it is easy to get into drinking during the photography sessions. Why do the models often hate themselves? Most of the male models think it is ok. But it's the women who have a prick in their mouth, who have to be tied up, who have to do everything so that a man can get his orgasm, who are exhibited as wet cunts and nothing else. I learned quickly to hate my body and myself for supporting capitalists and their easy money, and for supporting this society's decay. And I learned too that it is men who have the upper hand in this situation.

Who should I accuse because I was a porno model? Yes, I did it of my own free will, and the other women I talked to did too.

Nevertheless I accuse the government for making a law that supports a capitalistic patriarchal society with its ideology of women as sexual objects and nothing else; that gives life to men's sexual fantasies; that reduces women to passive objects to be abused, degraded, and used. I say that this is violence against women because now every woman is for sale to the lowest bidder, and for all men. I accuse the government for supporting the porno industry and for continuing to exploit women economically so that women still have very limited possibilities to control their own lives.

I believe that only by overthrowing this society will the violence against women cease. And I am prepared to use violence against an ideology that says that women are inferior to men. And I'm prepared to fight against a government and the capitalist economic system which strengthens such an ideology.

As the ex-porno model said, not only the models like herself are dehumanized, but so are all women, and young girls as well. Third World girls in particular are used in Denmark for the popular topic of "baby-love," the euphemism for collections of photographs of pre-adolescent girls having sexual relations with adult men, or of baby girls with their genitals displayed.

Witness 2: Denmark

The best evidence against pornography is a piece of pornography. We have a film here, and we would like to show it. It is very violent, it is about rape, and it might be uncomfortable particularly for those sisters who have been raped. This film is produced by the Danish porno industry. It is sold in many many shops, not only in Denmark but in Paris, in Amsterdam and in Berlin. It is exported to America and wherever it is wanted. It is also legal to see it in Denmark.

(The movie was then shown, but stopped after 2 or 3 minutes.)

We have met here today to talk about rape, about violence against women. The question is, how do we combat men's fantasies about women? In Denmark they have allowed men's sexist fantasies to flower, and this film is one of the products. It promotes the degradation of a woman. I am sorry it is so upsetting to see to what point male fantasies have come.

♀ ♀ ♀ ♀ ♀

The testimonies and reports concluded midmorning on Monday March 8th, International Women's Day. For the most part however we have followed the order in which crimes were presented at the Tribunal.

It seems appropriate to explain here how the Tribunal material was gathered and edited for the book. Everything said through a microphone in the plenary sessions of the Tribunal was tape recorded. To facilitate transcribing, after the Tribunal this was retaped onto smaller tapes. Because of retaping there are occasional losses of brief sections of speeches. All the material was transcribed and then translated into English. When translated, the coherence and articulateness of the unedited proceedings varied enormously. Often when the quality was poor we could not tell whether it was due to the woman speaking or the translator's interpretation. We must remember that many women testified in a language that was not their mother tongue and that the transcribers often were not transcribing in their mother tongue. There was also tremendous variation in translation skills, and even in the accuracy of typing or the legibility of the handwriting that we had to work from. For these and other reasons, about 10% of the testimony heard at the Tribunal has not been included here, and other testimonies have been edited considerably to include only what is comprehensible.

But our editorial eliminations were not just a matter of comprehensibility. Occasionally testimony was superficial, irrelevant or contradictory, and we saw no reason to include it to the detriment of other, more pertinent testimony. Also, in order to maintain the publisher's length limit and keep the book price within women's budgets, difficult choices had to be made about what to include in the book. We did not want to limit ourselves to what was heard in the plenary sessions of the Tribunal. We wanted to consider for inclusion all testimony or reports written for the Tribunal but not heard for one reason or another. In a few instances, we have included excerpts from letters sent to the Brussels Office by women from countries where there might otherwise have been very little material. These cases are footnoted.

Elimination of repetition or statements not central to the testimony, rearranging of paragraphs, and so on has been done to clarify and shorten where possible, without loss of an important point. In addition, we have separated proposals made during testimony and placed them in Part Two along with other such material which was presented on Monday afternoon, at the closing session of the Tribunal.

Part II

Solutions, Resolutions, Proposals for Change

CHAPTER 1

Proposals Relating to Particular Crimes

Any individual or group was free to make a proposal. Almost all the proposals were applauded, but none were voted on. The country mentioned after each proposal indicates the country from which the woman or women making the proposal, came. In some cases the proposals were formulated by international groups.

A MANIFESTO FOR OLDER WOMEN, U.S.A.

I want to present a manifesto for older women.

We older women wil no longer tolerate our invisibility. We will no longer permit ourselves to be shunted into the corner. We will no longer let ourselves be considered nonpersons who are just burdens.

We have something valuable to offer to the society as a whole, to our families, and to individuals. As older women, we have amassed a lot of experience, acquired a greater perspective. This can be invaluable in raising children, and getting a better historical perspective on the problems we all face, of getting acquainted with our roots and traditions that can give us not only greater insights of how to change our life styles and our society, but give us a greater ability to pursue our aims for a better life with greater vigor and more endurance. We do not, however, aim to impose our ideas on the younger generation of women, but rather see it as an opening of channels of communication both ways, thereby enabling us to learn from each other.

Among crimes committed against older women which have to be eliminated are the following: first, isolation. Grown children are too busy with their own lives. Our mates are often either dead or married to younger women. Old friends are scattered. Feelings of rejection and a turning inwards are therefore common.

Second, inadequate health care. We demand free health care, including glasses, hearing aids, dentures, etc. The elimination of carelessness and lack of interest on the part of the medical profession to giving adequate care to older women; and the cessation of the biased opposition on the part of the medical profession to the use of estrogen, a vital part of the female hormones that ceases to be produced by the ovaries and without which the older woman's health and mental capacity deteriorates rapidly.*

Third, media portrayal of the older woman. In contrast to the young woman who is viewed mostly as a sexual object, the older woman is viewed as asexual, the object of pity, as helpless, or domineering and unreasonable. We insist that we are individuals with a great variety of talents and needs, that we want warmth, companionship, and *yes*, sexual relationships. Yes, we are alive and want to be affirmed.

Fourth, economics. We want meaningful work with wages, not just volunteer work. Also social security benefits have to be revamped. In the U.S.A., young women raising families (alledgedly the most important job) do not accumulate credits towards Social Security. The claim is that the women will get Social Security as her husband's dependent. In more and more cases, where women are divorced after many years of marriage, this is no longer true. In the struggle to reestablish herself in the labor market, she can at best count only on low wages. Along with the many years with zero earnings, this means that her Social Security payments are very low.

Fifth, problems of the woman approaching menopause. Women who have dedicated their lives to the welfare of their children find themselves for the first time having to decide what she wants for herself, what she wants from life. At this time when her body is undergoing drastic changes and the children are on their own, the husband often leaves or dies. She has no economic base on which to build a foundation and no emotional base on which to build new relationships. Economic aid should be given to these women to enable them to get training in the field of their choice and to give them the opportunity to find out what they want.

This is only a partial list of the needs of older women. It's obvious that all women's fates intertwine. We need each other and in helping one segment, we help all the others.

ABORTION AND CONTRACEPTION, MEXICO

Who decided that at the moment of conception, women lost all their rights as a human being to dispose of her most inalienable

*Since there is growing evidence of a connection between cancer and taking estrogen some members of the U.S. Committee question whether opposition is not valid.

property—which is to say her own body? Why should we accept the "macho" idea which stipulates that the woman must accept all pregnancies to which her body falls vicitim? For many women, pregnancy constitutes an outside aggression because it happens against her will. Personally, I have heard women, mothers of eight and ten children, recognize bitterly that their capacity to love cannot satisfy the demands of all, and that undoubtedly some of their children will reproach them for not having been loved enough. As the European women said when demonstrating for the legalization of abortion, "My belly belongs to me!"

Concretely my proposition is the following: that women acquire, by means of an international campaign, the ability to exercise the right of control over our own bodies so that we do not have to ask for authorization in order to decide what we will do in case of pregnancy, and that the right of bringing it to term or stopping it shall remain completely ours. We would obtain these rights if we united in a true fight for them. We must stop being manipulated by governmental campaigns orchestrated by men who transform us into passive objects in regard to our creative capacities. It was the policy of the Nazi government that women must have all the children they were able to have in order to supply the State with soldiers. Today, in the Western countries, women are asked to limit their procreation. It is time to ask ourselves this question: for how long will we allow our destiny to remain in the hands of a male-oriented society?

WOMEN IN POVERTY, U.S.A.

I would like to give some examples of ways that we in the national welfare rights movement in the U.S. have gone about trying to solve some of our basic problems. One of the first things that we did was to list all our problems; for example, too low payments, no jobs available, the processing of applications too slowly, checks getting cut off for no reason. The next step was to analyze the problem, see where we stood with the law, and if the law was bad, we talked about how to try to change the law. We developed a legislative program. If the law was good but just not being enforced, we would take steps to force the department through confrontation to change their regulations. There were a number of different things we did, like welfare hearing campaigns, or credit campaigns where we demanded that credit be provided for welfare recipients. We put pressure on local merchants by going into places like Sears and Roebuck and taking foreign currencies (like pesos and pounds, and francs and pennies and nickles and foodstamps) and we'd try to buy clothes for our children with it. This way we would tie up all the lines and the cash registers and they couldn't sell anything to their other customers; therefore, they had to stop their business, and it was one of the ways we got recognition for our problem of not being able to buy anything on our low grants.

We also had something called an eat-in. In the state I come from in the U.S., they allow you 19 cents per person per meal when you're on welfare, but you can't buy anything for that small amount. An eat-in is when ten or 30 women, or whatever the number, go into a very nice, expensive restaurant and ask the people at the restaurant for their best meal. Then when the time comes to pay for it, you give them 19 cents!

We also have "pee-ins." We women in the United States have to pay to go to the toilet. So what we do is go in and pee on the floor, and then they open up the toilets for free.

The Welfare Department has refused to provide cooking stoves for people. So, what we have had are cook-ins. For a cook-in you get an electric hotplate and your pot of beans, or greens, or fish or whatever smells bad. You go down to the public office or the city council and you plug in your electric hot plate and you cook there! And then you might be given a stove. These are just some examples of the kinds of things that a few women with a problem can be creative about and change for themselves.

RAPE, FRANCE

We have heard the testimony of rape victims. We must now propose some solutions. I am from a group in Paris, of lawyers, doctors and other women who are working on rape. When a raped woman goes to the police station, she should not be greeted by men who take a malicious pleasure in listening to her evidence. She should not be in the position of being the accused. At the level of the courts, we must have women magistrates for cases of rape because it is apparent that women are still ashamed to describe the acts of which they have been the victims. Yet, they have to do so in great detail, which tortures them and makes them relive the entire experience. But having to do this in front of a man is even more painful. We propose that the jury of the Assize Court be composed of an equal number of men and women because women are more capable of understanding this problem than

Roswitha Gans

The opening of the International Tribunal

P. Bolsius—*Standard*

The media men's shortlived presence

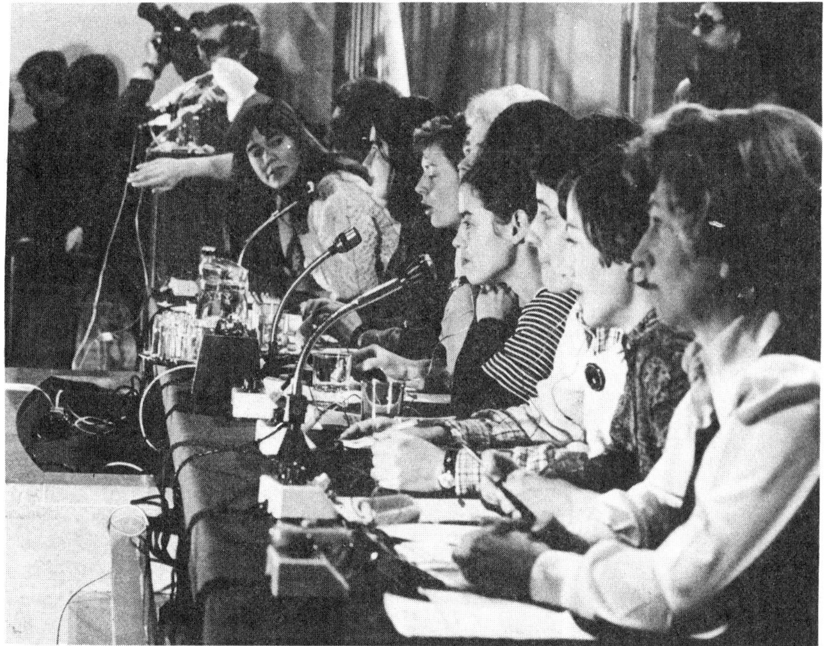

P. Bolsius—*Standard*

The Coordinating Committee, from left to right, Nicole Van de Ven, Diana Russell, Marguerite Russell, Elizabeth Natland, Lydia Horton, Miriam Bazzanella with Grainne Fanen hidden behind her, Erica Fisher, Moni Van Look (not actually on the committee) and Lily Boeykens.

Roswitha Gans

A Plenary Session showing three of the 5 interpreter's booths

Cathy Bernheim

The Tribunal participants waiting to hear testimony

Nancy Budd

A vote is taken on the issue of media men

Eva Besnyo

A lunch break is announced

Eva Besnyo

The testimony begins

men. At the moment in France, it is the Ministère Publique who must prove that the women did not consent, for it to be considered as rape. However, we demand that when the woman has been raped in circumstances which allow us to presume that she did not consent, that the burden of proof be reversed, and that the accused rapist has to prove that she did consent. The question of consent is extremely important because the current attitude among men is that a woman enjoys being raped, and that she therefore consents. In *M's* case (which you heard earlier and with which I've been involved as her lawyer), the magistrate did not seem to understand that when you have 70 kilos on top of you, the weight of a man, you can't defend yourself.

BATTERED WOMEN, INTERNATIONAL GROUP

In our workshop on battered women, we discovered that women of Japan, the Netherlands, France, Wales, England, Scotland, Ireland, Australia, the U.S.A. and West Germany have begun the fight for the rights of battered women and their children.

We call for urgent action by all countries to combat the crime of woman battering. We demand that governments recognize the existence and extent of this problem, and accept the need for refuges, financial aid and effective legal protection for these women.

CLITORIDECTOMY, FRANCE

The *exciseuses* (those doing the excision) operate without anaesthetics, with a curved knife or a razor blade, which must be well sharpened for the incision along the clitoris because the tissue is tough. Hemorrhage, tetanus, urinary infection and septic anemia are not infrequent results. The perineum (tissue) of those who survive hardens, and will tear in childbirth. Apart from the fatalities, women are victim to a particularly horrible consequence of excision, viz: the development of a nevroma at the point where the clitoride nerve is cut. This causes terrible pain if the area is touched even very gently. Millions of little girls (aged seven to puberty) are, at present, subjected each year to this sexual mutilation, hypocritically known as an "initiation ceremony," in the Yemen, in Saudi Arabia, in the Sudan, in Egypt, in Iraq, in Somalia, in Djibouti, in Ethiopia, in Kenya, in Togo, in the Ivory

Coast, in Guinea, and other countries whose representatives are seated at the United Nations and some of which pass for progressive countries.

Excision is but an extreme example of the oppression suffered by women in patriarchal societies. Because this torture is only inflicted on women, nothing is said about it. We state that we regard the excisions done on women as being on the same level and requiring the same action as other tortures which we have denounced, particularly during the wars in Algeria and in Vietnam; also in Brazil, Chile, Greece and elsewhere. We are at one with the women and men who rise up against these atrocities in their countries.

PORNOGRAPHY, INTERNATIONAL GROUP

This proposal comes from the workshop on pornography. This Tribunal has been concerned with violence against women—economic exploitation, sexual oppression, sexual torture, rape, physical and mental violence in general, the negation of lesbian women's lives and the expression of their love. All this exists in pornography; male reality and fantasy are one and the same. All these things are the expression of societies where hierarchy and power controls us all. It is pointless to just make a resolution condemning pornography, for with or without pornography, dominance of men over women still exists. The way men experience their sexual identity is oppressive to women because women's bodies are objects and their sexuality exists only in that it satisfies men's needs.

Our resolution is this: to ask all women to consider the consequences of what it means that their sexuality is defined by men; to see that when women's sexuality and bodies are owned, defined and controlled by men, social change alone cannot end our oppression as women. We resolve that all women should work towards a sexual identity that is a total expression of herself, her needs, sensuality, sexuality, and emotionality; a sexuality that is not fixed on genital sex, dominance and submission, that doesn't split a woman's body from the rest of her being; that women's bodies no longer may be used to support a social structure that dehumanizes all people. We condemn pornography for the violence against women it uses, for the sexual exploitation of women, and the sacrifice of women for the sake of male power, potency and domination.

PROSTITUTION, U.S.A.

Be it resolved that sexual acts in private between consenting adults shall be outside the purview of the criminal laws, that commercial sexual activities be recognized as a service business, not as a criminal act, and that it be treated as such, that women be as free to walk and converse on the streets of the world as men. All laws that discriminate against such activity by statute or by enforcement shall be eliminated, that women who choose to be prostitutes do so of their own free will after the age of consent and that no coercion by anyone be tolerated.

That prostitution be recognized as dependent on a repressive sexist socialization that can eventually be changed. Women and men who are free from sexual stereotypes and economic discrimination will be free from commercial sexual exchange.

CHAPTER 2

General Strategy Proposals

MEDICAL SELF-HELP, INTERNATIONAL GROUP

We have heard many negative examples of what gynecologists do to us women. I want to talk about self-help as a positive way of avoiding these abuses.

In many parts of the world, women have begun to regain control over their bodies and their sexuality through self-help. The basis for the self-help is self-examination and the sharing of our experiences. Since we were young, we have been taught to be ashamed of and feel disgust for our genital organs. Only men have access to our vaginas. Gynecologists exert power over us with their knowledge of our sexual organs. That is partly because as women we have had little possibility of gaining an understanding of our bodies.

Self-examination involves examining ourselves regularly with a speculum and a mirror. We use a plastic speculum, which can be locked open. This makes it possible for us to use it ourselves, and we can see more through the plastic than the gynecologist can see through a metal speculum (which is also very cold). During our examinations we can see, for example, that during the cycle, small red dots may occur on the cervix. Though many a doctor would eagerly cauterize these, they can be normal and disappear after a few days—so cauterization is totally unnecessary. There are women who are now able to determine the time of their ovulations through self-examination. In addition, we can find out about infections before symptoms like itching occur.

Through self-help we learn to reject a penis-centered sexuality. We get to know our own bodies, develop our own methods of treating gynecological disorders, and acquire skills like pelvic examination, breast examination, gynecological tests, menstrual extraction. We have been successful in using honey, garlic, yogurt, etc., for some disorders instead of vaginal medication, tablets, creams and cauterizations. In this way, we create a new health care which represents an attack on the established medical system, its representatives, the doctors, and on the pharmaceutical industry.

During the past years, women in the U.S. have created feminist self-help centers which continue to expand. Self-help groups exist now in many other countries, including New Zealand, Japan and Kenya. In West Berlin, we will soon open the first European feminist self-help center where we will do self-help courses and self-help presentations. We will build up information files for every woman to use, and we will start an international self-help newsletter. Women need power! Control over our bodies is a decisive step towards this power.

Women from Australia, Austria, England, France, Italy, the U.S.A. and the Federal Republic of Germany formulated the following resolution about self-help. As women, we have no allies in individual governments, in the male left, or in the male right, in corporate structures or in their cohorts, or in the population controllers, for all oppress and exploit us. Until now, we have done only cheap or unpaid labor. That is why we have to create our own institutions and structures, and realize and use the potential of our untapped and overlooked resources. These institutions are not alternatives, but the basis for the feminist revolution.

Control of our lives must begin with control of our bodies. This includes control of our sexuality. As lesbians and as heterosexual women, we reject the penis-centered sexuality.

We demand: (1) that it be a woman's choice whether or not to bear children; (2) the right to control our sexuality; (3) the end to experimentation and unnecessary surgery on women; (4) the end to forced sterilization; and (5) that drugs forbidden in one country be immediately forbidden internationally.

International self-help is more powerful!

WAGES-FOR-HOUSEWORK, ITALY

I think it's terribly important for all of us to fight against men's attempts to break up women's struggles into isolated aspects so as to control us more easily and to be able to play us off against each other. At this Tribunal, we've heard about lists of crimes without any indications of how we might fight against them. This is a defensive approach—it divides women according to the crimes, and it encourages women's movements to be set up to combat each crime. But women are fighting in the family against housework and against the authority of the family; they're fighting in the factories, they're fighting in their local areas, and the repression against these struggles is ferocious. They lock us up in psychiatric hospitals, they use brutality against us all the time, they put us in prison. The only way we can stay united and attack the roots of our exploitation is to look at the common basis of our oppression—the fundamental one which defines what it means to be a woman for us all. This is our job of doing the housework in the service of others. Even if some of us think we can avoid this by doing another job as well as the housework, being politically active, living in an alternative community, having fewer children, finding an understanding partner, we still won't escape. This kind of work cannot be rejected at an individual level or through our individual awareness of it because it's important to the capitalist system; it provides a labor force at low cost and therefore with maximum profit. All our efforts to cut down on housework or to change it in any way are attacked with numerous repressive instruments, as this Tribunal has dramatically shown. We fight constantly against this work but we have no power because we have no money. We're easily manipulated by the attacks of men, of judges, of employers, and of the family.

WAGES-FOR-HOUSEWORK, INTERNATIONAL GROUP

Wages-for-Housework Groups in Italy, England, Canada, Switzerland, and the U.S.A., decided that unwaged housework is robbery with violence; that this work and wagelessness is a crime from which all other crimes flow; that it brands us for life as the weaker sex and delivers us powerless to employers, government planners and legislators, doctors, the police, prisons and mental institutions, as well as to men, for a lifetime of servitude and imprisonment. We demand wages-for-housework for all women from the governments of the world. We will organize internationally to win back the wealth that has been stolen from us in every country and to put an end to the crimes committed daily against us all.

A STRATEGY FOR LESBIANS, ENGLAND

Some Spanish women said that we shouldn't speak as Black or white women. I presume they would also say that we shouldn't speak as lesbian or heterosexual women. They say we are all women, we are all sisters together. It would be very fine if that were true. Not only would it be fine, but there would be a revolution immediately. Because the way that we have been divided from each other is what prevents this. All women are not in exactly the same situation. Capital determines who is going to have jobs, where the jobs will be, who is going to have babies, who is going to be sterilized, who is going to have abortions, who will emigrate, where we will emigrate to. In South Africa we heard how they even plan what city we will live in, in Northern Ireland we heard how they plan where our children must go to school, and what jobs will be available afterwards. Not only do we have different situations, but we have different levels of power. White women have power over Black women, heterosexual women over lesbians, and it is for that reason that we have to organize autonomously as lesbian women, organize autonomously as Black women, in order to make sure that the particular situation that we are in, and the particular struggles that we have to make, are not slid over or subsumed in something that is supposed to be general, but that never includes us.

This does not mean that we should organize in isolation. Because despite the differences in the particular forms of our exploitation, fundamentally our situation as women is the same. Capital has one plan for us all everywhere in the world, and that is that we should do housework for free without a wage. The woman who spoke about welfare spoke about how vulnerable women are to poverty. What that means is that we are vulnerable to everything: to courts, to doctors, to rape, to all the agencies of the State. We need the money to have the power to fight against these crimes. These crimes can be committed against us because of our powerless position, because of the unwaged work we do at home. When we have organized as a women's movement, very often we have not organized against our powerless position, but around a particular issue such as abortion. These campaigns have been organized in many countries in a very racist way because at the time when many women are fighting against forced sterilization, these campaigns are fighting only for abortion, not for the money that we need to be able to bring children up when we have them.

To organize in that way is to allow ourselves to be divided precisely along the lines on which the state wants to divide us. To organize together for the time and the money that we need, all of us as unwaged workers at home, all of us in our particular situations, our particular interests, and our particular struggles, need to present a united front, and together fight against oppression and a system seeking to divide us.

LESBIANISM AS A STRATEGY, GERMANY

I would like to make clear what lesbian strategy is, by reading a statement which was worked out by a group of us. Lesbian women deprive men of their strength and their love. This strength and this love they give to women. They strengthen women and therefore themselves. They deprive their oppressors of their support. Many women will say: "We are not oppressed, and we love our men." But in these last few days, the most terrible crimes have been described which are committed every day in this world against women by men. I must tell you something which has just been sent to me from the interpreter's cabins. In Arabia, for example, women have been beheaded, their hands have been hacked off, simply because they escaped from a harem. These crimes are committed by men, and women are the victims. They are despised, scorned, beaten. These are not individual cases. Phallocracy, male domination, makes possible these crimes against women. It needs continually to create fear in us women. We can only fight against and overcome this fear together with other women—this fear which keeps us chained, this fear which forces us to let ourselves be degraded as objects. Women! We must give our love, our tenderness, our understanding to our sisters—in order to create a world for all of us in which we all can live. There is not much time left to keep this world fit for life. I want to stress that not all lesbians dislike children. For these children also, we have to fight against a male domination which has destroyed people and nature, and which will continue to destroy them. Women! We can only count on ourselves. We have to fight together, live together and learn to love ourselves. Only when we love ourselves can we love other women, and only then can we be strong.

Being lesbian means that you refuse to have anything to do with men, and this is something which will strike a capitalist and a patriarchal system at its roots, and it will be much more dangerous than any socialist movement we have had to date.

DANGERS IN STRUGGLING FOR ANTI-SEXIST DISCRIMINATION LAWS, NORWAY

Men and women are supposedly equal by law in Norway. Equality in the law is taken to mean that different treatment for the sexes is an evil that must be prohibited. But, if a real equality is to be obtained for women, the basis must be a redistribution of benefits. Men must put up with several forms of discrimination in favor of women if the situation of women shall be bettered. A law which does not accept this in principle is a male law and is calculated to strengthen the existing relations between the sexes. To eliminate discrimination against women, the law must treat men and women differently on a short-term basis, in order, in the long run, to give women the same possibilities and rights as men.

There are some protective laws for women in Norway. However, we start at the wrong end if we begin our struggle by repealing these laws. For one thing, it assumes that we should be like men; but we want the freedom to develop ourselves as women. We therefore do *not* want *equal* treatment, but *fair* treatment of the sexes.

It's rather fantastic that the law aimed at improving the condition of women in Norway prohibits women's organizations!

The law concentrates on single crimes, and not on structures, and cannot, therefore, improve our situation. Women need a law that totally prohibits discrimination against women. If the situation of women shall be changed, real material efforts need to be made. Sisters, the lesson that countries without antidiscrimination laws can draw from our experience in Norway, is that to obtain formal equality before the law is a blind alley.

FEMINISM MUST BE BROUGHT ABOUT POLITICALLY, BELGIUM

As a feminist, I appeal to all present to promote feminism together. Everywhere, in all countries, an international feminist movement will be found. We, as the United Feminist Party of Belgium, decided during our Congress to form our own political feminist party which will, through its participation in the politics of this country, introduce feminism in order to build a feminist society. This would require a social structure in which a human being is important as a person and no longer used or abused as a function of the economy, something which women are especially a victim of. This is the wish and the practice of the United Feminist Party. We appeal to the solidarity of all feminists present here and count on the support of all our sisters. After participating in this Tribunal for five days, we are more and more convinced that if women want to put a stop to discrimination practiced against them and make it disappear, this will not be given to them on a platter just because they demand it. If we, as women, do not want to be discriminated against any longer, we will have to do something about it ourselves. No existing institution is going to do it for us. A change in mentality comes about much too slowly and what's more, it is being held back by the ruling powers. Feminism must be brought about politically. That is why we appeal to all of you here. Our feminist struggle is also your struggle for universal feminism.

NECESSITY FOR UNITY AMONG WOMEN, PORTUGAL

We Portuguese journalists here at this Tribunal, reflecting on the experience we have had in our country during the past two years, want to alert all women to these following points. First, feminism is a progressive program of the left; therefore, the struggle for the liberation of women is also the struggle against fascism and against every form of totalitarianism and economic or political imperialism.

Second, the liberation of women is a revolutionary battle. But the revolution cannot be accomplished without developing a consciousness as a woman, and without being involved in the struggle for our own freedom. That is why women must unite to insist on our points of view, and to carry on our own struggle for the construction of a new world where women and men would really be free and happy and have dignity.

CHAPTER 3

Solidarity Proposals Relating to Women in Particular Countries and Geographical Areas

ARAB AND JEWISH WOMEN, ISRAEL

I have come here from Israel, and one of the reasons the women from Israel wanted me to come was so that we could see for ourselves and prove to people at home as well, that feminist politics is not the same as nationalist politics. Men and non-feminist women all said that we were crazy to believe this, as they say for everything else that we do. But we have seen here that we are *not* crazy. I would like to submit the following resolution to the Tribunal:

> Be it resolved, that the dialogue between Arab and Jewish women that has begun at this Tribunal shall continue within the framework of international feminism. As women, we understand that our oppression is by men and not by opposing nationalities. This Tribunal is the first international forum in which both Israeli and Arab women have each publicly condemned their own societies for their oppression of women, rather than condemning one another. This act on the part of the Middle Eastern women demonstrates that international feminism can rise above male-dominated nationalistic power politics.

WOMEN POLITICAL PRISONERS, IRAN

I would like to appeal to our sisters throughout the world to raise your voices and do something about your sisters, the women political prisoners of Iran.

I appeal to the sisters to condemn the brutal regime of Iran, to condemn its sadistic methods, to condemn the torturing of political prisoners, to condemn the torturing of Iranian women. I appeal especially to women journalists. Please break this conspiracy of silence. Put our plight in your magazines, in your papers.

Let the people know about Iran. Also sisters, I appeal for volunteers, doctors and lawyers in particular, because we are going to send a delegation to Iran. They are going to find out about the conditions there. This is being organized by the British section of Amnesty International.

WOMEN POLITICAL PRISONERS, INDIA

Considering the plight of hundreds of women presently detained in the jails of India for their militant political and feminist activities, taking into account the appalling conditions of detention in these prisons, especially the brutal and sadistic tortures to which these women political prisoners are subjected, those of us meeting here today vigorously condemn the repressive government of Indira Gandhi which commits such atrocities to retain its power; we call upon all the progressive and democratic forces to demonstrate their solidarity with their suffering sisters in India through concrete and effective actions, for the immediate release of all women political prisoners in India!

WOMEN POLITICAL PRISONERS, AND DENUNCIATION OF JUAN CARLOS, SPAIN

I speak to you as a member of the Popular Union of Spanish Women (U.P.M.), an organization that fights in the interest and rights of the women in all the cities of Spain. In Spain, we women fight hard for the rights which are denied us, against all kinds of discrimination, against all the laws that pretend to protect us, all of which, in reality, just degrade and humiliate us.

Everyday, as the repression increases, so does our combat. We have been detained; we suffer from being treated badly, vexation, physical and psychological tortures. The fascist "justice" no doubt will continue to condemn people to death, as it did two women (Maria Jesus Dasca and Concepcion Tristan) last September, although their sentences were later committed to life imprisonment. The government speaks of democracy and of liberation, but continues to be facist. It intends to bury these women for life, as was done with Beatriz Rodriquez who was sentenced to 110 years in prison. Also Luz Fernandez, Eva Forest and Jone Derrensoro have all served six months and have thirty years to go.

Sisters, we have united to discuss all the problems we have, regardless of the ideological and political differences between us.

It is necessary to unite with all the repressed women of the world in our mutual combat. The U.P.M. asks the International Tribunal on Crimes Against Women to include a resolution of censure against the monarchy and fascism of Juan Carlos, condemning him as inheritor and perpetuator of facism in Spain.

Long live the fight for the rights and liberation of the women of the world!

WOMEN POLITICAL PRISONERS, CHILE

The women from Chile propose to this Tribunal the following resolution: we repudiate and condemn the military dictatorship which governs Chile and which maintains a state of repression, of prison, of assassination and of torture of children, women, and men. We demand that the Chilean government stop immediately the violation of human rights used daily by their repressive agents. We demand the freedom of women political prisoners and of all political prisoners in Chile. We maintain solidarity with women who struggle for the liberation of their people in Latin America, especially Argentina, Bolivia, Uruguay and Chile.

CHAPTER 4

Solidarity Proposals for Particular Individuals

Violette in Belgium, International Group

Letter Addressed to Violette's Father:

> Sir:
> Alerted by a woman journalist of *Hebdo 76*, the International Tribunal has just been informed about the hunger strike, continued for 43 days, by your 15-year-old daughter, Violette. You opposed her legal emancipation and we understand that she prefers to die rather than remain under your guardianship. We do not think that the paternal authority gives you the power of life or death over your children, nor the power you already have taken by allowing the health of Violette to deteriorate in an irreversible way. Whatever your reasons for going so far in affirming your rights, we appeal to your sense of humanity in order to return to your daughter her life and her health.
> This affair has created a strong emotion among women of all nationalities informed by the Tribunal. We want to affirm our complete solidarity with Violette. You alone bear the entire responsibility for what has happened to her and for what will happen.
> We are counting on you to put an end immediately to this drama by emancipating Violette.

This letter has already been signed by Simone de Beauvoir, Benoite Groult, Luce Irigaray, Juliette Gérard, Claude Servan-Schreiber, Delphine Seyrig, Jeanne Moreau, Christiane Rochefort, Emilienne Brunfaut, Maud Frère, and Gisèle Halimi.

U.S. WOMEN IN PRISON OR FIGHTING PRISON SENTENCES, U.S.A.

Be it resolved that those present demand the U.S. Embassy to do all in its power to free Olga Talamonte from her unjust incarceration, and that those present support Inez Garcia in her struggle. We believe that women have a right to defend themselves. And be it resolved that those present support Yvonne Wanrow in her fight to remain a free woman. We repeat, we believe women have a right to defend themselves and their children.

MORGENTHALER, CANADA

In the name of women assembled at the International Tribunal, we deplore the unjust treatment of Dr. Henri Morgenthaler from Quebec. His only "crime" has been to promote legal abortions under safe, medical conditions for women from Quebec and from Canada.

We demand all the charges against Dr. Morgenthaler be dropped immediately, and we demand that the Canadian law on abortion be repealed.

CHAPTER 5

Action Proposals Still in Search of the Actors

SINGLE MOTHERS' ASSOCIATIONS, FRANCE

The Single Mothers' Workshop suggests that unmarried mothers get together and form associations in every country so that, instead of each one of us remaining isolated with her problems, we can support each other and fight together. Associations like this already exist in some countries, for example in Ireland. In the workshop we found that we were mostly women living in France, and we decided to form a group and start working on this idea immediately. The mailing address for this group is Groupe Mères Célibataires, Librairie "L'Echappée Belle," 1 rue Gracieuse, 75005 Paris.

INTERNATIONAL MEETING IN ONE YEAR'S TIME, U.S.A.

Whereas we have had documentation of the many outrageous, illegal crimes against women throughout the world; whereas we clearly see and acknowledge the commonality of our oppression as women; whereas because of the commonality of our oppression as women, we refuse to be divided on any grounds, nationalistic, sexual persuasion, ethnic or otherwise, therefore be it resolved that copies of the proceedings of the International Tribunal on Crimes Against Women be sent to feminist lawyers and/or appropriate activists in feminist groups worldwide. That after this material has been read and analyzed, an international meeting be held no later than one year from today of such lawyers and activists. The purpose of this meeting is to discuss strategy and begin litigation suits in the courts, and to organize other protest efforts to combat the crimes within each country, as well as on an international level. The governments of each country should be asked to fund the conference.

PERMANENT TRIBUNAL, CHILE

We propose that today, before the closing of this Tribunal, a permanent secretariat be formed to coordinate work on each of the categories of crimes discussed at this Tribunal. In the case of women political prisoners, we propose the formation of a coordinating secretariat which will centralize the information coming from all countries where there are women political prisoners. It will be responsible for the preparation of material on this theme for future sessions of the Tribunal, and it will additionally call work meetings periodically.

PERMANENT INTERNATIONAL COMMITTEE, INTERNATIONAL GROUP

This is a report from the workshop: "Outcome of the Tribunal":

The political power over women is maintained by sexist violence against women. Any attack against the integrity of the woman's body and her right to self-determination must be condemned, and must give rise to international action.

We represent a revolutionary force consisting of new forms of living, new forms of communication, new forms of relationships, new forms of political organizations, and new forms of using power. In our search for new structures of thinking and forms of living, we rediscover our creativity. This leads to a new definition of violence—that is, a definition which includes psychic, physical and social violence.

Sexist discrimination at work, in social behavior, and in legislation, is in all countries both general and specific; different types of societies and national traditions, customs and religions determine the different forms of patriarchy in all countries and the special forms of violence against women. Such violence includes among others: slavery (the selling of girls into marriage); polygamy (one man having several wives); clitoridectomy (amputation of the clitoris); rape (which is not only an attack against a woman's body, but also a negation of her existence as a woman); prostitution (in all its different forms); discrimination against lesbians; torture; femicide; and violence against women in medicine in general, and in gynecology and psychiatry in particular.

The women's movement in all countries is the expression of our collective resistance against violence in all its forms. This violence is a manifestation of men's fear. Our vulnerability to the use of power against us must be overcome by offensive action.

Forms of resistance already practiced by women include: organized resistance in the women's centers of all countries; self-help in various areas (e.g., clinics, organization of prostitutes, etc.); advisory centers for women; feminist therapy; centers for battered women; wages-for-housework; international protests against torture of women; utilization of international contacts for the mobilization of women; feminist research and science; the development of feminist culture (women's theater, women's cafes, bookshops, etc.); and feminist art (painting, music, etc.).

The Content and Structure of a Permanent International Committee

Our new forms of communication and living must be reflected in the content and structure of a Permanent International Committee. A women's collective from various nations must be elected for a certain period of time. This collective will coordinate, collect and publicize cases of violence against women. International contacts will be used for this purpose. The collective must be able to take immediate action.

This Tribunal has shown that we must work on two levels: an open tribunal for all women, and workshops. New forms of financing the committee must be found: contributions must be made by women's centers throughout the world, as well as by individuals and public institutions. The principle of open books must be followed.

Since existing legislation discriminates against women, we cannot give this committee a legal status, since the bourgeois-patriarchal laws would be used against us. Our new forms of thinking and acting and organizing must be expressed in the work of this International Women's Collective.

Sisterhood is powerful! Women of all countries unite!! International sisterhood is *more* powerful!!!

CHAPTER 6

General Concrete Action Proposals

LESBIAN NETWORK, U.S.A.

Be it resolved, that lesbians are an integral part of the feminist movement; that the Tribunal expresses its support of, and solidarity with, all lesbians who live in oppression all over the world; that lesbians at this conference form a communication network as a first step in organizing this support. All women interested in such a network, please write to me: Frances Doughty, National Gay Task Force, 80 Fifth Avenue, New York City 10011, U.S.A.

INTERNATIONAL NEWS BULLETINS, SWITZERLAND AND ITALY

The first issue of an International News Bulletin will be published in April of this year. The first issue only will be distributed free to all the feminist contacts we have. Subsequent issues will be available by subscription for $10 a year. There will be four bulletins a year. They will be available in Italian, French, German, English and Spanish.

Money may be sent in any currency to Post Office Account No. 12.22772 Geneva, Switzerland, in the name of "Service féminin international d'information et de communication—ISIS" (within Europe money may be sent through any post office). Or send money orders or travellers cheques to ISIS in Rome, Italy.

Addresses for ISIS: Via della Pelliccia 31—00153 Rome, Italy. Casale Postale 301—1227 Carouge, Switzerland.

INTERNATIONAL FEMINIST NETWORK, U.S.A.

I would like to propose that an International Feminist Network be set up. The purpose of such a network would be to facilitate the mobilization of the women's liberation movements on an international scale when needed. Such international mobilization occurred, for example, in support of the Three Marias in Portugal. Without the support of feminist actions in many countries, these women might not have been acquitted. Organizing support of this kind, whether in the form of fund raising, publicity, demonstrations, etc., will be greatly aided, I believe, by the kind of network I propose. Nicole Van de Ven has volunteered to be the coordinator of the IFN. Her address is: Rue des Scarabées, 11. 1050 Brussels, Belgium. Besides the coordinator, two or more volunteers for each country will be sought. It will be their task to distribute requests for international support sent them by Nicole to all the feminist groups in their country. Women needing the support of the women's liberation movement internationally should write to the coordinator detailing the ways in which women in other countries could help them. I hope that many of you will volunteer today, but if not, volunteers will be sought over the next months.

I also propose that instead of holding another International Tribunal on Crimes Against Women, interested women consider organizing an International Strategy Conference to combat crimes against women.

THIRD WORLD AND MINORITY WOMEN'S WORKSHOPS PROPOSAL TO SET UP A CENTRAL COMMUNICATION CENTER, INTERNATIONAL GROUP*

Women from 19 countries attended a series of Third World and Minority Women's Workshops. At our second session, we defined ourselves as falling into three groups: (a) *Third World Women:* women from underdeveloped countries in which most of the people are poor or oppressed (examples: India, South Africa, etc.); (b) *Minority Women;* non-white women residing in power-block nations which oppress minorities and women (in that order), such as the U.S.A., England, etc.; (c) *Majority Women:* all other women who join with our committee in the struggle against our oppression.

Considering ourselves a committee, we defined our purposes as follows: (a) To identify and analyze the crimes and oppression which most harshly effect us as Third World and Minority Women; (b) To develop a strategy to defend ourselves against

*This proposal was not actually presented before the plenary session, but at the press conference the day after the Tribunal. The Third World and Minority Women's workshop was the only one, to our knowledge, to come out with a written report.

those crimes and oppressions; and (c) To organize an international force which will develop the power to prevent the recurrence of these and other crimes and forms of oppression.

Activities

During the first nine months following the Tribunal, the committee members will devote as much time as possible to the development of several International Action Campaigns to illustrate the oppression of the Third World and Minority Women. Each committee member, upon her return home from the Tribunal, is to begin the development of the local, national and international plan. The steps were outlined as follows: first, inform women's groups within the homeland about the Committee, and try to get their support and participation. Second, develop local "crime committees" and assign tasks. Third, identify the resources needed to begin local committee functioning (money, space, paper, etc.).

The next step will be to identify the most oppressive crimes in the homeland.

Problem Identification

First, list all the issues that could be worked on. Next, analyze each issue in the following way: (1) What is the law? (good, bad, none, etc.); (2) What was the prior action against this crime (if any)? Why did it fail? Who else does it effect? How?; (3) Plan direct action: demonstration/confrontation, etc.; (a) Local action—what, when, where, who and why?; (b) Send information to the Central Communication Center (more about this later) and suggest what parallel action should be taken, including press releases. (Information must be sent five to six weeks before action to guarantee circulation and receipt of information by all committee members.)

The Central Communication Center (CCC)

The purpose of the CCC is to circulate information to the committee members; develop and maintain the committee membership and mailing list; develop a plan for publication and circulation of information and materials to committee members on a regular basis. Temporary location: 607 Quanckenbos Street, N.W., Washington, D.C. 20011, United States of America, c/o Catherine Day-Jermany.

Some Proposed Action Program Suggestions

International Days of Action: No Work Days—Don't get out of bed or, nothing days; *Occupation Day*—Women to occupy all male power positions in industry and home. Also known as International Role Reversal Day; *Pay Days*—Every activity performed by women must be paid for by any male beneficiary over the age of ten. (This should be repeated at least one day per month.); *Anti-Crime Days*—Embassy protest calendar will be developed so that each month one country's embassy will be confronted about its crimes against women. The protest will happen simultaneously at the country's embassy/consulate in each committee member's country.

Ins: There will be a series of -In's to demonstrate the problems of the various countries. Example: Eat-In's—to show the problem of hunger. These actions will begin in late 1976.

Crimes Conference: The committee hopes to hold an International Conference in the late summer of 1977 in Australia.

National Conference: Each country is to try to hold a national conference on the Oppression of Third World and Minority Women prior to the proposed International Conference. One of the purposes of the national conferences will be to plan action proposals, resolutions and strategies which can be adopted and carried out by and at the international level. In addition, each committee member is to work on the formulation of a proposed structure for the International Committee.

Part III

Herstory of the International Tribunal

CHAPTER 1

How It all Started

Every summer for the past few years, a collective of women belonging to the Danish women's liberation movement, the Redstockings, has organized a three-month, all-women's camp on Femø, a small island about four hours from Copenhagen. At least 12 days are set aside each summer for women from all countries.

In August, 1974, while participating in a workshop on international feminist strategy at Femø, some of us met every day to discuss what actions the women's liberation movement might undertake during the UN-declared International Women's Year. Most of us were highly mistrustful of what would be organized during this year by people unrelated to the women's liberation movement. Most of us did not subscribe to the espoused IWY goal of giving women equality with men in the system as it exists today—a system that requires radical restructuring, not the integration of women into its patriarchial structures. Besides, to eradicate sex roles *requires* such radical restructuring; the integration of women can never be more than token.

Nor did most of us believe that those voting for IWY and its goals seriously contemplated implementing such goals. On the contrary, we saw it as a hypocritical and token gesture which served to mask the fact that all the governments who voted for IWY are male dominated, and all maintain laws which sanction crimes against women, and in many cases, *constitute* crimes against women, to say nothing of their role in maintaining extralegal sexist practices. Half of those voting for IWY would not have their jobs if their explicit goal of equality were realized; they'd be at home minding babies and cleaning house. Probably only a few of them have any inkling of this and those who do, no doubt, feel safe enough knowing how far the grand sentiments are from being implemented. Were there to be any danger of implementation, most of these same men would show their true prejudices against women (minding babies is women's work, etc.) and fight for their immediate interest in maintaining the sexist status quo.

We therefore feared that IWY would, in all probability, achieve little beyond window dressing, and that, more seriously, it might succeed in leading women to believe that these patriarchal governments and the male-dominated UN itself have our best interests at heart. This could all too easily result in a co-optation of women's energy, a blunting of our anger at our true situation (as has happened in Sweden, for example), and a co-optation of the women's liberation movement, or sections thereof.

However, rather than putting our energy into criticism of IWY, we wanted to engage in counteractions that would be both radical and constructive. And some of us hoped to be able to use the publicity, resources and rhetoric of IWY to the advantage of women. The International Tribunal on Crimes Against Women was one of many ideas mentioned for the first time at our very last meeting on August 22nd. To develop and launch this and some of the other ideas that emerged, another international meeting was needed. Women from the Frauenzentrum in Frankfurt volunteered to organize one. Over 600 women, mostly from Western Europe, attended this International Feminist Conference on November 15–17, 1974.

The Frankfurt women had planned ten different workshops, based on a newsletter from the Femø workshop on International Feminist Strategy, their own ideas and input from other women they had received before the conference. The International Tribunal on Crimes Against Women was the subject of one of these workshops. These workshops met Saturday morning, Saturday afternoon and Sunday morning—very little time to give birth to totally novel international feminist events. Nevertheless, this is where the International Tribunal was born.

While none of us at the International Tribunal workshop in Frankfurt talked specifically about the Bertrand Russell Tribunal on Crimes Committed by the U.S. in Vietnam, I believe some of us had assimilated this event into our consciousness. It helped spark the idea that oppressed peoples have the right to dissociate themselves from those definitions of crimes which have been developed by their oppressors to serve their own interests. For purposes of the International Tribunal on Crimes Against Women, *all man-made forms of women's oppression* were seen as crimes against women. This conception implies a complete disagreement concerning acts defined as crimes by partriarchal societies.

Another idea fundamental to the International Tribunal from the start was the belief in the power of personal testimony to educate, politicize, and motivate. This belief in personal testimony is common in the women's liberation movement in many countries, though less where the movement is still very strongly influenced by the left. This method has been most often used in small consciousness-raising groups, although it has also proved effective in larger "speak-outs," for example, on abortion and rape in the U.S.A. By sharing personal experiences and problems, we come to see that these problems are not merely personal, but that they are caused or exacerbated by the way women are regarded and treated in general, and the situations and roles we commonly find ourselves in. We come to see that many of our problems are externally or socially induced, and hence, widely shared by other women. By talking honestly with each other, our isolation can be transformed into solidarity and our self-blame into anger, which motivates action much more powerfully than self-hatred!

A format in which the victims of crimes against women would testify regarding these crimes—the crimes and the victims to be chosen by each participating country—seemed to us much more powerful than the usual conference where so-called experts and well-known people propound their views. It seemed more powerful, too, than a conference where women from the women's liberation movements in different countries would debate about the causes of our oppression and the pros and cons of different strategies for change. Discussions about causes and solutions are, of course, indispensable to our struggle, both nationally and internationally, and the International Tribunal was always intended to include such discussions. However, our analyses, our syntheses, our proposals for action, must be informed by feelings, not just intellect. If we are to learn about the problem of wife battering in England, for example, let us hear from a woman who has suffered the experience, not just a researcher who can give us an abstract description and analysis of the problem.

The basic ideas underlying the Tribunal began to form 15 months before the International Tribunal actually took place. The rudiments of the organizational structure were set up already at the Frankfurt workshop. One volunteer or "national contact" was sought from as many countries as possible. The task of the national contacts was to see that a tribunal committee was set up in her country, either by initiating such a committee herself, or by finding others to do so.

The tasks of each national tribunal committee were: (1) to spread the word about the International Tribunal, and in particular, to try to get women from countries not represented at the Frankfurt Conference involved; (2) to try to raise consciousness about the crimes against women in their country and abroad; (3) on the basis of feedback from as many women and women's groups as could be contacted, to decide which three or four crimes women from their country should testify about; (4) to find women willing to testify about these crimes at the International Tribunal; (5) to prepare brief research reports on each of the crimes selected, to be read at the International Tribunal following the personal testimony; and (6) to raise money for the travel expenses of the women testifying, where necessary, and to help pay for other basic expenses. It was also hoped that money could be raised so that women from poor and/or unrepresented countries could attend.

At the end of the Frankfurt Conference, we only had national contacts for eight countries: Denmark, France, Germany, Holland, Italy, Norway, Switzerland, and the U.S.A., and a coordinator, Maureen Giroux, an American woman who lives in Paris. This baby was rather underweight, but, nevertheless, the Tribunal was born. The question was, would it live?

Shortly after the Frankfurt Conference, a French mail strike effectively prevented Maureen from coordinating anything or anyone. We had expected to meet mid-February to plan the International Tribunal further, and we had hoped that many more countries would have become involved by then. By the latter part of December, with the French strike still on, I wrote myself to the national contacts. The result was that our planning meeting was set definitely for the Easter weekend at the end of March, 1975, in Paris.

About 50 women from 20 different countries took part in our three-day planning conference in Paris. Any woman interested in the Tribunal was welcome to participate; no distinction was ever made, even when it came to voting on controversial issues, between women who were national contacts working with national committees, and those who were simply attending because they were interested.

Because of the amount of work, the time needed to translate everything into three languages (English, French, and Italian), and the size of the group, we divided into five subcommittees to work on the following questions: (1) the aims of the International Tribunal; (2) the locale; (3) how to finance it; (4) relations with the media; and (5) the Tribunal's format and program. A representative of each subcommittee then reported back to the entire group. The question of locale turned out to be the most controversial and time-consuming. Amsterdam, Lisbon and Brussels emerged as the three possibilities. Nothing could actually be decided until the Portuguese, Belgian and Dutch women investigated further in their countries the availability of a large hall and cheap accommodation facilities, the availability of simultaneous translation equipment and interpreters, and the willingness of women in the movement to work on the Tribunal. Nevertheless, there were strong feelings about the different cities. Some women

Palais des Congrès, locale of the Tribunal

Cathy Bernheim

Tribunal Posters torn from the Palais walls

Nancy Budd

Women gather in front of the Palais des Congrès

Cathy Bernheim

Women gathering in front of the Palais

Eva Besnyo

Inside the Palais: idealized mural figures contrasted with the real women participants

The Tribunal Information Desk beseiged

Roswitha Gans

Joy Chamberlain

The participants set up their own information desks

Women from the PFU, a feminist political party in Belgium

Nancy Budd

What's on at the Tribunal?

Eva Besnyo

One woman writes her testimony on improvised wall paper

Eva Besnyo

Joy Chamberlain

The video program

Joy Chamberlain

One of the many media women

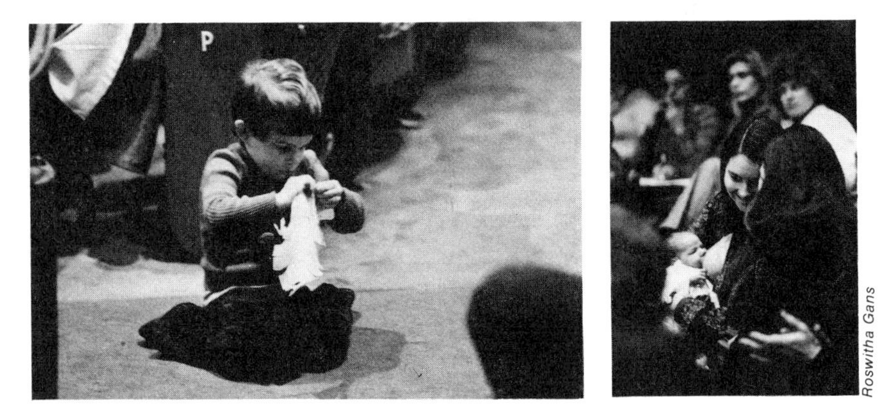

Roswitha Gans

Young participants, courtesy of the lack of child care facilities at the Palais

Nancy Budd

The much frequented Palais Restaurant and Bar

Nancy Budd

felt that having the Tribunal in Lisbon would be a courageous gesture of solidarity towards the revolution that was taking place in Portugal, and that it would be a great help to Portuguese women. Other women, anxious about the instability of the political situation in Portugal, did not wish the fate of the Tribunal to be tied to the political situation of one particular country. During the first vote on Saturday, the order of priority for location, other things being equal, was Brussels, Amsterdam and then Lisbon. By Sunday afternoon, a second vote changed it to Lisbon, Brussels and Amsterdam.

We had agreed, for the reasons mentioned earlier, that the International Tribunal should take place during IWY, and November was the chosen month. The specific dates were to be decided later by the women of the country where it would take place. Remarkably enough, the format and program worked out by the subcommittee at the Paris meeting remained pretty much unchanged from then on.

Interestingly enough, the question of whether to allow men to attend the Tribunal, either as representatives of the media or in other capacities, never became a controversial issue before the Tribunal actually took place. A defense of the policy to exclude men, the decision made at the Paris meeting, only became necessary just before the Tribunal was to take place.

The subcommittee on the aims of the Tribunal came up with the following statement:

> It is important to show that the oppression of women is the same everywhere, only different in degree; and that each case is not an isolated case, but typical of what happens in the particular country. The aims are to reach women everywhere, to reinforce solidarity between women, and to discover ways to combat crimes against women.

This was the first and last time that those organizing the International Tribunal ever agreed on its aims!

At the end of the planning meeting, the eight-woman coordinating committee was formed. This committee met again in September, 1975, in January, 1976, and on the eve of the International Tribunal in March, 1976.

Since the question of the Tribunal's location had aroused such strong feelings in Paris, tremendous care was taken to get as much information as possible from the women in Lisbon, Brussels and Amsterdam on the facilities and woman power each had to offer. Following a detailed report, the coordinating committee decided just prior to the Brussels meeting, September 16–18, 1975, to hold the International Tribunal in Brussels (the vote was six for Brussels, two for Lisbon).

Other major decisions made at this meeting were to postpone the International Tribunal until March 1976 because of lack of funds, and to reduce it's duration from five days to three days. Happily, the last decision was reversed to five days a month or so later. The official languages, it was decided, would be English, French and Spanish.

On November 20, 1975, the Brussels office informed us that the Belgian Minister of Dutch Culture, Rika De Backer, had agreed we could use the Palais des Congrès in Brussels for the duration of the Tribunal *free*. Since the Belgian committee had virtually no money at this point, this gesture transformed the International Tribunal from a hope into a reality. Our child now had a magnificant, albeit male-constructed, home. At last we had the place and dates quite settled—a bare three-and-a-half months before the event was to take place!

During those last three-and-a-half months, regular communications were sent from the Brussels office (BONs they were called, for "Brussels Office News") to all the national contacts. Each country was supposed to raise a minimum of $325, and wherever possible, they were urged to contribute more, to compensate for those countries unable to raise the minimum. However, numerous pleas in the BONs to send money to pay for office expenses (for example, down-payments for the youth hostels to house the participants, postage, office supplies, xeroxing, phone calls, etc.) produced little. Furthermore, deadlines for information about which crimes different countries wished to testify were not being met. Some participating countries still hadn't sent this information the night before the Tribunal was to start. Indeed, we didn't even know the exact number of countries that would be participating!

The idea had been that each country would inform the coordinating committee of three to five crimes they would like to testify about, and that the coordinating committee would then balance the amount of testimony on different crimes, by selecting, for each country, two or three out of the three to five crimes offered. However, this was not to be. The coordinating committee ended up playing no role in the selection at all.

At the coordinating committee meeting of January 24–25, 1976, the program was developed further. It had been decided previously that each country would contribute both prepared personal testimony (with a maximum of ten minutes per person), and a brief research report on the dimensions of the crime testified about (with a maximum of five minutes per report). After the prepared testimonies and reports about each crime, spontaneous testimony from other participants would be invited. The committee was concerned that there be as much time for spontaneous testimony as for prepared testimony (two hours of each for the first four days), since we felt it important that as many women as wished to participate should have the opportunity to do so. Unfortunately, at the actual event, time for the spontaneous testimony was constantly cut into.

Besides the four hours of testimony during each of the first four days, there were to be two and one-quarter hours each day for workshops on the crimes testified about: analysis workshops (to try to understand why the crimes exist and persist), and solution workshops (to discuss actions to combat the crimes). Participants would also be encouraged to initiate workshops on any topic that took their fancy.

By the meeting of January 24–25, 27 countries had indicated they were intending to participate. The number of countries was finally to grow to 40. Simple arithmetic made it necessary to limit the number of crimes each country could testify about to two. However, imposing this limit such a short time before the event was very difficult, since some countries had already selected more than two witnesses. In the end, this limitation was one of the many coordinating committee decisions that was simply ignored by many participants. Another policy decision that was sometimes disregarded was that women should always testify about crimes within their own countries—not in other countries.

Some of us on the coordinating committee were afraid that non-feminist groups would try to use the International Tribunal for their own non-feminist, political purposes. Two of us had attended the IWY Tribune in Mexico City, and we had seen this happen there. To try to prevent this from happening, the coordinating committee agreed that at registration, women should be asked to sign the following statement (available in the three official languages):

> I understand that the International Tribunal on Crimes Against Women will focus on the many ways in which women are oppressed in every country, and the ways in which we can struggle against these crimes. This should not be interpreted as a lack of concern about all oppressed people. However, I agree to concentrate our efforts at this Tribunal specifically on crimes against women.

The national contacts were asked to inform possible participants from the different countries about this statement so that those women who felt unable to sign it would stay away.

We also decided to have different moderators for each session at the International Tribunal, selected for their skills in insuring everyone equal time and avoiding long speeches, irrelevant testimony, etc. We asked each national contact or national tribunal group to consider who, if anyone, from their country would make a good moderator. This plea only produced one suggestion.

Simone de Beauvoir had been invited to open the International Tribunal after the Paris planning meeting in March, 1975, and she agreed, if the Tribunal were to be held in Brussels. The women in Paris said that her preference for this city was both practical (it is so much closer to Paris than Lisbon) and strategic; after returning from a trip to Portugal in the fall of 1975, she expressed the opinion that any feminist action there would run the risk of encountering indifference or even hostility. To our disappointment, when the Tribunal was postponed until March, de Beauvoir was not able to open it in person after all. This change of plan was also embarrassing, since some of the Tribunal publicity had emphasized her presence.

At the coordinating committee meeting in January, we were very divided about whether to invite someone else to open the Tribunal, and if so, who. Suddenly the whole issue of "stars" reared its head, and some committee members felt strongly that we should not exploit the star-system by inviting famous feminists. Others felt that a well-known figure would attract more media attention, thereby enabling the Tribunal to reach more women. Divided as we were, hasty invitations went to Elizabeth Reid from Australia, Maria Isabel Barreno from Portugal (though we don't even know if she received it), Gisèlle Halimi from France, and Mary Daly from the U.S.A. However none of these women were able to come at such short notice. Simone de Beauvoir's stirring message as recounted in the Preface was read and served the purpose remarkably well.

CHAPTER 2

Our Goals and Our Shoe-String Budget

In describing the *herstory* of the International Tribunal, I've said a lot about goals, both implicitly and explicitly. The slogan, "International Sisterhood is more powerful" captures well one of our initial assumptions—that our struggle must not only be conducted within nations, but across nations. We must not confine ourselves to *man-made* institutions. Yet after the Paris meeting, those of us organizing the International Tribunal differed sufficiently in our politics that we were unable to agree on a statement of purpose that could be used at its opening. Nicole and I therefore invited all the members of the coordinating committee to write up their notion of the purpose of the International Tribunal for inclusion in this book. Two members replied. According to Grainne Farren, the purpose was twofold: "To put the women's liberation movement on an international basis; and to raise the public consciousness about the crimes committed against women, many of which are unknown or ignored." Lydia Horton responded more indirectly: "Many experiences have convinced me that it is always to men's advantage that women be divided. Nationality, culture, politics, color, even age, are barriers to understanding each other. Difficult as it is to overcome these barriers, attendance at many international so-called feminist meetings (Cambridge, Paris, Mexico, East Berlin) has convinced me that our only hope of combatting them lies in demonstrating that our problems as women transcend them all, and that as women we have more in common with each other than anyone else in the world."

The statement used by the U.S. committee in our basic information on the Tribunal, expresses my own views on the matter:

> The aim of the International Tribunal is to reach and raise the consciousness of as many women in the world as possible regarding the extent and the depth of the oppression that women suffer in a male-dominated world. We see all forms of our oppression as crimes against us. In many societies these crimes have been going on for so many centuries they are considered natural events and are not seen as crimes. That is why we think it important to name them so as to increase awareness that they exist, and the determination to eradicate them. In many Western countries where there is already some

awareness of our oppression, there is often ignorance of the greater oppression of some Third World sisters, for example, in Arab countries. Knowledge of their situation should deepen our consciousness and strengthen our commitment and struggle. In other countries where there are no feminist movements and where the realization of women's oppression is still low, the Tribunal hopefully will strengthen the feminists both in and out of the closet in their enormous task ahead.

In addition, we believe that *international sisterhood is more powerful* and that this International Tribunal will help to bring us together as we discover how many crimes we share, regardless of our differences. The support that was given to the Three Marias in Portugal is just one example of how we can help each other in times of need. Hence, it should be clear that we do not see the International Tribunal as an end, but as a beginning. We want to see all crimes against women stopped in every country. As feminists we don't wish these goals to be interpreted as lack of concern for crimes against Third World men. We want to live in societies where there are no oppressed people. But in order for us to begin to control our own destinies and lift the yoke of male-supremacy and domination, we believe we must have our own autonomous organizations answerable only to women.

OUR SHOE-STRING BUDGET

When the International Tribunal opened on March 4th, 1976 approximately $5,000 had been received in contributions from different countries. Since approximately $7,500 had already been spent, we had a deficit of $2,500. Happily, however, many countries and individuals sent money after the Tribunal, including the Belgian Minister of French Culture who donated $1,102 for outstanding office expenses.

Belgium, then, is the *only* country that we know of where a member of the government contributed to the International Tribunal. It may be remembered that it was Rika De Backer, the Belgian Minister of Dutch Culture, and the only woman minister in the Belgian Government, who made the priceless contribution of the free use of the Palais des Congrès, together with all its facilities (print shop, sound technicians, bank, post office, telephone, telex, heat, electricity, maintenance staff, etc.).

The total expenses as of June 30, 1976, amounted to $14,421.

The actual contributions made by women in different countries amounted to $10,627. The amounts contributed by each country appear iun the Appendix. An additional $5,555 was collected during the Tribunal from the sale of posters and badges, collections, and the small registration fee.

(See Appendix for break-down.) Even if $14,421 underestimates the Tribunal's total expenses, the financing of such an event with this tiny budget is remarkable. This small sum in itself suggests how much energy and time must have been donated free. Marie Louise Coppens has tried to evaluate some of the time and services donated in monetary terms. It is certainly a minimal estimation, but interesting nonetheless. It also must be remembered that the Tribunal groups in each country had their own budgets, including many "gifts made in the form of free services."

Three entries constituting over one-third of the expenses, require some explanation. First, one youth hostel manager refused to repay the $1,000 deposit on the grounds that his hostel was not completely filled by women from the Tribunal, so he had had to sustain losses (he offered no proof that he'd turned anyone away, however). Second, other youth hostel managers claimed damages, which the Brussels office had to pay.

The biggest expense of all was the compensation for the lost and damaged earphones at the Palais. At the end of the Tribunal, thirty-four portable earphones were missing. Since each costs approximately $104, $3,546 went to replace them, and $228 had to be paid for damage to the earpieces of some of the installed earphones.

It is most unlikely that the earphones were stolen. During the proceedings, it was much more convenient to hang on to a set of portable earphones, available only in the 300-400 seats at the back of the hall, than to remain seated to get the simultaneous translations. Since the portable earphones were also a rather scarce commodity, many women hung on to them—some accidently, no doubt, but others on purpose. And then it was easy enough to forget to return them on the last day. Nevertheless, this bill was terrifying to contemplate paying before more money had come in. Before we actually received it from the Palais, we had understood it would be even higher.

Considerable press attention was given to expenses for damages during the Tribunal; they were even discussed in some detail at the press conference on March 9. We later learned that our portrayal as destructive and irresponsible women was quite unfair since our bill for damages was no higher than customary at conferences. However, volunteers in the Brussels office were initially worried, and sent out alarmed please-help-us memos. For once in the history of the Tribunal, these worked, so that by the end of June we actually had $1,760 in the bank. This money has been used to cover the expenses involved in writing and editing this book.

CHAPTER 3

Organizing the U.S. Committee*

The national contact of each country has, no doubt, a different story to tell about how she went about setting up an International Tribunal committee in her country, and with what results. One experience seems to have been common to most of us however, the difficulty we had in mobilizing energy and raising money. For example, the national contact from Greece, Margaret Papandreou, wrote the Belgian committee in January:

> Ever since I first made contact with you, I have been trying to get an organization of women here interested in participating in the Tribunal. On this I did not succeed. But in the process of searching, I discovered the tremendous need for an organization which would concern itself primarily with women's problems, and which would not be under the control of one of the traditional political parties. Thus we have organized the Women's Union of Greece.

What exciting news! We had hoped that the International Tribunal would facilitate the birth of women's liberation movements where none existed, and in Greece this happened. Hopefully, this occurred, or will occur, in other countries.

In the U.S. too, we had considerable difficulty in interesting women in the International Tribunal, though it inspired a lot of women to organize Tribunals on Crimes Against Women in different cities—New York, San Francisco, Los Angeles and Denver, or actions in support of them, as in Philadelphia.

As the U.S. national contact, I had the responsibility of initiating a Tribunal committee here. Based in the San Francisco Bay Area, our committee met approximately every two weeks, sometimes every week, with our numbers varying from 3 to 50, but averaging about 10. In spite of our small number, we did a tremendous amount. We mailed information about the International Tribunal to over 400 women's groups across the country, asking them for their opinion on the crimes that the U.S. should testify about, whether they knew of particular women who might testify, and so on.

*This chapter on the U.S. committee is included only because this book is being published in the U.S. It will, no doubt, be omitted from other language editions.

We tried to raise money in many other ways—by having an open house with drinks and eats and women's music; by organizing a forum on medical crimes against women and asking for money; by showing movies about battered women and the oppression of women in Latin America; by taking collections; by talking about the International Tribunal on the radio and explaining our financial needs at the end; by issuing a poster and different buttons; by asking people directly for donations; by putting ads in local and national magazines; and by having a feminist poetry reading and report on the International Tribunal after it was all over. To our dismay, most of these activities produced little money, except for post-Tribunal requests (some feminists gave us generous contributions to help clear up the debts we had incurred and the Methodist Church gave us $1,000), and post-Tribunal events (a poetry reading). And the buttons were a great success in Belgium. In fact, the sale of buttons in Brussels four months before the International Tribunal was the major source of income (and practically the only source) for the Belgian committee before the Tribunal!

Substantial interest in the International Tribunal only became apparent in the U.S. when women began to write saying they wanted to attend the Tribunal. Fortunately, a member of our committee suggested we ask every women from the U.S. who planned to attend the Tribunal to contribute $25 to help pay for organizing expenses. This ended up being by far the most successful fund raiser; most of the women were willing to do this, and some generously gave more.

We were especially concerned about money for three reasons. Since the U.S. is the richest country in the world and has the largest women's liberation movement, we felt it only reasonable that we should contribute more than the minimum requested from each country. In fact, I had *promised* that we would do so, and in the end I had to borrow money to meet the deadlines given us by the Belgian committee. Secondly, we wanted to be able to send poor, minority women to testify from the U.S.A., and we had to raise money for their air fares. Thirdly, we hoped to be able to raise money to pay for one or more women from Third World countries, who would otherwise be unable to testify at the International Tribunal. For example, we had corresponded with an Indian woman from India who was very enthusiastic about the International Tribunal and wanted to testify, but who could not afford the fare. Unfortunately, we were financially unable to help her out, and so she never came.

The U.S. committee originally chose four crimes for the U.S.

to present testimony on: (1) rape, an enormous problem in the U.S. and one on which we had some fairly good research because of the actions of the women's liberation movement; (2) femicide, the killing of females by males; the relatively high rates of extreme violence in the U.S. implies a high rate of femicide, and we suspected that if the U.S. did not present this crime, no other country would, since the sexual politics of murder has not as yet been generally recognized, even by feminists; (3) the poverty of women; in the richest country in the world, one which has the resources to eradicate poverty, the numbers of poor women are disproportionately high, particularly single mothers and elderly women; economic issues are often seen as entirely different from feminist issues, but the enormous disporportion of impoverished women reveals that this distinction is mythical. The U.S. committee wanted to expose both the problem and the myth; (4) the oppression of women in the home. Although rarely seen as a crime, we wanted to include discussion of the traditional division of labor in the home, where the man has all the economic and social power and the woman has a slave-like role and status.

When the coordinating committee limited the number of women who could testify from each country, we decided to drop the crime of rape from the U.S. testimony (since many other countries were clearly going to testify about this) and also the oppression in the home, since we understood this would be covered too. We invited Catherine Day-Jermany, a Black woman from Washington, D.C., who had personally experienced poverty and the sexism of the U.S. welfare system, to testify on this crime, and Pat Parker, a Black poet from Oakland, California, to testify on femicide. We had heard Parker read her poem "Womanslaughter" on the murder of her sister by her sister's husband and asked her to read her poem at the Tribunal. Both women incidently needed their travel expenses paid.

Before any limit had been set, we had also invited Joann Little, Inez Garcia, Yvonne Wanrow, and Mary Jo Risher to testify at the International Tribunal. Yvonne Wanrow accepted, and we promised to pay two-thirds of her travel expenses. (Yvonne kindly reimbursed us for this expense with money collected from sympathetic women at the Tribunal.) She testified as a Native American about the injustice of being found guilty of murder for defending herself and her children against a white rapist who broke into her home at 5 A.M.

The U.S. committee borrowed the money to pay for these fares, to pay for thousands of buttons (made in three languages), and to meet other expenses. Happily, three months after the International Tribunal ended, these loans were repaid.

About 50 U.S. women, some living abroad, attended the International Tribunal. As you will see from the testimony, several U.S. women other than those just mentioned testified there. Some did so in the periods of spontaneous testimony, and others because after the end of the second day, the limits set by the coordinating committee to insure time for spontaneous testimony were overrun.

Since three different travel agents were trying to put together package deals for women who wished to attend the International Tribunal, at one point we genuinely feared that the Tribunal would be overrun by Americans. Womantours of Los Angeles hoped to sign up at least 100 women. Signatures Travel Agency worked out a package that required a minimum of 23 women. A woman wrote us from New York mentioning that she was going to the Tribunal in a party of 20. Since we had been informed wrongly that the largest room could seat only 700 women (in fact, it could seat 1,400), even 100 U.S. women would be a terrible over-representation. We decided we had to discourage the travel agents, much to their annoyance, and introduced the requirement that women must apply formally through the U.S. committee. We warned the applicants that if more than 100 applied, we would have to give Third World, working-class and underrepresented women, as well as active feminists, priority for participation. All this must have created a lot of bad feeling, which we very much regret, but we were acting in good faith, even though it turned out to be a psuedo-problem. The travel agents, thinking the International Tribunal was going to be an IWY-type conference, unwittingly misled us. In fact, they were hardly able to find any women interested in going, and not simply because of the cold water we poured on their efforts.

To get more publicity and money for the International Tribunal, we sent out information and a fund-raising letter, to a number of well-known U.S. feminists. If they supported our goals, we also asked them if they would write us a letter to that effect. Like almost everything else, this didn't produce much money *before* the Tribunal ($100, in contrast to the $250 collected after it was over), but we received two fine letters. Robin Morgan had this to say:

> This is to let you know that I send my total support to the goals of the International Tribunal on Crimes Against Women. It is *past* the time that the more than half of humanity which is female began 'comparing notes," communicating, and thence rising up together to end the

crimes against us and to create a new and better means of existence for everyone.

My admiration goes to the organizers of the Tribunal for initiating a process which I am sure will continue for years to come and which will be of benefit to every woman alive and many to be born.

And on her way back from visiting India, Gloria Steinem wrote:

This is an important occasion for women all over the world: This Tribunal will offer the facts as well as the flesh and blood of some of the worst crimes against women. But not even the echo of Nuremberg and of American atrocities in Vietnam that are brought by this Tribunal can equal the suffering now being experienced by human beings simply because they were born female. We must have Tribunals on every continent and in every country until crimes against women are no longer a fact of everyday life.

I support the Tribunal and its goals, and I am very grateful to the women who have initiated and organized it.

In a personal letter, Gloria also wrote that she had hoped very much to attend the International Tribunal "all the more so because I have talked to so many women (in India) who could and should be testifying on so many of the crimes. I hope a glimpse of these (the startlingly higher death rate for female infants in India, for instance) will somehow be spoken for." Gloria then gave the exciting information that "there is considerable interest in holding in India a national version of the Tribunal."

A Tribunal on Crimes Against Women was held in New York the weekend before the International Tribunal, February 27–29, 1976. It was virtually ignored by the media. The opening statement of the New York Tribunal was read by Judith Friedlander who initiated this powerful event. She said:

The New York Tribunal on Crimes Against Women is one of several events taking place in the United States to support the International Tribunal in Brussels. Next week, March 4th to March 8th, women from many different countries will come together in Brussels to participate in a global speak-out. They will give personal testimony of the crimes committed against them and will call on their sisters around the world to indict and sentence the policies in their countries which perpetuate the social, economic, political, and cultural oppression of women. The International Tribunal is a great achievement as it is one of the first truly international feminist events planned by women outside the condescending approval of male-dominated organizations. In recognition of its sigificance, women in Los Angeles, San

Francisco, Denver, Philadelphia and New York have organized parallel speak-outs in our own cities during this weekend and next, so that we can add our voices to those participating in the International Tribunal.

Here in New York we are a coalition of individual women and organizations who are representative of different classes, races and political orientations. Yet despite the wide spectrum of our beliefs and backgrounds, we all recognize our common enemy: it is a society which sustains crimes against women, educating its people to consider such crimes as the natural way to treat women, frequently refusing, when challenged, to acknowledge these crimes as illegal or immoral acts. By means of this Tribunal, we will expose crimes unrecognized as such by the legal system and question the sincerity of a number of laws which pretend to defend the rights of women. The New York Tribunal is also a call for action, a call to our sisters and sympathetic brothers to continue the struggle necessary for changing a society that denies the seriousness of our claims.

The organizing committees of the New York Tribunal have functioned as grand juries and have made a series of indictments. Now, in the next two days, the evidence will be presented and at the closing session we will make our final judgments. The verdict is in our hands. Unlike a traditional Tribunal, there is no panel of judges, for we are all our own judges. We do not believe that a few individuals should have the right to make decisions over our lives, nor are we interested in judging individual criminals. We look to indict the system. Unlike the judges in that system who pretend to eliminate crime by scapegoating the less powerful, we call for a mobilization of our energy to destroy those structures which are in and of themselves criminal and serve to perpetuate our oppression.

Part IV

Critique

CHAPTER 1

The Controversy About Media Men

One of the most controversial issues in and outside of the International Tribunal was our policy not to admit male representatives of the media. Apart from the opening 45 minutes, no men were allowed in the main auditorium where testimony was given, or in the workshops. This is hardly a very novel policy in the women's liberation movement. Since women are, for the most part, isolated from each other by their relationships with men, they need to come together, without men, to break out of this isolation. The presence of men invariably blocks the development of our understanding of our oppression, and our struggle to overcome this oppression. Besides, few men are able or willing to relate to women as equals, let alone accept a subordinate role. This often makes it unproductive and even oppressive to work with them, particularly on the topic of our own liberation.

So, the Tribunal policy to exclude men is hardly surprising. "There's an important difference between oppressive discrimination and defensive discrimination," Erica Fisher from Austria pointed out at the final press conference on March 9th.

Most media men seemed to think that this policy should not apply to them. *We* thought, however, that female media personnel should have been sent to cover the International Tribunal. To have sent men instead, demonstrated how insensitive and sexist their newspapers, radio, and T.V. stations were. We had gathered together to denounce such sexist insensitivity as a crime against women. It would have been compromising for the Tribunal to denounce them on the one hand, then to cooperate with them on the other by allowing them into our plenary sessions and workshops. Furthermore, two of us had witnessed how the media men operated at the IWY Tribunal in Mexico, eagerly covering every disruption, and ignoring all demonstrations of solidarity among women.

Lily Boeykens explained our policy towards media men at the opening session of the Tribunal, mentioning, however, that a daily press conference would be held at 4 P.M. Three or four spokeswomen would give the press summaries of the day's events. She also said that the media men had free access to the entrance hall, the corridors and the garden. Media women were, of course, not restricted in any way. Needless to say, there was considerable grumbling, anger and incomprehension on the part of the media men—and some threatened to boycott the Tribunal and to withdraw media women where they had the power to do so. Since this issue caused so much feeling both inside and outside the Tribunal, and since it will continue to crop up at every feminist gathering of interest to the media, it seems important to document the entire controversy. Here the focus will be on what occurred at the Tribunal. The reactions of the press will be described more fully in the chapters which follow.

During the first day, various messages from media men, asking to speak to this or that witness were read out by the moderator. Many women found these messages intrusive, as well as the men's considerable presence in the halls and corridors (there really were a lot of them!). On Friday morning a Swiss woman interrupted the testimony with the following statement:

> We would like to bring up the question of which journalists have a right to attend the Tribunal. It was explicitly stated, that as an act of solidarity among women, only women journalists would be admitted to all but the opening sessions of the Tribunal. Additionally, yesterday morning it was said that women testifying did not want to do so in the presence of men. We note that in practice, the Tribunal is not sticking to its stated policy. While journalists are not admitted to the sessions, briefings have been organized to which they have access. I'm sure they all appreciate not having to be present all day long at our sessions, and receiving each afternoon all necessary information.
>
> Secondly, yesterday afternoon women who had testified were invited to go to these press briefings. As women, conditioned our entire lives, our comrades did not protest. But, is it easier to cope with male journalists during a press conference, than to cope with them while surrounded by the sympathy and indignation of several hundred other women?
>
> Thirdly, we were all struck yesterday morning by the number of male photographers and television cameramen who were present for the opening of the Tribunal. In these professions women are discriminated against and underrepresented. At least for five days, the Tribunal has a chance to tip the balance of forces in favor of women. It could have forced newspapers either to have to pass up news on an important event or to delegate women to cover the story. We think that on this important subject, the organizing committee alone should not have decided, but that it would have been more democratic to decide this question in a plenary session. We don't deny the importance of the newspapers to the Tribunal; but neither must we have any illusions about the way in which the press, dominated by men, have presented and will continue to present, our struggles. Therefore, the Swiss delegation demands that a decision as to whether or not to admit all journalists to attend the press briefings, or to allow only women journalists to attend, should be taken here this morning by the entire body of women attending the Tribunal.

Then a French woman jumped up to say: "I agree with my Swiss friend. As far as I personally am concerned, I have to file a report for a paper which is quite influential in France. However, this paper has sent a male reporter to the press conference, and while I'm participating in all of the proceedings of the Tribunal, it's his story which will make the paper—simply because he's been at the press conference for half an hour."

Without further discussion, a hand vote was then taken; a majority of those present were in favor of stopping the press conferences for men. A meeting of women journalists was promptly announced to discuss the new policy, and testimony was resumed. As a result of their meeting, some of the women journalists expressed the feeling that a momentous decision had been made very hastily, and that it was unfair to have only heard arguments on one side of the issue. In the midst of considerable tumult, a member of the coordinating committee intervened:

> There are a number of women journalists here who immediately came to the coordinating committee after the vote was taken saying they disagreed with the point of view that was expressed this morning. I think that the difficulty with this situation as regards the press is this: there is the political point of view regarding men attending the Tribunal, but there is also the tactical issue of press representation here. And I now speak as part of the British delegation. We have brought women here who desperately need publicity in England. If the papers that are represented by men at the press briefings are excluded, it means that what these women have to say will not be anywhere near as widely disseminated, and will not get to as many women in Britain as we would like to reach. That is the issue which each of you must think about. Because the political decision is a very easy one—none of us want men anywhere near the Tribunal.
>
> Now we are going to have a speaker for both points of view, and then I hope that we can reach a decision. The decision is up to you.

♀ ♀ ♀ ♀ ♀

First, an American journalist spoke in favor of the continuation of the press conferences.

> I am a woman journalist and I want to present this problem as it affects me in that role, and as I see it from that role. Now, it seems to me that there are two points that we have to consider. The first is: how important is press coverage of this meeting? Whether you think it is better to have lots of coverage or just minimal coverage? Because the minute you follow the decision you made this morning, that will largely eliminate press coverage by major organs—and not only those

who send men, but a number who send women where the publishers will refuse to accept coverage of this Tribunal from this point on.

An argument was put forward in the discussion earlier among the women journalists that what you should go after is quality of coverage. Here we have to accept the consequences of a decision that was taken before this conference began, the decision that men would be excluded from the hall. I have accepted that decision and think that it is probably correct. Nonetheless, if you have taken that decision, it seems to me unfair to then complain that a male's piece reflects only half an hour's coverage, and the female's piece represents an all day coverage. Because you gave the men no choice. So, you can't blame them for not being here at the conference, and for perhaps not comprehending it as clearly as they would have, had you let them in. Perhaps men would have written badly anyway, but you don't know that. Therefore, you must take the consequences of your decision.

Secondly, as a female journalist I face not only the question of feminism, I must also deal with the question of ethics. You said earlier when you explained your policy concerning the press that one of the reasons was to encourage women in journalism. However, I believe, along with a number of other women journalists, if not the majority who met this morning, that you are not helping us. You are damaging our cause as women in our profession by perpetrating something which runs counter to all the ethics of that profession. Liberalism in the journalistic profession and the right to free access is something the women in the profession have fought very hard for, and so have men. And if we do not allow men to cover this event to the extent of attending a press conference, then you do not help women journalists.

Uproar constantly interrupted and followed this speech. Then came a French speaking journalist who spoke against the continuation of the press conference.

Could I now present the point of view of those women who are in favor of the exclusion of the male journalists? I should like, first of all, to reply to the journalist who just spoke and who was saying, 'Don't complain!' I took that rather as a threat for us women. Don't complain if men don't write a lot about you because they weren't there. But I tell you this—men will not report widely on the Tribunal and they will not report it the way we want it to be reported. Secondly, the women are inside the hall the whole day, but whether they're there or whether they're not, not much of what they write will get printed. This is not a fact that we've invented; it's what we know from experience.

The female journalists have the right to be for or against the exclusion of their male colleagues, but it's the opinion of the women in this room on this question that is the most valid. No male journalist, and no female journalist, is obliged to write about what we are doing here. But if they want to do so, they'll do it following our procedure. Now what is the importance of reporting for our struggle? We say obviously "yes" to reporting, but we must say "no" to the terrorism of the mass media. We are greatly overestimating what can be said about us in the press. We all know that it's minimal. We've also been asked: do you want minimal coverage, or coverage which is wider? But I would like to ask you what *quality* of coverage you want? And do you want women to report on the problems of women or do you want men to do so? It is we, the women's movement, who must take upon ourselves the reporting of our struggles. It is we who want, for once, to have our say—to oppose male speeches about us with our female speeches. Men report about us only partly and partially. We know that, and we have to change it. This point of view is not only emotional, it is realistic.

We've also heard about technical know-how. I agree, men have technical power over us, but I should like to say to you that as long as we accept our dependence on them for technical things, we shall never be technicians.

And now I'd like to say that we didn't come to the Tribunal to discuss the problem of the press—male or female. This discussion is, obviously, very important; however, all the other things which we have to talk about are at least equally important. I propose that we end the discussion, take a vote, and that we stick to that vote. The male and female journalists will draw the conclusions that they wish from our vote; their conclusions are not important for the work of the Tribunal.

Finally, I should like to call on the solidarity of the female journalists who are going to report on the Tribunal not to name the women journalists who are in favor of the exclusion of the men. They are risking their jobs. We will keep a close watch on the papers to find out how the female journalists report what is said here, and if they have solidarity with other women.

The moderator called for a hand vote and subsequently announced that it was a tie. After considerable further tumult, a body vote was decided upon. All those in favor of a continuation of the press conference were to pass through one door, and those opposed, through another. The outcome of this vote was a majority in favor of stopping the press conferences for the men. A member of the coordinating committee announced the result, adding that since press conferences were not necessary for women journalists who could attend all Tribunal sessions, all press conferences would henceforth be discontinued. She added that the coordinating committee felt that each woman should decide for herself whether to give interviews to the male press. She continued: "The committee will ask the photographers who have been harassing some women not to take pictures without a woman's

Joy Chamberlain

Tumult during the media men controversy

Joy Chamberlain

A member of the Coordinating Committee attempts to keep order

Yuko Ijichi

Media men confined to the hallways

Yuko Ijichi

A media man anxious to find out what is happening inside

consent. If any woman still has a complaint about this, let us know and we will see that the photographer is expelled." This statement was made after a few incidents of male media men harassing women in the entrance hall were reported to us.

So that was the end of the press conferences. And the threatened boycott did not occur. By that time so much interest had been aroused in the Tribunal that the media men hung around the corridors gleaning what they could and interviewing women willing to talk to them. They also appeared in force (about 50 of them) at the press conference held the day after the Tribunal. The chapter on the International Tribunal Through the Eyes of the Media gives a fuller picture of how they reacted to the policy of exclusion. A few, at least, wrote the following statement of support:

> We, male journalists, although hindered in our work by our partial exclusion from the Tribunal, understand the deep import of the vote which led to this exclusion on the 5th of March 1976, viz., to give more opportunity to our female colleagues in our profession. This minor inconvenience is a first step toward equality between men and women in our profession.

However, an article published in *La Wallonie* on March 8th under the title "Reaction Against Feminist Sexist Decision" reported:

> The International Press Association in Belgium, representing over 250 international journalists, energetically deplores the discriminating and sexist decision of the International Tribunal on Crimes Against Women to ban the male journalists from its press conferences. Such a narrow-minded attitude must be totally opposed by everyone who believes in a free and democratic press, as well as by everyone who is in favor of equality between men and women.

CHAPTER 2

Further Controversy Within the International Tribunal

The mood of the audience at the International Tribunal could be described as calm only on the first day. I use the word audience deliberately because that is what it was on the first day. The coordinating committee had remained on the platform after the opening session, not by decision, but just because it seemed to happen. To me it felt more collective than to leave the moderator in complete isolation. And there was always the possibility that our help would be needed (for example, in counting a vote, keeping the time, answering questions from the hall).

After the opening session on the first day, the moderator, a Belgian woman fluent in Dutch, French and English, (who incidently, was not on the coordinating committee), sometimes had to ask a witness who had exceeded her ten minutes to finish quickly. The coordinating committee had discussed how to handle this situation before the Tribunal and we had decided that we should keep the witnesses to their time limits from the start so that women with long testimonies would be encouraged to shorten them before testifying. We also wanted to ensure that each country and each woman would have equal time. Furthermore, cutting off long speeches seemed fairer to the listeners, since it is usually much easier to listen to a number of people making brief speeches than to a few speaking for long periods. Finally, the more time taken by the prepared testimony and reports, the less time there would be for spontaneous testimony. So we saw the enforcement of time limits as an unpleasant but necessary duty.

However, interruptions that we considered necessary aroused a great deal of hostility in the audience, many of whom felt them to be insensitive and authoritarian. By the end of the first day considerable resentment and anger towards us had developed. We had scheduled a feedback and critique session at the end of the first day, and at this time the Spanish women suggested a total change in the Tribunal program. A Spanish spokeswoman complained that the testimony consisted either of mere "anecdotes," or factual descriptions. She felt that theoretical analyses of the causes of the crimes should be developed instead, and ways of combating them should be discussed.

A member of the coordinating committee pointed out that this was the objective of the workshops, and said that she felt that it was too late to restructure the entire Tribunal as the Spanish women suggested. Women had been selected by national committees to testify. Many had put a great deal of time and thought into preparing their testimonies and reports. Many had come a long way at considerable cost; the travel expenses of some women had been paid on the assumption that they *would* testify (the Norwegian lesbian, for example). She suggested that to implement the Spanish women's proposal would be unfair to these women and to all those women who had come to the Tribunal because they liked the idea of including personal testimony.

Some women saw this response as inflexible and authoritarian, and the Spanish women's point of view was to gain increasingly vocal support as the Tribunal progressed.

The second day opened with the controversy about the media men. Although the substantive disagreement in this controversy was important, I felt another important dimension was the need of many participants to feel that they had more of a part to play in what happened at the Tribunal. Thus, this conflict was also a revolt against the passive position they felt themselves to be in, and an effective show of power, vis-à-vis the coordinating committee, since obviously we had chosen at first to permit the press conference.

My description of the controversy about the media men earlier does not emphasize the tumult and even pandemonium that at times prevailed. At one particularly turbulent moment, the moderator, in panic, made the disastrous mistake of trying to close the session by ordering the microphone turned off, then leaving. This, of course, only added fuel to the fire and channelled hostile feelings towards the coordinating committee as a whole, though we had not participated in this decision at all. Women swarmed onto the platform to find out who was responsible. The male technicians (yes, men!) controlling the microphones would not turn them back on except at the moderator's request. Some of us tried to find her, and others to persuade the technicians to turn the microphones on again without her instruction. After 20–30 minutes, the microphones went on again and the fury continued. The entire coordinating committee was blamed for this "fascist act." From then on, we could do nothing right.

A Swiss woman had this to say about the incident:

> When the women behind the table cut off the mikes this morning, we were forced to be mute. We have been mute all our lives. The work at

this Tribunal happens within masculine structures. A small number of people have power, mainly technical power, and we others are only here physically. But you may be sure that without us this Tribunal would not occur. It would be funny, a Tribunal on women with six women. It is the 1,000 women present here who constitute the Tribunal. We have gathered the money for the Tribunal, we have gathered the cases for the Tribunal, and they stop us from speaking!"

After several more denunciations, the new moderator had this to say:

I do not think it is correct that you go on accusing us concerning this affair with the microphones. This afternoon we have already apologized twice for this unfortunate incident. The members of the committee do not agree with what happened. It was an action taken by a woman in the course of confusion and she has apologized.

We would like to stress that we do not want to exert power over the women present here, and that we have worked very hard on the Tribunal, in particular the woman who gave the order to switch off the microphones. She has been doing an *enormous* amount of work for this Tribunal. So, I do think we should finish this question. We have formally apologized and we would like to get on with the work.

Not content with this statement, another member of the coordinating committee added:

It is really a very, very strong feeling of the committee that we totally condemn the switching off of the microphones. It was not a thing that should have happened at a feminist meeting. We do totally condemn it. We are sorry, but we had no idea why the microphones had gone off. But I think we should all accept her apology and you might all try to trust us a bit more. We really want to work with you, and I do hope that you will accept our apology. We do condemn her act with you, but we can't undo it now.

However, as you will see, these statements did not have much impact. A considerable part of what was left of Friday was spent criticizing us and the Tribunal program. A lot of criticism being repeated over and over again; for example, a Swiss woman repeated the criticism made on Thursday by the Spanish women this way:

Cases are being presented one after the other, but cases are boring for everybody. All the women here know about these sort of things. We all know what it is to be raped, to not have the right to abort, etc. It is not important to describe these cases. What is needed is to know how to analyze their causes, and how to start solving them. We want to form

> a small group that will write a text that will be submitted first thing tomorrow morning in the plenary session, and the group that is directing the Tribunal should not interrupt us.

In an attempt to meet these criticisms, a Spanish woman suggested five working groups on the following themes, "Woman and Sexuality," "Woman and Work," "Woman and Politics," "Woman and Education," and "Woman and the Family." Each working group was to analyze the causes of problems occuring within its theme, and to consider solutions to these problems. Each group would report its conclusions to the entire assembly. "At the end of each theme at the end of each day, the microphone would be left free for an hour or an hour and a half so that each feminist group or each different ideology could give its opinion regarding the conclusions." This proposal was never picked up by anyone else.

A little later, a very articulate Australian woman speaking for "a group of Australian women attending this conference" made the following statement:

> We realize that the coordinating committee has put in a great amount of time and energy into the organization of this conference. But we think that the structure of the Tribunal should change to include less individual testimony and allow more dialogue and interaction between women speaking and the audience. We feel that there are a lot of people here who feel dissatisfied with the superficial nature of the testimonies. The present form of testimony allows for no examination of the specific crimes within their particular context, and a formulation of strategies for change. One way to change the structure of the Tribunal is for the coordinating committee to leave the podium and allow women's groups who have worked on certain issues to occupy the stage for short periods of time. We don't think that it is enough for the coordinating committee to suggest workshops while still remaining at the central place of this conference.
>
> There is obviously a great amount of aggravation and dissension among the women listening to speakers. For far too long women have been expected to passively listen and contain their anger or their dissension. Confrontation should not be prohibited in a conference like this. There are differences among women despite our common oppression and it is constructuve and essential to discuss these in order to understand each other. Looking at crimes in terms of nationalism simplifies the real differences within countries and obscures the similarities all over the world. The Black woman representing Australia sees herself as having more in common with her Black sisters than with white Australian women.

A Swiss woman responded:

> I would like to answer the comrade who just spoke. She said that the coordinating committee has worked a great deal. I would like to complete what she said. *We* also have worked a great deal. We have sent reports. We came. And at any rate, the aim of this meeting is not to compliment one another. What we want, is to analyze the methods of struggle which are used in each country, and develop a feminist strategy. No one negates the work done by the coordinating committee, but this work must not stop us from going ahead. Therefore, we want to change the format of work at the Tribunal. I would like to suggest that the testimony and reports be stopped now. Women who want to give their opinion on the proposals that have been made should be able to have their say now.

However, none of the proposals made were ever put to a vote. A large number of women seemed united against the coordinating committee and our program, but when it came to suggesting alternatives, this unity disintegrated. Although the dissatisfaction of many women was apparent enough, few were able to come up with really concrete proposals. The Spanish proposals to divide into five different work groups on different themes was perhaps the most concrete. But no proposal caught enough women's fancies to even get close to implementation. So, the criticism continued. A woman who apparently spoke for several others said:

> We, a group of women from Switzerland, from Spain, from Portugal, Mexico and Sweden, denounce the Tribunal because it does not at all go into—from a feminist point of view—the political, social and ideological structures which are the basis of discrimination against women. As a result, the Tribunal has testified on a whole series of problems that we are all aware of on a personal level, and does not bring out the political, socio-economic aspects which block the way of women towards their liberation. We are taking a stand against the continuation of this Tribunal because it has not elaborated the basis of a common struggle for the women's organizations from the many countries represented. Hence, it is not truly feminist. And we question the authenticity of the democratic process of this Tribunal. We invite the assembly to express its feelings on this statement.

Then an Irish woman spoke:

> My name is Nuala Fennell. I come from Ireland. I am one of you. I had the money and the raised consciousness to come here. I came to this Tribunal because Irish women need support and solidarity in their fight for liberation. This afternoon you will hear personal testimony about the life of one Irish woman less fortunate than I, or than most of you. She truly represents thousands of Irish women and millions of oppressed mothers all over the world. We came here because

> we liked the proposed structure of this conference presented to us. We *still* like it. We came too because we felt the warm sisterhood from the women who worked for years to organize this Tribunal. I salute them for their work and their loyalty to us, hundreds of faceless females. And above all, I salute them for their patience and endurance with our squabbles since we started. Make no mistake. *We* were not the workers for this Tribunal. They were. And the interpreters are. Please listen to me. I listened to all of you. I suggest, with some humility, that no one person, no one country, no one ideological group, holds the secret of liberation for all women. Some may think they do, but to force this idea aggressively on this Tribunal is to obstruct the true course of liberation for most women. Allow us to develop at different levels. To express our feelings. To decide our needs. Do not impose your kind of dictatorship. This week from the floor I have seen female dictatorship. Please, listen to me! I'm one of you and I find what is happening here frightening and sad. This is a unique opportunity. Please, let us trust one another. Please, let us show some understanding and some patience.

Finally Friday came to an end. The double oppression of Third World women had been scheduled for Friday afternoon, but no time remained to hear their testimonies. After Friday, the coordinating committee did not occupy the platform again, except intermittently. Some women criticized us for leaving, and permitting a basically anarchistic situation to prevail, though none said so publicly. But the majority seemed to prefer it that way, and we did too. However, still concerned that women who had been selected by their countries get a chance to testify, we continued to prepare a daily program, even though it was rarely adhered to.

On Saturday morning the Third World women, who had come together at a Third World and Minority Women's Workshop the day before, organized their own panel. It was magnificently chaired by Catherine Day-Jermany, a Black woman from the U.S. The testimony was so fascinating, and the perspective of the Third World women so much appreciated by the mostly white audience, that nobody seemed to mind the complete disregard of the time limits.

Near the end of the presentations of the Third World women, the Swiss woman who had spoken so articulately the day before tried again to argue for the replacement of testimony with analysis and strategy proposals. This time there was little reaction for or against her suggestion. With the coordinating committee out of the way, the urgent desire to change the whole program of the Tribunal seemed to have dissipated. However, this did not mean that disruption and conflict had ended. Saturday afternoon was full of it: the lesbian demonstration, the bomb scare, the

Eva Besnyo

Just prior to the lesbian demonstration

Eva Besnyo

The lesbian demonstration

Nancy Budd

Singing a lesbian song

Eva Besnyo

Two women fear recognition

Yuko Ijichi

Annie takes over the mike

Nancy Budd

The Older Women's Workshop

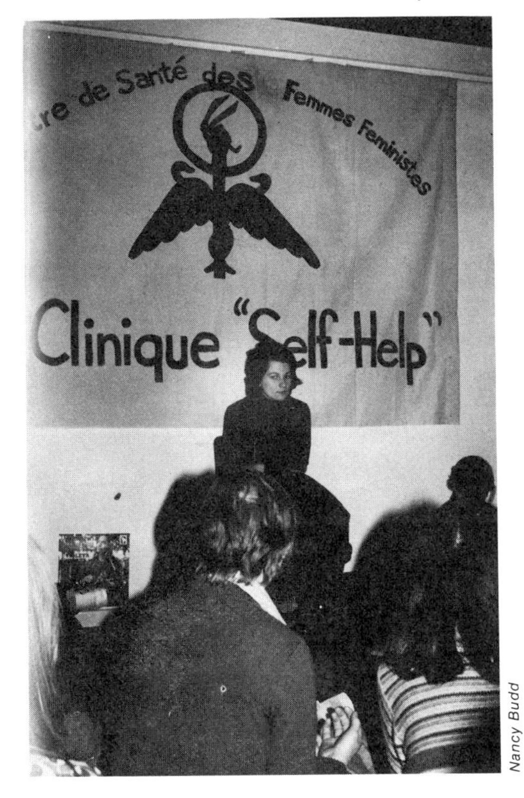

Nancy Budd

The locale of the Self-Help Workshops

Nancy Budd

Workshops everywhere and anywhere

A Palais worker gets in on a workshop

Christina Perincioni, Christa Branz, Agnes Thomas, Henriette Lührmann

"The Flying Lesbians": as photographed on the cover of their first record album

Christina Perincioni, Christa Branz, Agnes Thomas, Henriette Lührmann

"incident" involving Annie, and finally, great upset about the showing of a pornographic movie as part of the testimony against pornography. A few women decided to leave the Tribunal because they couldn't tolerate seeing women so set against one another.

To quote a report written by some British women, "The structure of the conference had undergone a radical change." By the fourth day, there was a situation "where the most organized groups who felt they had something important to say took control of the proceedings so that power, in effect, had passed from the committee to the floor." Miraculously, most of the women who had come with prepared testimony were able to speak, though this meant that testimony ran on into Monday, the day intended to focus on solutions and strategy.

The Monday morning session was moderated by the Swiss woman who had been one of the major critics of the Tribunal. After the testimony had ended, she then proceeded to read the following report.

> I would like to read the text that we have prepared. The title is: "Some Constructive Criticisms Concerning the Tribunal." A group of women from various countries have been working since last Friday on this. We would like to establish the following work process, which can be used in future meetings. We demand that all women present reflect on these points and continue to discuss them with the women's groups in your countries.
>
> First, the press and mass media. Male journalists will be excluded in the future from all of our meetings. However, we have considered that in the interest of spreading our work and information to women in other countries who are not here, we should have press releases which have been edited by us, and which are issued daily to all members of the mass media.
>
> The second point concerns finances. Finances should be made public. The books of the committee of the organizers will be open.
>
> The next point concerns daycare centers. A daycare center will be organized and will be mentioned in the invitation sent to all women and to all women's groups.
>
> The next point concerns rooms. A sufficient number of small rooms are needed for workshops, meetings and individual actions, so that women wanting to testify in front of a small group will be offered this opportunity.
>
> The next point concerns the daily schedule. Although most of the day will be reserved for work in smaller groups, we would like time to be reserved for a discussion on the output of these work groups in a plenary session in the evenings. Contributions should be kept short and precise. This is necessary in order to leave time for questions. Several microphones will be available in the plenary room. The presiding group will be renewed daily.

All technical means of communication—that is microphones, video tapes, means of technical reproduction, e.g., typewriters, copying machines, etc., as well as the administrative office—will be available to all.

The committee responsible for preparing the next Tribunal should inform potential participants of the program planned with the necessary details some months in advance so that comments and exchange of ideas, suggestions for change, etc., can be done before the beginning of the Tribunal.

Authoritarian structures will be avoided. The podium where I am now sitting will have only an organizational function.

The program should incorporate the following points: (1) flexibility to absorb unexpected cases as you saw happen this morning (with Annie); (2) more time must be reserved for personal and social contact; (3) daily information summaries of previous events and points will be posted relevant to the Tribunal. For example, where the lavatories are located or where to find a particular place in the city.

The second part of our critique concerns content. The main theme must remain as limited as possible in order to allow the most intense work possible.

Criticism concerning the functioning of the Tribunal: first, the emphasis was, unfortunately, laid much too often upon personal testimony. This worked out to the detriment of necessary political analyses of the cases presented. In addition, we would like to have concrete analyses concerning the means of resistance already utilized and developed in different countries, which can be revealed to other women, so that these points can be taken into consideration. Recognition was not given to the women's movement all over the world in this regard. This should be one of the themes in the next Tribunal so that we may gather information concerning the number of members in the women's movements, their internal tendencies, their structures, their means of communication as well as their particular methods and strategy.

The coordinating committee returned to the platform for the final afternoon session on proposals for change. However, we did not use up the little time remaining by trying to respond to the many points made in the critique group's report.

♀ ♀ ♀ ♀ ♀

EDITOR'S RESPONSE TO THE TRIBUNAL CRITICS

The preceding account of the various criticisms of the coordinating committee and of the Tribunal is far from complete. But I have tried to convey both the variety and the similarity of the criticisms, and to let the women speak for themselves.

Having given our critics so much space, now I'd like to take my turn.

First, I will take up some of the points mentioned in the critique group's report which have not been dealt with elsewhere.

The suggestion in the report that the finances of a future Tribunal should be made public suggests that we did not do this. This is totally untrue. At the Tribunal, as well as before and after, we informed anyone interested—and many who were not interested—particularly the national contacts, about the details of the financial situation. And our books were never closed to anyone.

Of course there should have been childcare available. The Belgian committee who assumed almost all of the practical responsibilities of organizing the Tribunal, did not forget about childcare or ignore its importance. The Palais des Congrès, which would not permit childcare in its buildings, is situated in the administrative center of Brussels. We couldn't find a private house nearby to be used for this purpose. The pre-Tribunal deficit of $2,500 prevented the Belgian committee from renting a place. This was a problem that they were simply unable to solve.

The suggestion that small work groups be the basic structure for a large gathering of women from many different countries sounds great. But it presents the problem of finding a tremendous number of interpreters, or of working within language groups, or of spending enormous amounts of time finding out how many languages are needed, and then doing consecutive translations.

Regarding the suggestion that a sufficient number of small rooms be provided for workshops and other meetings, I completely agree. One of the greatest misfortunes of the International Tribunal was that only a few rooms were available for workshops, they were often difficult to find, and they had an environment as alienating as the hierarchical structure of the main hall: most were large and formal, and the immovable seats were often arranged in lecture formation. While there were marvelously spacious corridors everywhere, the Palais manager told us repeatedly that because of fire regulations, it was illegal to sit in them, and he threatened several times to turn off the electricity if women persisted in ignoring this rule.

In addition, the simultaneous translation in five languages available in the large hall was only available for very few workshops. As a result, the general sessions where the testimony was heard became the focus of the Tribunal, rather than the workshops.

The Palais was not constructed for a feminist conference. Our dependence on technical equipment—all the greater because the Tribunal's international participants—made overcoming these male structures even more impossible.

Small groups, in which all present have the opportunity to participate, have long been the preferred mode of meeting among feminists. The passivity enforced on the majority in large gatherings is anathema to us. Nevertheless, to put all the blame for the imperfections of the Tribunal on the structure of the Palais des Congrès would be a mistake. Because of the communication problems inherent in international meetings, there is no way to satisfactorily accommodate our preference for working in small groups. However, the frustration arising out of this situation was enormous.

It is impossible for videotapes to be made available to all. Each one costs about $12, to say nothing of the equipment. Typewriters and reproduction facilities were available to all.

Ever since the Paris planning meeting a year before the Tribunal occurred, we informed potential participants of the program, and asked constantly for feedback and alternative suggestions. The critique groups were obviously uninformed about this. We cannot be held responsible for all the women in the world who didn't know about the Tribunal and the program worked out over a year and a half. This is not to say that women who didn't know about the Tribunal are responsible. It's not a case of blame on either side.

I think that we *did* use our position on the platform merely as an organizational function—as the critique group recommended. We also showed considerable flexibility in removing ourselves from the platform when this was suggested, even though it was never established by a vote that the majority agreed with the suggestion.

So much for the report, which was at least expressed in a constructive spirit, unlike most of the spontaneous criticism.

In general, I think the portrayal of us as a power hungry, authoritarian group of individuals was grossly unfair, incorrect and extraordinary. The truth is that we rarely defended ourselves; *we* were much more mute than our critics, and less articulate. Not one of us from the platform attacked anything anyone said or did, except for the single incident when the microphone was turned off by one member of the committee. Frankly, I think that the accusation that we were weak and wishy-washy would have been more valid. We were so taken aback at being treated like The Enemy that most of us were somewhat paralyzed. Certainly I know I was.

The *herstory* of the Tribunal shows clearly that we had our reasons for choosing to focus on personal testimony. The irony is that many women, in the first two days in particular, did *not* testify about their personal experiences, but gave second-hand reports of facts and figures instead. Regarding the claim of some women, that they already knew about everything that was being said, I simply do not believe this. How many women know what it's like to be a porno model, to have their sister murdered, to be battered by their husband, to have received a 25-year prison sentence for shooting in self-defense, to require open heart surgery after a knife attack by a rapist, to be a Black woman in South Africa or Australia, to be forcibly incarcerated in a mental hospital for trying to escape a brutal husband, to be beaten up for being a lesbian, etc., etc.? To dismiss completely what can be learned from the women who have experienced these crimes themselves seems to be quite contrary to feminist thinking. Of course, we do need analyses and solutions. We planned on having both at the Tribunal.

I think an international feminist conference focusing on how to combat crimes against women, and not on the crimes themselves, would be great. Indeed, I proposed this on the last day. But this wasn't the conference we had organized on this occasion, because we liked the idea of a Tribunal. To come to a conference that women have worked on for months and years, and then to try to transform it almost immediately into a very different type of conference—now *that* seems authoritarian to me! If those who put most of the work into the conference and who feel responsible to the participants attracted by the planned program don't immediately applaud the idea of changing it totally, do they really deserve to be denounced as inflexible and authoritarian? I object to this criticism, particularly since not a single practicable proposal was ever made to replace the testimonies.

It's like going to a conference on teaching women's studies in the university, and then denouncing it and its organizers because it isn't changed to a conference on self-help. The critics may believe self-help to be more important to the feminist struggle than women's studies, but does that mean that all feminists have to agree? Does it mean that women's studies conferences must be obstructed?

Another thing that I found extraordinary was that, despite all the denunciations of the Tribunal, women kept proposing future Tribunals, even the Spanish critics! Why not propose a strategy conference, or a conference on theories of women's oppression?

Everyone seemed wedded to the word Tribunal, and everyone seemed to think that someone else would organize the future Tribunals according to their stipulations. There were lots of suggestions but not a single volunteer.

Before the Tribunal, we wrote to all national contacts that "We don't want to have two classes of women: those who make the Tribunal possible with their labor, and those who enjoy the fruits of this labor. Every woman can help in some way(s). We will need volunteers for translation, interpreting, typing, office help, moderating, childcare, selling buttons and posters for the Tribunal, putting out the daily news sheet, helping with registration, answering questions and providing information. It would be helpful if women coming to the Tribunal be informed about this ahead of time." The need for volunteers was reiterated at registration, and from the podium. Hardly any women volunteered. Most of those doing the work were women living in Belgium who had signed up ahead of time. Many of them were unable to attend a single plenary session or workshop. Many of these women complained about the way they were treated by others during the Tribunal. They felt their work was taken for granted and, like the coordinating committee, they received many more complaints and expressions of dissatisfaction than appreciation or offers of help. They felt that some women saw them as servants, or perhaps mothers—not as sisters working for free. We were only a few women putting on an enormous event, but every imperfection brought criticism and denunciation.

♀ ♀ ♀ ♀ ♀

So much for counter-criticism. Now it's time for analysis. *Why* did so many women feel so hostile towards the organizers of the Tribunal?

One fascinating aspect of the Tribunal process was that after we had left the platform and other groups had taken over, frustration and antagonism seemed to emerge from the audience at the end of each session, directed to each new moderator. Initially at least, some of these moderators seemed to get away with behavior not tolerated in the coordinating committee. One moderator, for example, used a bell to inform people that their time was up; another tried to cut Pat Parker short a couple of times when she was reading her poem on the murder of her sister, even though she was well within her time limit. A Japanese woman simply wasn't allowed to read a report on forced prostitution in Korea except during a lunch hour when barely anyone was there to hear her, even though neither Japan nor Korea had exceeded the minimum amount of time alloted for each country. I know at least two witnesses (from Israel and South Africa) who never got to give their prepared testimony, and I am sure there were more.

My point isn't that the new moderators were poor ones. On the contrary, I thought that most of the time they were excellent. But to begin with, the women listening seemed to tolerate behavior in them that they would not accept in us. However, even this tolerance usually wore thin by the end of the session. This appeared to be an almost unavoidable hazard of the moderator role, and of course, the constant change of personnel was the most effective solution.

How can the greater tolerance towards the new moderators be explained? I believe it was because they were seen to have emerged from the floor, from "the people." They were usually women who had most articulately criticized us and the Tribunal, and so had established their credentials as women who were anti-power. We, on the other hand, had never established any credentials. We were anonymous. Few knew who we were—and, of course, we were in no way chosen by those present to represent them. With the awesome facilities of the Palais, and us sitting on high up there, viewing us as sisters was apparently impossible.

For example, one member of the coordinating committee expressed her own opinion during the media men controversy (it is included in that chapter) and people were outraged. The British women who wrote a report on the Tribunal—women who, incidentally, knew this member of the coordinating committee well, and had worked with her up until the Tribunal, reacted as follows: After one speaker had spoken for either side, "The committee member arbitrarily expressed her personal point of view, thus erasing any semblance of democracy." (Incidentally, she said her piece *before* the two speakers.) Others were outraged that some committee members voted on the issue. We were supposed to be the only disenfranchised women there.

Most feminists have a healthy suspicion of those in power, but the misperceptions and intolerance on this occasion seem far from healthy to me. Another member of the coordinating committee, Lydia Horton, analyzed "the revolt," as she calls it, as follows:

> "This hostility to management of any description crops up in many different countries and cultures, and reflects perhaps women's typically underdog mentality which assumes that anyone in any kind of authority automatically is going to try to rip women off. In addition,

> the security of an enclosed, all-woman meeting is conducive to the expression of long-repressed frustrations. And finally, many feminists are deeply concerned with problems of authority and power and the need for us as women to discard male models of organization. So I feel the suspicion and hostility surrounding this revolt was peculiar to our stage of evolution as women.

Having said all this, I should add that I think the Tribunal improved greatly during the last three days—for several reasons. The testimony became more personal and first-hand. The topics were less well known. And it also worked very well to have sessions run by those testifying on a particular crime.

More important than any of these points is that the passive audience of the first day had changed into active, involved participants. The Tribunal had come alive. This involvement contrasted strikingly to the passivity of the audiences in more traditional conferences, such as the World Congress in East Berlin. There, many members of the U.S. Delegation literally fell asleep in our seats on the first day and we were awakened by T.V. camera men gleefully photographing us in this comprising position. Women at the Tribunal were deeply emotionally involved, sometimes shouting in anger, sometimes clapping and booing, or crying, or being intensely quiet. One never knew from one minute to the next what would happen. This surely was why the Tribunal had such a deep impact on so many women.

Was the scape-goating of the coordinating committee a necessary condition for this intense, dynamic gathering? I like to think not, but I really don't know.

CHAPTER 3

The International Tribunal Through the Eyes of the Media

Brussels has an International Press Center (the I.P.C.). The Brussels office realized early that contacts through this Center would be extremely important in reaching worldwide audiences. Consequently, when we were informed that we could stage our Tribunal at the Palais des Congrès, we called a full-scale press conference at the I.P.C. on December 9, 1975 informing the media of the place, date, format and aims of the Tribunal. The Belgian press printed these bare facts widely, using our own words. Only the *Metropolitan*, a provincial daily, felt immediately threatened, and stooped to denigrating us as "the last isolated pocket of survivors of feminism," concluding with the arrogant statement that "Luckily, we already have experience of this type of tribunal, and that, on more serious subjects!"

At our second press conference on February 15th, again at the I.P.C., we made the announcement that men and consequently male journalists were to be excluded from the plenary sessions and workshops. We gave our reasons for this decision: the possible embarrassment of witnesses giving intimate details in public about violences committed against them; the need to respect the anonymity of those testifying about crimes against women political prisoners; the false reporting and distortions by male journalists in accounts of previous feminist meetings. The first of these three reasons was readily accepted. The second was met with astonishment: if women journalists were going to respect witnesses' anonymity, then why would men not? The third reason was seldom picked up, and when it was, no comment was made on it. It was all too easy, at this second press conference, for the men to pick up one of their favorite old cudgels, the freedom of the press. They were unanimous in deciding that we would harm ourselves in excluding them, but it was obvious from the compromise they suggested—that their female colleagues should hold back on the release of information until the time of the daily press conference—that they were mainly concerned with being scooped.

While before the Tribunal, coverage had largely been left to the wire services, reporters, both men and women, began flocking to Brussels from all parts of the world for the opening of the Tribunal. On March 1st, already *Le Nouvel Observateur* (France) had opened its columns to Simone de Beauvoir writing about the Tribunal. *Le Monde* (France), *The Times* (London), *The New York Times, Der Spiegel* (Germany), *Il Messagero* and *La Stampa* (Italy), to name but a few, all followed, sometimes with extensive coverage of the opening.

But the events of March 5th, concerning the exclusion of male journalists even from press conferences catapulted the Tribunal once and for all into the headlines. This decision caused an immediate, antagonistic and virulent reaction in the world media. We were threatened with total boycott. For example, a U.P.I. man said that they had originally assigned a woman to cover the event but when they found out that men weren't allowed, they took her off the story as a matter of principle, adding that his organization was trying to break away from the tradition of women reporting solely on women's events. Clearly, the question was very controversial, for most of the women journalists at the Tribunal themselves regretted the decision, calling it emotional and hasty. Suzanne Van Rockegem, reporting in *Le Soir* (March 6th) wrote: ". . . A motion has been signed by more than 40 women journalists from the different countries represented. They declare their solidarity with the women's liberation movement," and ". . . they protest the decision of the majority of the Assembly . . . preventing, as it does, women around the world from having access to the widest possible information." In *Het Volk* and *De Nieuwe Gids* (March 7th) Suzanne Van Houtryve agrees that "we have strong doubts whether the sectarian discriminatory path taken by radical feminists can ever lead to feminist goals, that is, a society where women and men enjoy the same rights." Tillie Stuckens, writing for *De Standaard*, attributes the cause of an "irresponsible decision" to "the youth of the majority of the participants." Alone of the Belgian press, Hilda Uytterhoeven expresses a supportive opinion in *Wij:* "Let us hope that they will learn a lesson from the bitter fact that, simply on the basis of their sexual characteristics, they were judged, condemned and excluded. For centuries, women have lived with this bitter reality."

One male journalist lived the "bitter reality," and has described it vividly. Roberto Giardina, writing in an Italian daily, the moderately-left *Il Giorno,* describes in these terms the raising of his consciousness: "I consider myself a feminist, but I can't accept this discrimination against me. Much to my annoyance, I find that this decision is a just one . . . I keep telling myself that the only thing bothering me is that my female colleagues will be able to file better stories than I can. I am irritated, as a journalist. Not as a man. As a man, I 'understand' absolutely. How many times have I gone ahead of female colleagues just because I was the strongest, the quickest, or simply because the person I was interviewing preferred a man to a woman journalist? Now it's my turn to be discriminated against, and between 'understanding' this, and 'experiencing' this—there is an enormous difference. In the first case, you feel intelligent and generous; in the second, you resort to trickery and scheming. I try to pick up information from women and make them speak. Am I deceitful? Perhaps this is the state that men have put women into. I am obliged to use ambiguous methods, to be accepting, to smile and to suppress my anger."

Jerome Grynpas, in the Belgian leftist weekly *Notre Temps,* objects in the name of Marxism: "It is a fascist attitude, at best infantile, to inculpate various anthropological groupings: men, women, whites, Arabs . . . Marxism and common sense have always rejected such attitudes." *La Cité* also took refuge in insults: "This ostracism is not only extremely rude, but stupid too."

From Spain comes the voice of Soledad Balaguer in an article devoted to journalism at the Tribunal. Addressing male journalists, she writes: "You understand nothing, nothing at all about what goes on inside a female mind, which is different from yours, thank God. We, yes, we understand what's going on in yours because we've had to suffer its consequences for centuries. As a woman and as a journalist, I know all about subtle discrimination, 'unimportant' little incidents which build up over the years in the profession until finally they get you down. In the press room, in the workshop, the top person is always making remarks about the good looks of the woman journalist 'whose presence brings joy to his sight,' and he can't resist finding out whether or not she is married, and if the opportunity presents itself, he makes a pass at her, either verbal or tactile." That's enough, dear little males," she concludes, "things being what they are, all men out!"

Despite the threat of total boycott, in the two weeks before and after the Tribunal 165 articles appeared in the Belgian daily and weekly press alone—a remarkable number not entirely due to the fact that the event was taking place in Brussels in the Palais des Congrès. The national and local radio and television stations also covered the Tribunal, both live from the Palais at the opening session, and in recorded interviews with participants.

The extent of the Tribunal's impact on the world press is difficult to evaluate precisely. The national contacts had been asked to collect clippings in their own countries or to employ a clipping service. For a number of reasons, only a few national committees could afford the latter, but many sent us what clippings they had gathered themselves. These reveal the extensive coverage accorded to the Tribunal by the press in many parts of the world. Obviously, many articles published were not picked up, and we feel, therefore, from what we have already received, that a major crack in the bastions of male domination of the press has already been achieved . . . because of, or in spite of, the exclusion of male journalists?

Both the right and left wing press, both the establishment and the feminist media have taken up the Tribunal. The most favorable articles were not always penned by feminist women; the most sexist, alas, not always by male chauvinists.

U.S.A.

In the United States, the *New York Times* published two descriptive articles on the Tribunal on March 3 and 5, underlining that it closed "with a sense of accomplishment," that "the 60 or so American participants remained in the background during the sessions seeking to avoid the criticism that arose in past gatherings about better organized Americans taking over," and that "the most striking testimony came from the relatively few women at the conference from the Third World."

Although *Time* and *Newsweek* delegated correspondents to the Tribunal, nothing appeared in their columns on the historic events taking place in Brussels, preferring to ignore them in favor of masculine world politics.

For the *Women's Press* of the month of May, Marianne Oktober wrote: "By almost any standards of judgment, the International Tribunal on Crimes Against Women was an astounding success. When most reports from women attending conferences are negative and emphasize the problems in working together, it is a pleasure to be able to report that at this conference, while the differences among us were recognized and dealt with, they were far outweighed by our similarities, our agreement on feminist principles, and our dedication to struggle for the freedom of all . . . Women attending had an extraordinary chance to learn at first hand what life is like for Australian Aboriginal women, South Africans, for women in Spain, Portugal, Japan, Israel, Syria, Korea, India, and so on." "On the other hand," Marianne admitted, "listening to so many personal stories of oppression, maltreatment, and misery was a physical and emotional strain on us all."

To Marianne: "One of the most satisfying features of this conference and one of its unique characteristics was that the structure provided for every woman's views to be expressed, and criticisms of the proceedings were incorporated into the conference, not dismissed or left to be dealt with later." Marianne "came away from the Tribunal with a deepened respect for my sisters around the world who struggle against overwhelming forces," and "the deepened conviction that the feminist movement must transcend the national boundaries erected to prevent the powerless from uniting to overthrow our oppressors. World sisterhood is not a dream but a reality."

AMERICAN PRESS IN EUROPE

Covering the five days of the Tribunal, Susan Heller Anderson reported in the *Herald Tribune* on what she described as the "biggest international feminist event in history." She emphasized that "since reform will take a long time, it was a pleasant surprise to see some immediate results after the dust had settled from the Brussels conference. Succeeding where previous feminist gatherings had failed, the Tribunal confronted three troublesome issues that have divided and often stalled the womens' movement—the press (male), homosexuals (female) and power." Referring to the male journalists as being "accustomed to being handled with kid gloves," she noted how women had resented their intrusion when they "found themselves surrounded by male camera crews, wire service reporters and photographers on the opening day. And they resented what they saw as the insensitivity of news organizations for seemingly not caring about getting the best story, and not sending women to cover it." She strongly underlined the fact that the ban did not stop reporting of the event, by saying: "Not only did the Tribunal demonstrate that it did not need male reporters, it made the decision pay off." At the end of the Tribunal, Anderson commented, "the participants' euphoria at just having survived all this was palpable. The women's willingness to absorb the blows of the press, militant lesbians, and their own dissatisfied sisters, and make them part of the Tribunal's business, was a source of hope that the women's movement has come to terms with some of its internal problems."

BRITAIN

Of the countries about which we have information, coverage of the Tribunal was poorest of all in Britain. Michael Hornsby of *The Times* could only bring himself to write 150 words, preferring to use two-thirds of his space to write about another topic. So, virtually the entire responsibility rested on Jill Tweedie of the *Guardian,* who attended the Tribunal for all but the last day. "No one nodded off through boredom," she wrote, "only through complete mental and physical exhaustion. But by its own yardstick," she continues, "the Tribunal came somewhere near a failure."

"The women's movement," Tweedie continues, "suffers from a surfeit of democracy. It is controlled so much by women that it is no longer for the women, only for those with the loudest voices and the most obsessive grievances. Priorities of suffering are lost in the melee, as the strong trample the weak, as the wounded victim whispers while the merely bruised, screams. Those appointed to defend priorities stand down, more terrified of being accused by the power of dictatorship than reproached by the weak for betrayal."

About the elimination of the press conferences for men, Tweedie had this to say: "The spotlight of the world flickered and died. Third World women, battered wives, all those who desperately wanted their cases heard beyond the walls of the Palais des Congrès, were outvoted to protect some of the most articulate women of the West. 'Is there such a word in English,' said a Danish woman to me, 'as sister-fuckers?' 'there is now,' I said."

Tweedie also had some scalding comments about the lesbian demonstration: "Imagine a Tribunal of Black people protesting their oppression and allowing Black homosexuals an entire morning and many long interruptions to state their case. If being a lesbian is a problem, sisters, how does it line up with torture, prison, endless pregnancies, starvation, dying children, rape, a lifetime of brutality from a violent husband?"

Tweedie ended up her article with a completely negative view about the potentiality of international feminism. "Reluctantly, now, it seems to me that any international meeting of women is more likely to produce division than cohesion. Our problems are too disparate, too tied to our particular societies, to be solved outside. International action is only effective on relatively trivial issues—demonstrations against the film *Story of O,* for instance . . . Better, then, to stay at home and work out our problems there."

The unfortunateness of Tweedie's negative conclusion regarding international feminism goes beyond the fact that it was the only article in the non-feminist press in Britain. It was also republished in Israel and South Africa, and probably elsewhere as well. Yet her ascerbic negativity seems to be belied by some of her own statements. For example: "No reasonable man who had been allowed to listen to such testimony could have failed to feel bitterly about his fellow men, could have failed to want change. The Catholic Church, a male institution if ever there was one, emerged as one of the prime instigators of crimes against women, indicted time and again by women from Catholic countries as the dictator of their bodies and minds, the instantly traceable source of every horror from rape to femicide, whether in Ireland or Puerto Rico, Belgium or Spain. In Rome, the men sit and debate the saving of souls. At their feet, the ruined women lie, souls in the Czarist sense. The Pope's serfs."

IRELAND

The four long articles written by Nell McCafferty for the *The Irish Times* form the most detailed, the most complete, the best documented (with long excerpts of testimony), coverage of all the world press on the Tribunal. She has followed everything, been everywhere and said everything with a precision that in no way stifles her emotion: "After five days of such testimony, from 10 in the morning till 6 at night, I came away feeling totally assaulted. I didn't want to hear about women's bodies anymore, or about women's condition . . . The reaction was to call for silence. I didn't want to hear anymore. But, the Tribunal pointed out, these things are happening all over the world to millions of women. That they are not spoken about is part of the shame we have to face. We have to take cognisance of the total horror of our universal condition . . . And then the question was posed: what to do about it? The Spanish delegation intervened in the proceedings continuously to ask for analysis of why these things happened to women, and discussion of what to do about it. First, came the answer, we have to document the fact that it happens. A prerequisite of action was a sense of need for action. The need for action is best encouraged by refusing to deal in abstractions. And so we went back to personal testimony."

In the *Irish Press,* Nuala Fennell goes into detail about the human exchanges from the moment of her first contacts in Brussels: "Friendliness and familiarity exuded from women who had never met before," and this sentiment permeates her entire article, which she concludes by enumerating what the Tribunal has brought to Irish women. "For the first time, it provided a platform for the cause of Irish women to be internationalized, as Simone de Beauvoir suggested, without governmental mandates or bias. It has given the world feminist movement an insight into our lives, as it gave Irish delegates who attended a new perspective on the problems of other women. Some of our sexual inequalities and abuses emerged as uniquely Irish, in which case global evolution alone will not alleviate them, but many other issues were classically defined as traditional, universal oppression, or non-development of women. In these instances, we have a common interest with women of other nations. Such a high-level conference throws into relief the course of change in other countries, and it would provide a blueprint for future developments here, while at the same time giving us the opportunity to avoid the mistakes and the excesses made elsewhere."

FRANCE

A quotation of Simone de Beauvoir's article in *Le Nouvel Observateur* appears in the Preface to this book. For Evelyne Le Garrec, in *Politique Hebdo,* another left wing review, the hour is right for analyses and strategic development alone, and not for a "boring and endless litany" or a "lament on the misery of being a woman." Mentioning raped, battered and aborting women, in which she sees simply "history repeating itself, a mere statement of an oppression from which there is never any escape," she asks whether "even in a hundred years we shall still be making lists of our oppressions."

Biased, sectarian *Paris-Match* offers its readers, in two pages with a few photos, a defamatory picture of the Tribunal, "a huge psychodrama from which emerges, above all, incoherence." It goes on to quote a taxi driver: "I would shove them all into a crematorium oven," and a hall porter at the Palais: "If you want my opinion, it would be better to lock them in a country brothel. That would calm them down." It offers these two quotes, significantly, without comment.

Le Monde, under the signature of Pierre Devos, talks about "anarchy which has rarely been equalled," "testimony of women coming essentially from rich countries," but also of "the establishment of touching bonds, for example those between Arab and Israeli women." These are the only comments in his account, where crimes were merely catalogued by name, the case of Violette capturing most of his attention.

HOLLAND

More than 30 articles have reached us from Holland, mostly from the establishment press. A feminist analysis of this coverage was published in No. 14 of *N.U.B.*, a leftist student publication written by women who had participated at the Tribunal. They deplore the fact that the announcement of the Tribunal they had passed to the Dutch news sevice ANP *(Algemene Nederlandse Persagentschap)* was published in one daily alone, as far as they know, and that the ANP radio service did not utter a single word on the Tribunal, neither before, during nor after. On the other hand, they commended the articles written by women themselves for the *Haagse Post*, the *Nieuwe Linie* and *Vrij Nederland.* They stress that in Holland the predominant picture of the Tribunal portrayed by the media was one of hatred for men. For them, the major point to emerge from the Tribunal was the futility of trying to separate political issues from individual experiences: "We must, as the Tribunal did, begin at the beginning—by how we feel, and by how we live. Indeed, our menstruation and our orgasms are politically significant, however insane this may seem to those who are not yet feminists."

Gemma Pappot, at the end of a very long article in the *Haagse Post*, emphasizes that "Brussels showed how much support women can give to each other and how similar their problems are. When one hears their first-hand accounts of rape victims, then, in the name of God, is it still possible to believe that women bring this on themselves . . . ? I leave the Tribunal with the absolute conviction that it has fulfilled its purpose—to denounce the crimes committed against women—and that it has given an enormous impetus to action already started, as well as to international cooperation and solidarity."

Also in Holland, in the days following the Tribunal, Emmy van Overeem and Judith Esser brought out some long articles on self-help; they both saw in this a means of changing not only the social position of women, but also society itself.

PORTUGAL

Three issues of the Portuguese women's magazine *Mulher* describe, in 15 or so pages, and many photos, the Tribunal as seen by Susana Ruth Vasques and Maria Antonia Palla. For the latter, "the main result of the Tribunal, where each participant was able to express herself freely and give evidence, lies in the condemnation of the oppression which has weighed on women for centuries." The themes of abortion, the right of women over their own bodies ("My belly belongs to me"), single mothers, the unpaid ("invisible") work of housewives, the testimony of Lidia Falcon, and rape, are the subjects of her article. Susana Ruth Vasques describes the Tribunal in three articles—one of which is devoted to wages-for-housework. She repeats the Portuguese journalists call to the women of the entire world reminding them that feminism is progressive, "but that the liberation of women can only take place if they themselves fight for their own liberation." The author asks that the next Tribunal be redesigned to arrive at more definite conclusions: "Simple awareness of our oppression," she says, "is not enough to stop the exploitation to which we are subjected." The author holds the opinion, prevalent among some of the Spanish, Swiss, Italian and French participants, that a socio- or politico-economic analysis of the crimes would have been preferable to the testimony.

SPAIN

The great majority of the 25 articles from Spain are by women. They reflect broadly the criticisms of the Tribunal voiced in some of the plenary sessions, and taken up again at a press conference on the return of the Feminist Collectif Seminar to Madrid: "The theoretical planning of the Tribunal was correct, but the fundamental error resides in the lack of an analysis of the background to each actual case and in the excessive repetition of testimony on each theme." The exclusion of the male press was justified for the Spanish feminists by the fact that we cannot forget "that the male press has made a travesty of other feminist encounters." They give as an example of this distortion the "sensationalist nature" of the description of the lesbian demonstration at the Tribunal as a "power takeover"—this for a demonstration which "lasted for only an hour."

Under the title "Sex Instead of Politics," and signed L. Albeniz, the magazine *Posible* denigrates the Tribunal entirely, except for the lesbian participation (". . . the most coherent of all"). To him, the Tribunal was "brought together by the art and magic of God knows whom," "a real disappointment, as if it had been organized by . . . people trying to strip all prestige from the feminist movement."

ITALY

A dozen articles were published in the conventional press in Italy. With the exception of *La Stampa* (moderate right) and *Il Tempo* (extreme right wing), they appear in left wing dailies and magazines.

A particularly long and prominent article appeared in *La Repubblica* on March 6th: "Disagreement showed up among delegates: some gave priority to illiteracy and poverty, others to abortion and sexual freedom . . . On one point, however, all were agreed—the damage caused by male power." This same woman journalist is enthusiastic about medical self-help ("revolutionary" and "liberating") and is impressed by the way participants are able to flaunt fashion and convention: "From whichever country they came, they all have a common and different feminine form: the refusal to improve their appearance . . . in order to conform to commercial criteria or male fantasies of womanhood. Not one of them uses makeup, almost all have long, beautiful and natural hair, their clothes are cheap, practical, way-out, gayer than the gloomy costumes of high fashion . . . Of their poverty, women at the Tribunal are very proud . . . nearly all of them got here by chancy means: hitchhiking, trains or student charters. They are lodging in youth hostels. They eat tinned food and biscuits which they've brought with them. At most, they buy themselves a sandwich."

Among the countless Italian women's weeklies, only one, *Annabella,* wrote about the Tribunal (four pages of text and a dozen pictures). This publication, like *La Repubblica,* also emphasizes the physical appearance of the participants, (a sure sign of one facet of the writers'/readers' conditioning!). On the cases themselves, the author, Paola Fallaci, picks out "as the most cruel," political imprisonment, rape, Yvonne Wanrow's testimony, the treatment of elderly women, and clitoridectomy. She concludes that the "verdict" reached at Brussels is "a hard and passionate document against the injustices towards women," and that "the deepest meaning of the Brussels trial lies in its spirit of revolt and sisterhood."

Writing in *Il Messagero,* Franco Ivaldi expresses the typical masculine reaction to testimony on battered, beaten and raped women: "It is clear," he says, "that the feminists' accusations cannot be levelled at all men, but only at that limited section of wrongdoers, to be found all over the world."

In the column, "Civil Rights," of the weekly *Expresso,* a full-page article with the flamboyant title "The Phallocrat is a Multinational Monster," appeared on March 14th, and a week later another page and a half was devoted to lesbians at the Tribunal. The latter article, often sympathetic, for the most part objective, nevertheless fell into the well-worn groove in its very last sentence: "Perhaps, who knows, they will return to loving men?"

Noi Donne gives the opinion of some communist women in Italy: "Comprehensive and effective in its presentation and denunciation of the cases, the Tribunal was less convincing on the action to be taken, the need to establish priorities, the methods to be adopted, and the global strategy for the struggle. To hope for all this would not have been realistic," says the author, "for the assembly was too diverse, and this not only because it was the first big feminist meeting of women and groups from so many countries—each one of them with its own problems within the general one, each with its favorite themes, and its own level of elaboration—but also because the oppression we suffer varies in degrees. And that is not a small thing."

Carmela Paloschi's criticism of the Tribunal in the feminist publication *Limenetimena* and in ISIS is very similar to that of the Spanish women, but she adds: "Lack of organization often means chaos and I have seen more than one feminist meeting end up in nothing, without having reached any conclusion because even a little self-discipline was rejected. The meeting in Brussels succeeded in arriving at a compromise: on the third, fourth and fifth days, the organizers were no longer sitting on the stage, nobody followed the organized programs (even if the proposed subjects had been carefully planned) and there was no confusion at all . . . "

NORWAY

From Norway came the following report by the participants at the Tribunal: "We were almost completely neglected by the mass media! No Norwegian journalists attended the Tribunal. We sent a press report to our biggest press bureau and the biggest newspapers. No response. The biggest newspaper in the labor press printed a male chauvinistic article. It told how the lesbians at the Tribunal had disturbed and destroyed the testimony from rape victims. We reacted very strongly to this way of putting the facts, and our lesbian witness wrote an article to the newspaper. It was never printed. The results of all our efforts are limited to a couple of small articles in the socialist newspaper and a student newspaper. *Sirene*, the only feminist magazine in Norway, has published a long report of which the headlines are: "Women are Slaves All Over the World," "There is a Women's Politic Which Crosses All Country Borders," "The Oppression of Women is a Universal Fact," and "We Have to Make Injustice Known."

JAPAN

News of the Tribunal in the big circulation media in Japan apparently reached the astonishing number of 20 million readers, the combined circulation of the three giants *Mainishi Shinbun, Asahi Shinbun* and *Yomiuri Shinbun,* plus the provincial daily *Kyoto Shinbun* and the most popular women's magazine *Josei Jishin.* This wide circulation is the work of our national contact, Yuko Ijichi, who placed, together with her photos, three articles (one of which in the *Kyoto Shinbun* was picked up in over 70 local papers). Yuko was also interviewed by the *Asahi Shinbun* and the *Josei Jishin,* and did TV programs on the Tribunal. She wrote that the Japanese media, which usually does not cover women's movement events in other countries unless they are organized by governments, like the IWY conference in Mexico, took the Tribunal unexpectedly seriously. Indeed, Yuko said that she was quite satisfied.

INDIA

Although we have not seen the articles which appeared in the Indian press, we may presume, from a letter we received from New Delhi, and dated March 10, that there was some coverage there. In a letter, our national contact expressed enthusiasm for the success of the Tribunal and the resolutions which it passed, and that she was "very glad to read about it in the newspapers."

LUXEMBOURG

"Jews had their Nuremberg and other trials . . . women, who are half of humanity, have not yet had their justice," wrote Albert Montjoie in the *Republicain Lorrain,* a leading daily in Luxemburg. The author felt that "one has to be a man to make fun of this Tribunal, one has to be a woman to feel its importance, its horror." Mentioning that "in a peaceful and civilized little country like Belgium, at least 25 women were killed by men in the course of the last nine months" he sees "no vain words but conrete facts" coming from the Tribunal where "women, direct victims of sexist crimes, testified personally." Summarizing the five days' events, he further commented that "men have not yet understood this spontaneity, this disorganization, this constant effervescence, this sincerity, these tears, this exuberance, this creativeness, all this richness; all this they consider weakness because it doesn't fit their stereotype, their rules—because it bothers them." "But," he continued, "this cry from a thousand throats already bears fruit. Across the races, languages, and frontiers, for the first time, women have found themselves victims, in various degrees and forms, of the domination, the oppression, the violence of males." "This Tribunal," he concluded, "is the beginning of international feminism. Greeted by Simone de Beauvoir as an historical event, it is, no doubt, as she said, the beginning of a radical decolonization of women."

DENMARK

From Copenhagen, our national contact reports: "We received unusual press coverage in Denmark, maybe because only women journalists, with the exception of one male photographer, were sent to Brussels. Both radio and T.V. had short reports in their news programs about the Tribunal. Every day articles appeared in nearly all the newspapers. One morning paper had one and a half pages of testimony, and all references were positive. The negative points were mostly written by those who were not present in Brussels, or those who were not concerned with the problems dealt with at the Tribunal."

GERMANY

In Germany, the Tribunal was the subject of over 150 articles in the daily and weekly press, and numerous radio and T.V. programs were dedicated to it, both at a national and regional level, and we received 18 press clippings. The *Suddeutsche Zeitung*, a big national daily, with a circulation of 400,000 covered some of the crimes dealt with at the Tribunal quite adequately in three different articles. *Der Spiegel* (March 15) opens its report with the vivid description of a dramatic moment of emotional outburst at the Tribunal that stopped the projection of a Danish porno film (part of the testimony). "The hall was darkened, the projector began to whiz and across the screen flickered three men, intruding into a house and brutally raping a naked woman. More than a

1,000 sex-mates of the tormented sat in the auditorium, and reacted terrified. 'Stop it,' 'Lights on,' was yelled through the auditorium: It was too close to reality: before this viewing, women . . . had described for four hours how they themselves had been raped. . . ."

Der Spiegel then mentions that the participants had come to the Tribunal without any support from the established institutions: "Raped, battered, tormented and tortured came to the microphone. They accused their governments and their husbands, the police and the church, judges and doctors, procurers and porno producers, family men and sex violators."

Der Spiegel reports that the lesbian demonstration was greeted mainly with applause. "Contrary to this," they note, "one participant was booed altogether. She was of the opinion that aggressions against men did not make sense ('We should rather try to earn their respect"). The French feminist Annie Cohen obviously hit the prevailing mood much better . . . when she suggested women should think of 'declaring war instead of love!'."

Der Spiegel seems to take all this remarkably in stride, even comparing the Tribunal very favorably with The World Congress in East Berlin in October 1975, and with the IWY Conference in Mexico in July of the same year: "Contrary to the other meetings where official women speakers veiled the misery of women in either patriotically or socialistically tinged speeches, this time the persons present articulated their experience plainly."

SWITZERLAND

In Switzerland, over a dozen articles came out on the Tribunal in the conventional press, articles announcing the international feminist event. In addition, *Schweizer Illustrierte* and the national press agency covered the proceedings, as did the Swiss T.V. (S.K.G.) who conducted live broadcasts from the Tribunal. Interviews in German as well as in English went out over four radio channels.

ISRAEL

While coverage in the Israeli press was minimal during the Tribunal, the event was later extensively recorded in *At*, a leading womens' monthly, *Davar,* a labor daily, and *Yediot Achronot*, a leading evening paper. All published excellent, well-documented articles. Their author, Joanne Yaron, describes the atmosphere at the Tribunal as "charged with excitement mixed with rage and even sorrow" where women "indicted their societies and the world as a whole for the continuous and systematic legal and social degradation of the female half of the human race." In disagreement with Jill Tweedie's negative evaluation of the Tribunal, published in Israel as well as the British *Guardian*, Joanne concludes that: "Rather than division, the Tribunal was a great step forward in creating an atmosphere of mutual understanding and solidarity among women everywhere." In particular, Joanne felt that the Tribunal had succeeded in "reaching across language, political, national and cultural barriers." She said that a private conversation with a Syrian woman had "strengthened the belief that geniune feminism could cross political barriers."

"Despite some organizational setbacks," Joanne wrote, "the Tribunal . . . maintained a constant air of unrestrained excitement and hard work." At the end of these days, the author's feeling is that "The Tribunal ended on a note of hope. As the many women trailed out of the elegant building, followed by the tired over-worked simultaneous translation crew (all women), hordes of journalists (all women), and finally the Palais staff, it became apparant that international feminism could become the greatest force for social change ever to sweep the world."

SOUTH AFRICA

There was a complete silence about the International Tribunal in South Africa while it was taking place. When the two South African participants, Sindi Sayedwa and Anne Mayne, arrived home some weeks later, however, there was coverage at last—in "Black Woman's Burden," an article published in *The Argus*, one of Capetown's two most widely read newspapers, Sindi talked in some detail about the oppression of Black women in South Africa. Needless to say, this is not a common topic in the white-owned newspapers! The fact that she testified at the International Tribunal gave Sindi a platform in South Africa that she would not otherwise have had. The article ends on a powerful note: Sindi is quoted as saying that "Via the IFN (International Feminist Network), women throughout the world can be mobilized into action in only one day."

Anne Mayne wrote that she had been interviewed by *Sarie Marais*, an Afrikaans women's magazine, *Fair Lady*, an English women's magazine, and the *Johannesburg Star* and that she and Sindi were able to talk about the Tribunal on the radio.

CHAPTER 4

The Impact and Consequences of the International Tribunal

One of the achievements of the International Tribunal seems to me to have been the breaking of some new ground in developing alternatives to the male conference model. Many people, particularly from the media, asked before the Tribunal started what its conclusions would be. Consider the assumption lying behind such a question: that the conference cannot transform ideas and hopes into something different, that the participants are there to rubberstamp previously worked-out conclusions! Yet, people often thought it was a sign of inadequate philosophizing or poor organization that we didn't know what the conclusions would be until the end.

However, because of the limitations imposed on us by the structure of the Palais, our dependence on technology, etc., we couldn't transcend the male conference model sufficiently to satisfy many women. Yet I personally have never been to a conference where the organizers were so willing to accept a basically anarchic situation, nor have I previously experienced anarchy working so well.

It is rare for conferences to be as alive and ever-changing as the Tribunal was. Many women literally described it as one of the most fantastic and meaningful experiences in their lives. On the other hand, there were others who found it one of the worst, and who were deeply disturbed by it.

It is, of course, impossible to assess accurately the consequences of the International Tribunal only four months after it ended. In fact, we will never know its full consequences. What we know is only the tip of the iceberg.

Carmela Paloschi, wrote that "after the Tribunal, lots of women were interested, probably because the magazines talked about it." A long newspaper article in the Italian newspaper, *Il Giorno,* reported that the testimony of Italian women about the brutal treatment of women giving birth at a Ferrara hospital made headlines back home one day after the Tribunal was over. "It was discovered" wrote the male journalist "that a good part of the denunciations brought forward by the Ferrara feminists hit the target." "In fact," he continues, "the 'j' accuse' of the woman,

Dr. Antonella Picchio, raises the question: Why hasn't anybody ever had any hint of these facts before now?" He points out later that "the facts are already a year old." The bad publicity abroad certainly seems to have strengthened the feminists' struggle in Ferrara, Italy.

A Norwegian woman, Asta Magni Lykkjen, wrote that "four of us are editing a pamphlet on the Tribunal," of which one to two thousand copies will be printed, and that the women who attended the Tribunal have been giving talks about it. As a result, one women's group has decided to try to start a refuge for battered wives and a rape crisis center in Oslo. In addition, a wages-for-housework group has been formed. Asta also wrote that "we realized that crimes against women are crimes against *us*—against all women. As for myself, I felt that all the pieces suddenly fit in the worldwide patriarchal puzzle."

Barbara Schleich wrote from Germany that the German Minister of Family Affairs, Katharina Focke, was so impressed by a TV program about the Tribunal that she gave $150,000 for a refuge for battered women. This is ten times more than the total budget of the Tribunal!

As a result of the International Tribunal, women in Munich organized a city-wide Tribunal on June 25th which was attended by about 1,000 women. Many of the crimes denounced at the International Tribunal were discussed and analyzed, and the texts have already been published by a feminist press called *Verlag Frauenoffensive*. In this publication, the International Tribunal is referred to as having constituted "a very important step in the international women's movement." A manifesto formulated by the International Tribunal workshop on the outcome of the Tribunal was read at the Munich Tribunal.* A national meeting is planned for November 27–28, also in Munich. All the feminist groups in Germany had been invited to attend the Munich Tribunal to discuss the organization of this national meeting. "The subject of this national meeting is not strictly crimes against women," Doro Carls wrote, "but you can say that Brussels had some impact on the questions to be discussed at this meeting. The general subjects will be: repression of the women's centers, questions of strategy, goals of the women's movement and how to bring them into realization."

In answer to our question on the impact of the International Tribunal in Ireland, Nuala Fennell wrote: "Very con-

*This resolution appears under the heading "Permanent International Committee" in Chapter VII B 5 d.

siderable . . . a successful public meeting was held with the two delegates as speakers. There was a wonderful response from the audience. As both delegates were also journalists, articles were published in national papers, a feminist journal, and a medical journal. There was also good radio coverage. But the most positive spin-off is a mini-Tribunal organized for Dublin on the evening of May 31st which will follow the structure of the Brussels conference."

Judging from a long article about the mini-Tribunal published in the *Irish Independent*, June 8th, it was most successful, as reported by Marianne Heron: "It was the scene of a human rights hearing. Evidence covered violence, neglect, torture and brutality, which permanently affects the lives and health of women and children, born and unborn. The cases concerned five women who had between them 39 children, and whose total suffering had lasted for more than one hundred years. There was nothing extraordinary about the women. Their kind of suffering is commonplace and has in the past been accepted as part of marriage Irish-style."

Marianne Heron then summarizes the horrifying experiences of the five women, which were heard "by a packed audience of over 500 who were at times visibly moved. Then, "each of the cases was summed-up and the remedies—or present lack of them—outlined." These included an appeal for refuges for battered wives.

Regarding her personal reaction to the International Tribunal, Nuala Fennell said that she disliked the disruptive, destructive element, and she regretted the ban on male journalists. But: "after all that, the Tribunal for me was like a baptism, an awakening, a happening all at once. It was emotionally tough, tender, stimulating, and disturbing—all combining in a strange way to give me a greater understanding of being female. If I needed justification for working in the women's movement I got it in Brussels. I got understanding, interest, and a true sense of what the term "sisterhood" really means. I know women are a wonderful and special species. More than ever I wish to liberate their distinct talent, which can only be an influence for good."

Less than a month after the Tribunal, Joanne Yaron, who presented the report on the sexist marriage laws in Israel, replied to our question concerning the Tribunal's impact:

> For me personally, the Tribunal was an extremely moving experience, since it was the first time I had come in contact with feminists from many countries. It was good to know that there are so many of

us out there. I also felt that the bringing together of women from so many countries was a magnificent expression of the universality of our oppression, no matter what form it takes.

In addition, many personal friends were made at the Tribunal, creating an informal feminist network all over the world. However, there were moments of profound disappointment on my part, particularly when the French woman took over the microphone and caused disturbances; also, some of the testimony seemed to me not really on feminist matters. But in general, I feel that I learned a great deal, much of which I am trying to bring back to the women here and to the general public. There was tremendous interest on the part of the women to hear what I have to say. To date, I have spoken to four groups, reaching perhaps 150 women which, for us, is a lot. I was also given the opportunity by the local press and the leading women's magazine to write major articles on the Tribunal. This for us is a tremendous step forward since we feminists have never had a very good press.

As for the impact the Tribunal has had on the country—that is, as yet hard to measure. I believe we will see here a long-term effect due to my raised consciousness, being passed on to more and more women. This would be the same for Marcia* who meets with women in Haifa and Jerusalem and is doing the same. We were both particularly impressed by the self-help clinics and hope to introduce the idea here. To my amazement, the reaction to my initial, timid suggestion on this matter was very warmly received.

According to Grainne Farren, "Here in Paris most of the women I spoke to individually were happy about the Tribunal on the whole."** But at a meeting of between 30 and 40 of the women who had attended, "it was mostly the negative impressions that were talked about. For example, not enough discussions, too much of a speaker-audience relationship and the fact that the Palais had been designed for traditional, formal and profoundly masculine events." Also, "several women were angry about Annie's intervention and the row that followed. They said it made the French movement look silly . . . so it turned into a fascinating discussion about what was wrong with the movement in France . . . If there are more discussions like it, they may lead to profound changes in the movement here. And it was the Tribunal that sparked off all that."

Speaking for herself, Grainne wrote: "It was an intensely emo-

*Marcia Freedman, the other woman from Israel.

**Margot de Labar, one of the national contacts for France, taped a number of interviews of women (including herself) concerning their reactions to the Tribunal. Sadly, these tapes were lost in the mail en route to us.

tional experience, both because of the testimonies and because of all the contestation, discussion and power struggles. There were moments when I was afraid the whole thing was going to degenerate into a brawl . . . But in the end, the whole thing was much more dynamic than if we had just tamely followed the prepared program."

Susan Heller Anderson, who covered the Tribunal for *The Herald Tribune*, wrote that a direct consequence was the formation of a women's journalist association "to try to educate our own colleagues about sexism in the news media, and to improve employment of women journalists in France."

In Austria, 2,000 copies of a feminist journal entirely devoted to the Tribunal have been published. In addition, Erica Fischer and two other women have signed a contract with a German publisher to do a book on the Tribunal. Swiss women are also reportedly working on a book about it. The first issue of the International Feminist Bulletin published in March was devoted entirely to the Tribunal, and distributed free to women all over the world: 1,500 copies in English, 1,000 in Italian, 500 in French, and 500 in Spanish. Women in Britain also brought out a lengthy report including a lot of testimony, which is being sold within the movement.

Belgium is another country where women have been inspired, as a result of the Tribunal, to set up a center for battered women. A member of this group has already traveled to England and Holland to see how the centers are organized in those countries.

And what of Violette, the 15-year-old Belgian woman who had been on a hunger strike for 43 days? Her case caused considerable emotion at the Tribunal, and got enormous press attention, particularly after Delphine Seyrig took up Violette's case. According to the journalist Chantal Gras, who brought the case to the Tribunal, Violette stopped her hunger strike 12 days after the Tribunal ended and returned to school, but is living with friends, not her father. The judge has promised to arrange a consultation with the Youth Tribunal when Violette has finished her exams, and the man involved was released from prison on June 20th. What the judge and the Youth Tribunal will recommend is not known, but Chantal believes that the International Tribunal made a great difference to the case. The solidarity shown for Violette broke her isolation and discouragement, and the publicity raised consciousness and applied pressure on all who were involved in the case. Chantal's opinion is that without the support from women at the Tribunal, "nothing would have happened."

Many women from Holland were tremendously moved by the

testimony of Yvonne Wanrow, the Native American woman, unjustly sentenced to life imprisonment for defending herself. When they returned home they started a campaign to raise money for her, and got 2,000 signatures on a petition which they sent to the governor in the State of Washington, U.S.A. They brought out literature and posters in support of her struggle, told other women about it, and sent her defense committee $375.

Dutch women were also inspired by the resolutions of the Third World and Minority Women Workshop to think about organizing a women's strike in Holland. "As a warm-up, we are organizing a national weekend on May 21st and 22nd in Amsterdam on the subject 'striking for women'" wrote Loes Emck. However, they decided they would prefer to coordinate a women's strike with an international strike day. When and if this will take place, we don't yet know. Meanwhile a Dutch feminist press is eager to translate this book so that Dutch sisters who couldn't attend the Tribunal can at least read about it.

Sindiwe Sayedwa from South Africa said of the Tribunal that "it was a tremendous learning experience for me." She feels strongly that any Black woman who could possibly afford it should try to spend time away from South Africa. "The kind of education you can get outside this country in three weeks is more than you will probably get if you live here to be one hundred," she said. As a Black South African, just being able to sit in a restaurant with whites was a new experience for her, as was seeing women living together and being so mutually supportive.

Sindi's overall impression of the Tribunal was that "most women were prepared to be tolerant and accept differences. While I was in Brussels, I felt, *in a physical way*, the birth of international sisterhood, and I became very optimistic. I felt if we could keep that going it would be really meaningful and supportive. But returning to South Africa has sobered me up, and the physical realities of my situation here are beginning to hit home. Like, how on earth am I going to be able to keep in touch with women outside the country when I can't even afford the postage? However, if the worst came to the worst, I feel I would be in a stronger position now, having made personal contact with all these women."

Anne Mayne, the white South African woman who attended the Tribunal, shared Sindi's feeling of being in a stronger position after the Tribunal. "Lydia Horton and Nicole (Van de Ven) both said to me in a very strong and supporting way that if anything happened to us when we returned to South Africa, they would swing everyone into action. This has given me courage to do things that I wouldn't have normally dared to do. International sisterhood is real to me now." Anne also felt that "because we were there, we brought South Africa home to people in a very real way. They are more likely to take a personal interest in the country now."

Both Sindi and Anne emphasized the importance of learning by seeing and experiencing, rather than reading and hearing. For example, Anne said, the existence of a woman's center in Cape Town "is due to the fact that three of us have been exposed to the American experience, so we *knew* it would work even when it didn't seem to at the beginning."

In the U.S., as in Italy, there was much greater interest in the Tribunal once it was over, but chiefly among feminists. The national committee distributed about 2,000 copies of a short report to the feminist media all over the country, and to women who had shown an interest in the Tribunal before. Those of us from the San Francisco Bay Area and Los Angeles have given several talks about it, including a few on radio and T.V. Women seem to be interested and sometimes really excited by news of the Tribunal. The most enthusiastic response to our short report must surely be Adrienne Rich's: "The report on the Tribunal is one of the most moving and exciting documents I have ever read. Clearly, the international feminist movement has found its voice and will not ever be coopted again by either the Right or the male Left. I am filled with admiration for what a handful of women, working within the usual limitations of women's poverty, have been able to set in motion."

In spite of the U.S. interest, it is hard to say what the impact of the Tribunal will be. I hope, particularly with the publication of this book, that it might increase U.S. women's interest in, and feeling for, the oppression of women in other countries. Partly for reasons of geographical isolation and the sheer size of the country, Americans are often rather parochial and chauvinistic. In the U.S. women's liberation movement too, it is common for women to think that they have more to teach women's movements elsewhere than to learn from them. This is unfortunate. Many other movements are far more advanced in their internationalism, especially in Europe. How many feminists in the U.S. know anything about the movements in Canada or Mexico, let alone the rest of the world? I like to think that the Tribunal will help to stimulate a greater sense of international sisterhood in the U.S. movement.

Two of the longest telegrams I have ever seen were sent to the Brussels office from Iran. The President of the Association for the

Protection of Prisoners took 351 words to say how false were the charges of "a young woman claiming to be Iranian." "There are only 400 not 4,000 women prisoners," he claims, "there is no torture, but rather Iranian prisons offer opportunities for education, sports . . . training courses, films and concerts."! The other 296 word telegram is from "the Secretary General of the Women's Organization of Iran." She too claimed that "the allegations of torture are completely unfounded." Furthermore: "There is much of which we are proud concerning the role of women in Iran, that can be presented before any international gathering. Yet your Tribunal has chosen to turn a blind eye to all this. Iran has been among the most active countries in the cause of women during International Women's Year. Its measures, both domestically and internationally, speak for themselves. Yet the Tribunal, ignoring these activities has allowed itself to become a sounding board for unfounded allegations and pernicious slander." The Iranian witness at the Tribunal testified about the great efforts those in power in Iran have put into trying to improve their image. These telegrams certainly corroborate this.

The Status of Women committee in Cairo also sent a telegram offering to the Brussels office "our firm support to you" in your "pioneer action for women's dignity and social justice."* The New Women's Union of Greece telegrammed their "Congratulations for excellent idea of Tribunal." And women from a communist union group in Germany said in their telegram: "You have our full support, as does any initiative that supports the fight of proletarian and working women against their double oppression and wants to bring closer a real improvement in women's situation." There was also a telegram from Birmingham, England, reading: "Help. Help. In your deliberations remember the West Indian urban woman in Britain." These are just some of the many telegrams received.

Many countries have been omitted in this brief sketch, not because the Tribunal has had no impact, but because no one has written us about it. With regard to the impact on women personally, I have so far quoted from only one of the organizers, Grainne Farren. Here are the feelings of Lydia Horton, an American woman who has lived in Belgium for 11 years.**

---

* The Minister of Social Affairs in Egypt (a woman) was considering sending two representatives to the Tribunal, and a woman editor of *El Ahram* wanted to attend, but unfortunately none of them were able to come.

**We invited all members of the coordinating committee to inform us about the impact on them, but only heard from these two women.

> For me, participation in the Tribunal was a privilege. The testimony I heard, the people I met, the new concepts I encountered, the sisterhood I shared combined with the self-knowledge I gained, add up to a uniquely significant experience. I shall hear echoes of it all my life.
>
> The proof that inexperienced, moneyless, overworked and understaffed women really could produce such an important, large-scale international exchange, overcoming all the obstacles that paralyzed fainter-hearted women, is in itself perhaps the greatest contribution of the Tribunal. The money was raised, the services were provided, the resolution of differences was achieved. The communication we effected, the actions we stimulated, all will stand as a monument to the power of women. Some of us always thought we could do it. Now we know.

With the considerable coverage in both the feminist and the establishment press, we can be sure that the Tribunal has been heard about by millions of women all over the world. (This is in striking contrast to the International Feminist Conference in Frankfurt in 1974, about which almost nobody in or outside the movement has heard.) Merely the *idea* of an International Tribunal on Crimes Against Women, completely organized by and for women, is radical in and of itself. Even when the press has been negative, even when the women who attended have been extremely critical, this doesn't mean it has not had a positive impact in their countries. A British woman, in touch with the women's movement in Spain, told me that the Tribunal had had a very positive effect on the movement in Spain. Unexpectedly, large numbers of women turned up to feminist meetings after the Tribunal, and the Spanish participants had been challenged by the opportunity to meet and experience women from other countries where women are less oppressed than in Spain.

As the South African woman pointed out, an important function of women from many countries coming together is that they can make personal contacts through which the situation of women in different countries becomes more real, and of much greater concern. Such ties include the sharing of solutions, to problems encountered in particular countries. For example, British women have done a lot of work with battered wives and refugees, many Italian women have mobilized around the issue of wageless work in the home, and American women have been very active on the issue of rape and helping the victims through rape crisis centers. Now, in dealing with the issues, women don't have to start from scratch, but can benefit from the thinking and struggling of women in other countries. Not that the same strategies will always work, but at least there is an example to consider. This cross-fertilization doesn't require conferences, but they certainly facilitate the process.

We don't need direct feedback to imagine the impact of the testimony on lesbian persecution on many women from countries where lesbianism is still taboo, even in the women's movement. I was told that women from Spain, Portugal, Ireland and Italy wrote anonymous testimony about their closeted lives as lesbians for the lesbian workshop, being too afraid to testify in front of the whole Tribunal. Some Spanish women were even too afraid to attend the workshop, but sent a spokeswoman instead. The demonstration by so many women that they felt good about being lesbians and wanted to proclaim it to all present, must have had an enormous impact on some women; so much consciousness-raising in less than half an hour! The same could be said for women exposed directly to the concept and experience of medical self-help for the first time.

The most exciting action proposal to emerge from the International Tribunal seems to me to be the Central Communication Center (C.C.C.) set up by the Third World and Minority Women's Workshop.* However, the only information I have received about this since the Tribunal from Catherine Day-Jermany, the coordinator of this center, is that she hasn't heard from many of the women on the committee. We hope that these women will reemerge, and many others will join them to bring some of these important and audacious ideas to life.

With regard to the International News Bulletins**, the Tribunal cannot take credit as the birth place of this important new resource. Some of the members of an international working collective, whose name in English is Women's International Information and Communication Service, known by the initials ISIS, were present at the Tribunal. They describe their work as "providing services of information, documentation, communication, contacts, dialogue, and exchange among women and women's groups on six continents." The work group consists of ten women in Geneva, 12 in Rome and about 20 women contacts throughout the world. They have been working together for some time, gathering materials, resources, and contacts, from women and women's groups and indexing them with the use of an optical computing system. They concentrate "mainly on the things women themselves are producing in their local situations—newsletters, bulletins, films, videotapes, songs, poetry, research, books, photographs, magazines, art work—information that is not readily available through the established communication

*See Part 2, Chapter 6.
**See Part 2, Chapter 6.

channels or widely available outside local situations. A great deal of this material is actually available at the ISIS Documentation-Resource Center now open in Rome, but "an important part of our service," they say, "is also to be able to inform others where material and human resources are available, and to refer women directly to other women."

ISIS is also building a network of contacts. At present they have approximately 5,000 addresses of groups and individuals in 90 countries all over the world.

Funds permitting, they now intend to send out special news bulletins whenever necessary to mobilize support and solidarity for women quickly. The women's movement in Australia already asked for such a bulletin to generate international feminist pressure concerning a rape victim who had been convicted of "falsely accusing her rapist"!* Since such news bulletins are identical with those planned by the International Feminist Network (IFN)** proposed at the Tribunal, ISIS and IFN will work together. The network of key contacts being developed by IFN will simplify and economize on the distribution of ISIS bulletins.

I believe that ISIS, IFN and the Central Communication Center proposed by the Third World and Minority Women Workshop are concrete indications of a growing internationalism in the women's movement. The women who organize the next international feminist conference will surely not meet the indifference and resistance that so many of us experienced before the Tribunal, working in our separate countries.

Aside from these and other proposals formulated at the Tribunal, many other ideas were discussed without being developed into resolutions. For example, there has been talk about organizing a national Tribunal in India (according to Gloria Steinem), in Japan and in the U.S. There was talk about organizing International Tribunals that would be limited to one particular crime against women, for example, battered women, women political prisoners, immigrant women, rape, Third World women, persecution of lesbians, economic crimes, etc. Some of these ideas are sure to reach fruition.

♀ ♀ ♀ ♀ ♀

Women's struggle to combat all man-made crimes is an international struggle, and the International Tribunal on Crimes Against Women was a giant step towards recognizing and actualizing this fact.

---

*On July 6th, 1976, we heard from women in Australia that Irene had "won her appeal, largely due to the mobilization of women both here and overseas."

**Part 2, Chapter 6.